Personnel Management in Polytechnic Libraries

Personnel Management in Polytechnic Libraries

Edited by
Don H. Revill

Gower
in association with
COPOL

Published by
Gower Publishing Company Limited
Gower House, Croft Road
Aldershot, Hants GU11 3HR
England

Gower Publishing Company
Old Post Road
Brookfield, Vermont 05036
USA

British Library Cataloguing in Publication Data

Personnel management in polytechnic libraries.
1. Libraries, University and college— Great Britain—Personnel management
I. Revill, D.H. II. Council of Polytechnic Librarians
023′.9 Z682.4.C6

Library of Congress Cataloging-in-Publication Data

Personnel management in polytechnic libraries.
Bibliography: p.
Includes index.
1. Library personnel management—Great Britain.
2. Libraries, Technical college—Great Britain—Administration. 3. College librarians—Great Britain. 4. Library employees—Great Britain. I. Revill, Don H.
Z682.2.G7P47 1987 023 86-31813

ISBN 0 566 05268 7

Printed in Great Britain at the University Press, Cambridge

Contents

Figure and tables

Figure

Tables

Contributors

Graham Bulpitt, MA, Cert Ed, ALA
Deputy Librarian
Hatfield Polytechnic

Maureen E. Castens, MA, BSc, ALA, DMS
Deputy Head of Library Services
City of London Polytechnic

Graham K.L. Chan, MSc, BSc, ALA
Library Project Leader
Liverpool University

Angela Conyers, MA, Dip Lib, ALA, DMS
Site Resources Officer
Brighton Polytechnic

John Cowley, BA, FLA
formerly Head of Library Services
Middlesex Polytechnic

Ken R. Graham, BA, Dip Lib
formerly Library Assistant
Liverpool Polytechnic

Jean Higginbottom, MLS, ALA
Senior Subject Librarian
Manchester Polytechnic

Christine E. Moon, BA, ALA
Assistant Head of Learning Resources
Brighton Polytechnic

Don H. Revill, MA, BSc(Econ), Adv Dip Ed Tech, FLA
Polytechnic Librarian
Liverpool Polytechnic

C. Barry West, BA, Dip Lib, ALA
Deputy Polytechnic Librarian
Coventy (Lanchester) Polytechnic

Introduction

Despite the impact of the computer and information technology in general, libraries are still about people. Libraries serve people. They try to help. People are a library's most important resource. Libraries will be labour intensive for many years to come not only because so much routine is manual rather than automated but also because libraries are in the people business. A library may be 'poor' in many objective ways yet if the staff are receptive, helpful and skilled much will be forgiven. It is something of a failure of academic libraries that institutional managements and controlling bodies seem not to recognise this fact, preferring generally to put books and buildings first. Important as these things are, good library service depends more on the numbers and quality of the staff than on 'mere' physical resources. Access to information can often be obtained without the necessity of possession. Interpretation of need is frequently necessary. Explanation and personal assistance are valued by library users.

The themes recurring throughout the book are those of change, service, participation, effectiveness, morale and motivation. People are important yet they can also generate many problems. At least one school of thought believes that all problems can be solved by discussion, arbitration or compromise. However there are degrees of reconciliation and acceptance while it is possible for two parties to maintain totally incompatible positions. These ideas are explored in several chapters.

Although chapters are numbered consecutively there are three identifiable parts to the book. Structure and staffing processes come first. Chapter 1 covers the problems in designing and achieving an appropriate organisational structure. Chapters 2 to 4 follow a developmental sequence, covering the recruitment and employment of staff, through their training and considerations of effectiveness, to staff management and communication.

Chapters 5 and 6 discuss mergers and retrenchment, which are major features of public sector higher education in the UK. They are not unknown in many other parts of the world, nor are they concerns only of the past. Mergers and financial stringency continue and are equally likely in the future.

The latter part of the book examines four significant and important staff roles or positions that are common, albeit under different titles, to all academic libraries. The library assistants' view is featured. The published literature says very little about the role and perceptions of library assistants, yet it is recognised that no library could survive for long without them. They largely represent the library to its public. Their actions constitute our actual policy regardless of what the written policy says. They are the people who are 'managed'.

A large literature has been devoted to the role of the subject librarian. No apology is given for including it in this volume. The subject librarian is vital if services are to be oriented to readers' needs. The library assistant provides the basic infrastructure. The subject librarian adds the sophistication. It can be argued that no library can reduce its services and costs to such an extent that it is merely a basic 'good' warehouse, supplying what is required when it is required. The ideas are contradictory. To supply what is needed necessitates an ability to anticipate and predict. A warehouse will have a history of demand for a limited range of items. Library material tends to be more numerous, unique and somewhat unpredictable in the demands made upon it. A degree of sophistication is needed in order to discover, via the academic staff, what is likely to be required in the future. Library staff require extra sensory perception or an information technology solution where a message is sent to the library from a 'bug' on each classroom and study wall whenever a library related notion is mentioned. Ideally the message should be transmitted two to three months before it is originated! This is the realm of the subject librarian.

Systems librarians are a fairly recent feature of library staffing. They and their skills will be needed for a long time to come – until the electricity is cut off. Their role and skills may become more generalised and distributed among many professional staff.

This volume concludes with a view of the role of the polytechnic librarian who must be concerned with all the matters covered in earlier chapters.

It is hoped that readers outside the polytechnic sector, principally those in further and higher education in the UK but also librarians in multi-disciplinary institutions throughout the world, will find something of value in these pages.

We have more in common than perhaps we are willing to admit.

Contributors have been largely free to adopt their own preferred style including use of masculine and feminine pronouns. Where the majority of staff in a role being discussed are of one gender then normally the appropriate pronouns will apply. Otherwise the reader should assume that plural includes singular, male embraces female. The merit or faults in individual chapters should be attributed to their authors. The editor accepts responsibility for the structure of the book and having invited the participants.

Don Revill
Liverpool, June 1986

1 Organisational structure

MAUREEN E. CASTENS

Every organisation has some sort of structure. It is usually illustrated graphically by a 'family tree' type of chart, which shows who reports to whom, how the people within that organisation are grouped together to perform various tasks and functions, and the primary communication pathways. By itself a chart gives only a partial view of how the organisation operates. It does not show the supporting structures of formal and informal groups, committees and working parties which carry out certain tasks and make or influence decisions affecting the functioning of the organisation. Beer (1985) has referred to the organisation chart as 'geological genealogy'. His view is that it merely rationalises the structure after the event, and has little to offer the manager beyond a procedural method of blaming somebody for whatever has gone wrong.

There is undoubtedly some truth in this view. However, the organisation charts of twenty-nine polytechnics reproduced in the Council for Polytechnic Librarians (COPOL) Working Papers Series (1983) do provide a valuable insight into the organisational structure of polytechnic libraries. In the introduction Russell reported that some polytechnics could not readily supply charts when requested, or had to update them, suggesting that such charts are not commonly used as a basic tool for the analysis of library operations. If this is the case it is a pity. If nothing else they provide an invaluable guide to new staff entering the library service, allowing them to see at one glance how the various components of the service fit together on one dimension at least, and where they as individuals stand in relation to the other staff.

Analysis of polytechnic library structures

Russell has commented that on the evidence presented by the organisation charts it is difficult not to be surprised at the degree to which the structures resemble one another. Given the broad similarities of their history, size, technology, goals, environment and the type of people they employ, it would probably be more surprising if they differed widely. There is unfortunately as yet no companion volume outlining the supporting committee structures, although Sidgreaves (1985) has reviewed some of the more common decision-making groups.

Since these charts have been published there have been a number of changes including some minor restructuring of the National Joint Council (NJC) Grading Structure used for many of the professional and all the non-professional staff employed in the polytechnics outside the Inner London Education Area (ILEA), and a rather more substantial restructuring of the ILEA salary scales for all library staffs. The former grade titles are shown at each hierarchical level on the charts. There have also been some other structural changes such as the decentralisation of a number of technical services functions in some polytechnics. These changes do not as yet substantially alter the overall picture.

One major conclusion to be drawn from an analysis of the organisation charts is the high degree of structural complexity which operates both vertically, with up to sixteen different salary bands, and laterally, with up to thirteen specialist positions at the widest part of the structure at one polytechnic. Of the twenty-nine organisation charts studied, there were an average of thirty-one positions separately identified. This average conceals a wide variation of between fifteen and forty-eight unique positions, but given that the majority of polytechnics employ between forty-five and fifty-five staff the picture is of highly complex hierarchical and differentiated structures. There is little apparent danger of any member of staff being in the position of breaking the rule that only seven people should report to one person. The problem is much more likely to be one of over-control and poor communication.

The reasons for complexity

Specialisation is desirable in some situations where the tasks to be carried out are diverse and different in nature and where specialist skills are required to solve particular types of problems. It can, however, lead to fragmentation, boredom, and difficulties in communication. It certainly presents problems when organisations are faced with major changes such as automation or contraction. What are the reasons then for the high degree of complexity observed in most polytechnic library structures?

Four factors appear to be particularly influential: the complexity of the systems maintained by libraries; the diversity of tasks carried out within the library; the predominantly multi-site nature of polytechnics; and the grading/salary structure. Other factors traditionally identified by writers on organisational structure and design, such as history, size, technology and objectives, are also relevant but in the framework adopted for this analysis they are seen as contributory rather than determining.

Libraries are in themselves complex organisations. The COPOL *Statistics of polytechnic libraries 1984/85* showed that on average libraries contain about 300,000 books, 70,000 audiovisual items and purchase over 2,200 journal titles a year, as well as some 13,000 new books. They issue over 260,000 items a year to some 10,000 registered borrowers, deal with over 6,000 inter-library loans and maintain services for some sixty hours a week on several sites. The figures in themselves are not particularly meaningful in isolation, but they become more important when the nature and records of the stock are considered. Although there is some duplication of individual titles, on the whole each book, periodical issue, slide or video is unique in either its information content or method of presenting and structuring the information. Libraries have had to develop complex and highly inter-dependent systems to acquire and arrange the stock in a logical and systematic way, and to control its movement in, out of and around the library.

Complexity of systems

Such inherent complexity enourages the formation of specialist teams of staff to deal with the variety of systems necessary to support the wide range of services offered by the typical polytechnic library. These systems generally demand the application of professional judgement at certain critical points and a high degree of accuracy throughout. Systems are also required for the management of the library service. The centralisation of the technical services functions of book acquisitions, cataloguing, indexing and processing which was commonplace in the seventies is a good example of one particular type of organisational strategy and structure developed to deal with a particular sub-system. The acquisition of audiovisual materials and serials has not been centralised to the same extent. At the time, the rationale for this appeared to be self-evident as polytechnics were usually formed from the merger of disparate colleges, and struggled to integrate their systems and stock. The case for a centralised unit to co-ordinate and deal with orders, exert financial control and create a uniform union catalogue or database of the stock holdings available to all parts of a dispersed organisation was overwhelming for most polytechnics.

The trend was accelerated both by external pressures from the Council of National Academic Awards who were anxious to ensure that students within the institution could benefit from the access to all the resources of the library service, and by the appearance on the market of a number of automated cataloguing systems. These provided assistance with the difficult task of retrospective conversion of the records of highly dispersed systems, and the task of current cataloguing by making the records of the British National Bibliography (BNB) and the Library of Congress available in machine readable form. Their most immediately useful service, however, was the production of multiple copies of the catalogue on microfiche, on a monthly basis if required.

Although it was always possible to have maintained the cataloguing and classification functions at individual sites, even in the early days of the automated systems it was much simpler to build up a small specialised team of staff whose primary task it was to learn about the systems and prepare the records for inputting, particularly as the systems themselves were untried and untested and were being continuously modified in the light of experience and technological developments. The specialist cataloguing staff were themselves actively involved in this process, either by developing an in-house system or, more usually, by participating in the development of the services provided by the cataloguing co-operatives such as Birmingham Libraries Co-operative Mechanisation Project (BLCMP).

Even in the mid-seventies when the mood was very much of the bigger the better in library terms, and there was a general commitment to the arguments of economies of scale, functional specialisation and centralisation, some libraries reserved their position either by refusing to centralise their technical services or by only standardising on certain aspects such as cataloguing, but retaining local control over classification practice. The degree to which this happened varied from institution to institution, but at one extreme individual site libraries even retained different classification schemes or at least used local versions and editions of a single scheme. A few polytechnics at the other end of the spectrum insisted that in order to maximise the benefits of automation and access to externally provided records, standard BNB classification practice should be adopted wholesale.

New, integrated stand-alone systems now coming on to the market are designed to provide multiple and dispersed online access to a database comprising all the records traditionally handled by technical services, including orders, financial reports and catalogue records, as well as the issue record traditionally accessed at the issue desks. There is now potential to reverse structural decisions on centralisation and specialisation of particular functions. Database creation and amendment is technically possible at many more points of the system if individual terminals are set up to handle such transactions and the proper security codes are known.

System-wide standards have now generally been established and the expertise built up over the years can potentially be shared around the system. As and when polytechnics purchase such systems they will be in a position to decide whether or not to decentralise. Some institutions, such as the Polytechnic of North London, have already moved in this direction, disbanding their central units and moving the staff to sites.

The newest technology facilitates this strategy but does not in itself determine it. In the context of declining staff and material resources, transferring staff from 'behind the scenes' administrative units to the point of service is an attractive option. Most polytechnics are reporting increased issues and reader services activity despite stable or declining student numbers and far less new material is being acquired. There has also been a history of tension between technical and reader services areas. Centralisation as distinct from specialisation was not always popular. Subject staff have complained that they no longer know what is happening to crucial book orders and that they are not able to influence policy decisions on cataloguing, classification and subject indexing. As a result, a number of them have become deskilled and less effective at exploiting the catalogues and indexes.

For some, and perhaps all, of these reasons, decentralisation is a live issue. In the short term it is likely to be a popular strategy. In the longer term it will be effective only if site teams are able to ensure that backlogs do not build up and that standards are maintained to a reasonable level. The size of central teams and the number of sites in many polytechnics is not sufficient to allow all site libraries to gain their own personal experts from a dispersed technical services unit. This is likely to present problems in training site staff who may never have had to catalogue or classify since they left library school, particularly if they joined polytechnics after centralisation. If subject librarians are to assume responsibility for classification for example, they will need training and additional support as will technical services specialists if they are expected to undertake a broader range of tasks at site level. It is the age-old problem of having either a large number of staff operating at a certain level of competence, or less flexible specialists able to concentrate on doing certain tasks at a high level of skill. In order to manage such a major structural change effectively, manpower planning is essential.

Although there were a large number of technology-led reasons for the creation of central technical services units, it should also be borne in mind that there were managerial considerations. Centralisation was seen by polytechnic librarians as an integrative strategy, allowing them to break up and bring together in new groups staff who had formerly worked in the constituent colleges and site libraries. It was believed that the experience of working together on common tasks of benefit to the polytechnic as a whole would help to replace college or site library 'think' with polytechnic 'think'. It also provided a specialised taskforce of staff who could cope with the problems of catalogue revision which faced so many of the polytechnics as they absorbed a number of institutional mergers and the subsequent rationalisation of stock holdings across the institution.

The situation has now changed. Polytechnics have become mature institutions each with a unique blend of courses and specialisms. There has been a massive shake-out of the smaller colleges across the country but further institutional mergers on the scale experienced in the seventies seem unlikely. In the present economic climate it is more likely that there will be closures of smaller colleges and some rationalisation of particular courses rather than expensive mergers.

A possible exception is the proposal that a few polytechnics might merge with neighbouring universities.

The optimal structure of any library service is that which facilitates the effective performance of the primary tasks of the organisation at the lowest cost possible, in an atmosphere that satisfies clients and in which staff give of their best. The centralisation of technical processes has been discussed above as a structural option which at the time appeared to optimise the effective performance of those tasks. It was also held by some to be the lowest cost strategy in terms of staff time as it allowed managers to identify those tasks necessitating relatively expensive professional staff time, and ensured that other routine tasks such as filing were carried out by the cheaper non-professional staff or were automated. There were also held to be economies of scale. To date there is no conclusive evidence to that effect, although it is likely that polytechnics would not be in the position to benefit from the new integrated systems with their enhanced capabilities if they had not adopted this strategy.

Diversity of tasks

There is plenty of evidence that many routine, relatively low level clerical and even manual tasks remain to be carried out in any library, despite the heavy investment in automated systems that have done away with filing catalogue cards and Browne issue tickets, and writing numerous overdue letters and postcards. The library literature is full of articles discussing what sort of staff should be concerned with such tasks. Everyone who has ever worked in a library will have encountered problems on what is or is not professional and whether professional staff should, for example, do their 'fair share' of shelving. The discussions are usually confused by accusations of élitism or exploitation. At first sight this is an unexpected debate given the plethora of grades and apparent hierarchies within the average polytechnic library. Such complex structures suggest that all the activities within a library have been carefully analysed in terms of their volume and the level of skills necessary to carry them out. On this assumption there should be a very clear idea of who does what, and sufficient staffing of the right level to ensure that it gets done. This should be a particular concern of any library manager who has a duty to ensure that staff time is deployed cost effectively; this includes ensuring that there is sufficient clerical and assistant staffing.

The problem is a complex one. Firstly, there appears to be a great deal of embarrassment about acknowledging the extent to which work within a library is routine. Secondly, there is as much, if not more, embarrassment about admitting that staff doing such jobs will be cheaper to employ and that libraries should run at the lowest cost possible whilst remaining effective. Thirdly, the discussions on what tasks are non-professional and what are professional have been substantially confused by issues of low pay and lack of a career structure for non-professional staff. Fourthly, it is difficult to separate the non-professional and professional tasks which together contribute to the maintenance of library systems and services. This is particularly so in the multi-site library system characteristic of so many polytechnics. Sites often vary considerably in size and no amount of careful work analysis and measurement could ensure the optimum mix of staff at any one time.

These problems have not prevented polytechnic libraries from identifying a wide diversity of tasks and assigning them to staff at different levels within the organisation. A close study of the organisation charts reveals that different judgements have been arrived at by different libraries in what tasks they have chosen to specify, and to which level of staff they have assigned these tasks. For example, eight polytechnics have identified staff in their organisation charts who have specific responsibilities for inter-library loans. The two single site polytechnics have specified responsibility at the library assistant level, one at NJC Scale 1/2 and one at Scale 3/4. All the others have identified professional posts graded from Scale 3/4 to Scale 4/5/6. Other tasks specified relatively infrequently and at different levels on organisation charts in descending order of frequency include circulation librarian, systems or automation librarians, planning or development or research librarians, and publicity librarians. Technical services staff are universally specified in one way or another, but media and audiovisual librarians are specified as such on only sixteen charts. This presumably reflects different approaches to the distribution of responsibilities for this work both within the library and the individual polytechnic.

Subject librarians are identified in one form or another in practically every organisation chart, although they appear at a variety of different levels with a similar diversity in their job titles. This is partly because there is far less similarity in practice between the mix of tasks carried out by subject staff in different systems than for many other posts. There is an extensive literature on what is meant by the subject librarian role. Practice will vary from library to library but it is probably fair to summarise the common components as being responsibility for the selection, maintenance and exploitation of stock relevant to the needs of a group of courses or subject disciplines specified by the job description. This can include to a greater or lesser extent liaison with departments and faculties, serving on committees and groups concerned with curriculum development, teaching user education and information handling skills, online searching, handling enquiries, preparation of various publications to assist users to exploit the information resources of the library, and identification of items of stock for inclusion in specialist loan categories. Cataloguing and classification may also be undertaken.

In some libraries certain elements such as user education and online searching may be assigned to some staff and not others, and other elements may be dealt with outside the subject team. Aspects of the work may not be done at all or only done for some user groups and not others. The way in which this work is structured will depend upon the priorities of the service, the organisational structure and the resources available. An important dimension of the resources available is the seniority and experience of the staff involved as well as their quantity and quality.

A number of polytechnics have developed structures with faculty librarians at the second or third tier of the library's management structure supported by a team of subject or assistant librarians at a slightly lower level. Another model, which usually reflects an institutional decision to differentiate academic units more specifically than at faculty level, is to have a larger number of subject librarians (sometimes called course resource officers, school librarians or tutor librarians). Such subject librarians can again be located at more than one level in the organisational structure and may be supported by more junior professionals with some subject responsibilities. In these cases they may be co-ordinated by a reader services librarian at the second or third level in the hierarchy.

It is practically impossible to describe adequately the enormous diversity of structural solutions to the problem of locating the subject work tasks, although a broad distinction can be drawn between those systems that separate subject teams from technical services and user services/circulation teams, and those that superimpose subject responsibilities on to staff who are primarily dispersed around the system according to a functional remit. This aspect is discussed in greater detail in a later chapter, but it is worth noting that decisions about the distribution of this work among professional staff also has implications for non-professional staff. In some cases they can be specifically assigned to subject teams, and in others they have little contact.

Number of sites

The fact that the majority of polytechnics have a number of sites is a major contributing factor to the complexity of their organisational structures. House (1985) has recently discussed the various problems inherent in managing such systems and identified two broad categories of organisational structures in terms of the large central site library with smaller outlying site libraries versus the more federal systems with sites of a similar size. There appears however to be significant variation between the organisational charts of the libraries within the same broad grouping. The number and size of sites contribute to the lateral complexity of polytechnic library organisational structures, but they do not in themselves determine the structure. They do however lead to another type of organisational specialisation, the post of site librarian, which can vary widely in scope and level of responsibility for both services and staff. This has implications for staff who may wish to gain managerial experience. In highly multi-site systems the site librarian's job is far too often seen as administrative rather than managerial.

Grading and salary systems

The majority of polytechnics use two grading/salary systems: the Burnham scales for Teachers in Higher and Further Education and the scales determined by the National Joint Council for Local Authority Administrative, Professional, Technical and Clerical Services (normally referred to as NJC APT & C or Purple Book Scales). The five Inner

London polytechnics use different scales determined by the Greater London Provincial Council of the NJC which have salary bands specifically for professional and trainee-professional library staffs. As a discussion of the different systems and a review of the arguments for and against Burnham versus NJC are covered elsewhere in this book, the present chapter will consider only the implications for organisational structures of the use of two different salary schemes within the relatively small managerial unit of a polytechnic library.

There is little doubt that their co-existence has contributed significantly to the proliferation of hierarchies. Given that polytechnic libraries employ two major categories of staff, professional and non-professional, the use of two types of salary structures would appear to be logical, and could even be regarded as functional. The situation is not as simple as that. With the notable exception of Birmingham, Brighton and Leeds polytechnics whose professional staff are all on Burnham scales (Council of Polytechnic Librarians, 1985), and Kingston and Wolverhampton where all staff are on NJC scales, Burnham and NJC scales are used for both groups of staff. NJC scales are invariably used for non-professional staff.

The two salary structures differ with regard to the length of scales, salary levels, criteria used to determine gradings and conditions of service. The NJC system is a multi-banded scheme with a relatively large number of short scales typically end-on to one another, whereas Burnham is a broad-banded scheme with fewer but longer and overlapping scales. Salary levels on the NJC scales are generally lower than Burnham when both are used for similar jobs. NJC scales are typically used with a job evaluation scheme which determines the appropriate scale for a job according to the number of points awarded for factors such as supervisory responsibilities and involvement in policy matters; Burnham scales are based on different criteria such as the level of course dealt with. NJC conditions of services relate to a normal working year of fifty-two weeks with a sliding scale of annual leave entitlements and a normal working week of about thirty-six hours; Burnham conditions are based on thirty-eight working weeks a year and a thirty hour working week. Most library staff on Burnham salaries work NJC conditions of service. The trend is to replace Burnham posts with NJC posts.

The purpose of a salary structure is 'to attract, retain and motivate'. It is 'meaningless except in the context of manpower decisions about such things as the kind of employee the organisation needs to employ and in what numbers and whether it is proposed to fill senior posts by internal promotion or recruitment from outside' (National Board for Prices and Incomes, 1969). It is therefore likely that the use of two systems for professional staff will inhibit the achievement of that purpose. Which staff and which posts should be put on Burnham scales and which on NJC scales? One scale encourages staff to stay, and the other encourages staff to look for other posts within a fairly short time of appointment. At the time of low staff mobility NJC scales can be useful in limiting the costs associated with incremental drift.

Most polytechnics inherited a mix of grading practices from their constituent colleges with senior tutor and college librarians having been on Burnham scales. As they expanded their staffs in the seventies, they tended to recruit lower level professional staff on NJC scales which were cheaper and are used in the public libraries of the constituent local authorities. Some polytechnics managed to keep their local authority establishment branches at a distance or persuaded them that college libraries were different from public libraries. Others were less successful and have had to try to integrate both schemes for their professional staff with mixed success. Organisational structures have sometimes been severely distorted in order to give some semblance of credibility to the existence, for example, of some staff on the Senior Lecturer scales doing much the same jobs as others on much lower NJC scales.

Individual polytechnics have attempted to join separate NJC scales together in order to achieve longer scales similar to the Burnham ones and thus simplify their structures. Often, however, in order to satisfy the requirement of establishment offices, it has been necessary to have individuals regraded from one scale to another by 'adding on' specialist responsibilities rather than by linking grades with automatic progression between them. This has had the effect of further complicating the organisational structure. One polytechnic library for example regraded thirty-seven staff in a four-year period between 1979 and 1982 (excluding internal promotions) that is, 12 per cent of their staff a year (Castens, 1983), at a high cost in management time. The effect on morale was damaging: for every satisfied regraded member of staff there were always several actively dissatisfied.

Where Burnham and NJC scales are mixed because of the differential rates of pay, staff on the Burnham scales appear at the top of the hierarchy. It is possible to argue that the use of the NJC multi-banded structure at the initial stage of professional experience is functional. Theoretically it allows for the positive selection of 'good' staff who are moved up through the structure fairly quickly by a series of internal and/or external promotions. Less good staff are held at the lower levels. The better and more experienced staff will eventually arrive at the top levels when they can be transferred to the broad-banded Burnham scales occupying the specialist professional or leadership posts where a reasonable degree of stability is desirable. There is a certain superficial attraction in this argument, but this is not how the system actually works.

The wide variation in the distribution and use of Burnham and NJC scales between polytechnics makes any hope of this type of systematic career planning problematic. The situation has been made more difficult by the contraction of staffing levels and subsequent lack of movement within and between libraries. Where Burnham vacancies have occurred they have often been deleted or replaced by NJC scales. Where Burnham scales have been extensively used, staff have tended to stay in post. There has been very little alleviation of the problem by the interchange of polytechnic library staffs with those in other libraries, either in the public or academic sector.

Much of this discussion has been confined to the salary structures for professional staff, although over half of polytechnic library staffs are non-professional. At this level there is again evidence that the short multi-banded NJC scales have influenced organisational structures. The majority of polytechnics have senior library assistants as well as library assistants and other clerical staff at lower levels. The notable exceptions are four of the five ILEA polytechnics which use a single much longer scale at this level. It may be that such distinctions are useful where the duties or responsibilities of assistants are genuinely differentiated, but given the average ratio of professional to non-professional staff of 1:1.25 and the dispersion of assistants across a number of sites and specialist units, it is difficult not to suspect that some of the differentiation is superfluous. Where libraries have separated the bulk of reshelving work and employed shelvers or have library porters or machine minders, there is obviously a case for a separate salary level, but there is limited scope for such specialisation even where part-time staff are used. These comments do not take into account the issue of using non-professional staff further up the hierarchy than is currently customary to carry out substantial administrative tasks. There is little room for this type of development in the average-sized polytechnic and this will continue to be so unless there is a substantial change in the ratio of professional to non-professional staff.

The consequences of complexity

The general impression is of library systems imprisoned by their complex organisational structures which have been largely determined for them by their history, by earlier decisions on structures often arrived at in order to accommodate existing strengths and weaknesses of current staff, by the inherent complexity of library systems and the multiplicity and diversity of their tasks, by the numbers and relative sizes of their sites, and by their inherited salary and grading structures. Major restructurings have tended to occur either in the context of rapid growth and expansion of services or with the introduction of new technology. Such changes have sometimes coincided with the arrival of a new chief librarian whose appointment has legitimised a rethink on structures. In the seventies restructuring tended to take the form of centralisation of technical services. The signs are that in the eighties the even newer technology could well be accompanied by a similar restructuring but in the opposite direction, although it may prove to be more painful in the context of retrenchment.

A worrying aspect of many of the structural changes is that they have been system led. Lip-service has been paid to the user services side of the work, with some notable exceptions. A rather less coherent pattern of provision and supporting structures has appeared. The literature on reader services is patchy and uneven in coverage. Staff working in this area have other tasks such as running site libraries or staffing counter and enquiry desks. They simply do not appear to have sufficient time or mental 'space' to engage in the creative tasks of developing the services required to meet the needs of their diverse user groups.

It may be that the second or third generation automated systems will at long last provide some real assistance. There is considerable potential to extract a large amount of management information from these systems about exactly how and to what extent different groups of users make use of the stock and services. If this could be provided as a matter of course to subject librarians they would be in a far stronger position to identify real areas of need and concentrate their energies at that point. It is likely that libraries will have to develop rather different structures to facilitate the delivery of systems and services which are more responsive to existing patterns of use and non-use and to future requirements. In one sense existing structures reflect what can easily be provided. The need is for structures supportive of the actual requirements of users.

Manpower planning

As Turner (1984) has said 'grading, salary levels, structures and training are inter-related and should be dealt with by properly integrated staffing policy'. Classically this is built up from an analysis of the range and volume of tasks to be performed. Such an analysis enables the organisation to determine the quality and quantity of staff required, the appropriate gradings and training needs. Although task analysis is the basis of manpower planning at this level, it has to be carried out in the context of clear understanding of the aims and objectives of the library service and a critical approach to the validity of each task. There is too often an uncritical acceptance that certain activities or tasks are necessary. Turner has suggested that if the task analysis has been properly carried out and grouped sensibly into individual posts a structure will emerge naturally from the groupings of the posts. He acknowledged that there will be several possible groupings and that 'some will be directed by physical considerations'. Sufficient has already been said to indicate that this approach may be by no means as simple to adopt as is suggested.

There is a danger in thinking that such planned approaches are merely theoretical abstractions of little real utility. A good and well thought out manpower planning approach which incorporates an audit of existing and potential staffing resources should make a significant contribution to ensuring that an organisation reacts to its internal and external environments in such a manner that it can command now and in the future the numbers and qualities of people who are required to enable it to achieve its output within 'whatever cultural constraints of efficiency that may be imposed on it' (Thomason, 1981, p.132). Polytechnic libraries are increasingly required to work under constantly shifting 'cultural restraints on efficiency'. There is a tendency to respond in an *ad hoc* way to such apparently random shifts. Such strategies may be all that is possible in the short term but they are counter-productive in the long term. Systems tend to stagger on with an outdated structure and a commitment to providing a range of services that they are less and less able to deliver in any consistent manner.

A long hard look is required at the real demands for services, including demands for services that are not currently provided. For example most polytechnics are reporting increased requests for weekend opening including Saturday afternoon and Sundays particularly from part-time students on professional and business courses. More users are requiring access to text and bibliographical databases, and changes in teaching and learning strategies within the institution are also beginning to change demand patterns. These changes require regular monitoring and systematic review of implications for the numbers and types of library staff required. There may be limited or zero scope for additional staffing resources but staff are highly flexible resources and can be retrained or redeployed to meet changing patterns of demand. If they are imprisoned in complex structures or restrictive job descriptions, it is certainly more difficult to achieve change in the short term, but in the longer term it is possible to prepare the ground so that full advantage can be taken of minor changes such as individual vacancies or requests to reduce hours. Staff training and development programmes can be designed to create an atmosphere supportive of such changes. In some cases a review of the use of part-time staff, term-time contracts, job sharing, job exchanges and staff deployment practices can be productive. There is perhaps less than ideal room for manoeuvre, but there is some. A manpower plan can identify that scope.

On the whole, library staff are highly motivated to provide a good service, and changes centred around real demands for particular services or from specific user groups will gain a positive response from staff. Too often structures are centred around the maintenance of particular system and sub-systems rather than directed towards user groups. It is sometimes necessary to make hard decisions about some activities and simply cease to do them, or do them in a simpler way.

Staffing levels

One of the outputs of manpower planning is the determination of the numbers of staff required at each level within the library service. There is very little evidence in the literature of this approach having been adopted on a systematic basis by polytechnic libraries. Much more work has been done in the public library sector with, for example, the publication of the LAMSAC study of public library staffing in 1974, which generated a number of formulae for determining staffing levels for particular tasks and methods at local, area and headquarters levels. Revill (1977) applied a series of norms for site libraries based on various measures of stock size and predicted activity levels related to the size of the client group. The derivation of these norms is not explained in terms of unit times for particular functions or tasks but he has suggested that they made sense in the context of Liverpool Polytechnic Library Service at that time. The unit time approach has never been generally applied to determine staffing levels because of the difficulties of accounting for different working practices between systems, and the work required to generate such unit times.

McLean (1982) has suggested the minimum staffing levels for site libraries offering a basic range of services as being four or possibly five staff, but again this is not justified except in terms of providing adequate coverage for 'reasonable' opening hours including some evening access. Conyers (1985) has indicated that on the basis of a study on the costs of the multi-site library service at Brighton Polytechnic, multi-site operation accounted for 31 per cent of the existing staffing of eighty. In a single site system of fifty-five this would give a library staff to student ratio of 1:98 which she suggested is the informal target of other polytechnic librarians. This approach, which assesses staffing needs on the basis of student numbers, is a common one in academic libraries. The National Association of Teachers in Further and Higher Education (NATFHE) College Library policy statement in 1982 recommended a ratio of 1:80 for a single site with unspecified additions for additional sites, as did the Library Association's College Libraries Guidelines. The Library Association stated that their guidelines were based on a consensus view of good practice in libraries and indicated the level currently demanded by validating bodies.

The adoption of norms ratified by existing levels of provision rather than bottom-up assessments of needs appears to be a reflection of the current economic climate. COPOL's *Statistics of polytechnic libraries 1984/85* showed a further deterioration in staffing levels with an observed mean ratio of 1:117 full-time equivalent (FTE) students, but it is difficult to assess what this means without data on changes in the number of sites, opening hours or levels of services offered. Physical restrictions on the layout of libraries will also affect the number of staff required to maintain services. Some libraries have no choice but to maintain more than one staffed issue point or enquiry point if all parts of the collection are to be effectively controlled. Similar considerations can also determine the scope for decentralising staff.

Organisation cultures

Each organisation has its own distinctive atmosphere or culture. Anyone who has worked in a number of different organisations, even if they were all polytechnic libraries for example, will have been conscious of this. Attitudes to work and users differ as do problem-solving styles, levels of energy and individual autonomy. Handy (1985) has pointed out that there is a close inter-dependence between different organisation structures and their cultures. He described four cultures in terms of their typical structures: the power culture, centred on a central power source with a web structure radiating out from it; the role culture, which he compared to a Greek temple resting on a series of pillars; the task culture, which is job or project orientated and tends to have a net structure; and the person culture, which is the least common, comprising typically of clusters of highly autonomous individuals such as in an architect's partnership.

Recognition of the cultural dimension is important. Some cultures are particularly suited to certain types of tasks and people and others are not. Any organisation needs to have a clear idea of the sort of cultural and structural mix it needs in order to be effective. Such considerations can affect staff selection decisions. It is important to choose people who will fit the culture, unless they are selected deliberately as change agents.

At first sight libraries are predominantly bureaucratic, role-dominated organisations. Normally, there are clear procedures for assigning roles such as the use of job descriptions with specified levels of authority, procedures for communications between different parts of the system, and rules for the settlement of disputes on matters such as dealing with defaulting readers. Rules and procedures are major methods of influence. Libraries typically score high on measures of specialisation, standardisation and formalisation, particularly in the highly specialised and functional areas such as technical services. Staff from other parts of the system who work for a period in such a unit will often comment on how relatively quiet and formal they are, just as users may make the same comment of their site library. It is all a matter of degree.

Such role cultures offer a degree of security and predictability to the individual, and tend to reward the 'satisficer', the member of staff who is concerned with doing a job up to standard, but not necessarily any more than that. Compulsive achievers or staff with high work self-actualisation needs are not likely to be happy in such a culture unless they are able to progress very quickly up the pillars of the structure to the 'pediment of the temple'. In practice, most organisations develop a number of structures within their prevailing structure to deal with particular situations, and although most polytechnic libraries exhibit a primary role culture and structure, they have also evolved a number of semi-permanent or temporary structures to support those aspects of their operation that are not suited to this approach.

Role cultures are highly functional where the organisation has control of its environment, where its market is stable or when the product (such as the provision of a library service) has a long life-cycle. They can fail when the product, or the market for the product, changes. By their nature they are slow to perceive change or to react. It is difficult to envisage a polytechnic that will cease to have a need for a library service which acquires, stores, displays, retrieves and disseminates relevant information and stock to its staff and students, but libraries are much more than simple purveyors of undergraduate texts or providers of convenient study places. Although such activities will continue to account for the bulk of staff activity for the foreseeable future, libraries will also need to be responsive to demands for new types of information and learning support services, and shifting patterns of demand for existing services.

The task culture is far more productive when flexibility and sensitivity to the market or environment is important, or where a new project such as a new library building or the implementation of an automated system is undertaken. The culture and its supporting structure brings together people with the relevant specialist skills or knowledge at the appropriate level in the organisation, to work on the tasks. If the right people are involved, such a structure emphasises their strengths and minimises their weaknesses. It fosters commitment to the objectives of the organisation and is by far the most popular culture, as a personal choice for middle and junior professional staff. It fits in well with the behavioural views of organisations.

Libraries have recognised this and where possible have tried to make use of such cultures in, for example, the formation of subject teams of staff involved in providing in a creative and reactive way a range of services to particular user groups. The somewhat Byzantine appearance of so many organisational structures, where for example they have established technical, circulation and subject teams interacting with one another and operating in parallel, is evidence of these efforts, as are the proliferation of committees and working parties set up to deal with matters such as staff training, the selection of photocopiers and library publications. A problem of such task-centred structures is that they are difficult to control on a day-to-day basis. A high degree of mutual trust is essential, and they are easier to support when sufficient resources are available to meet all reasonable requests. When resources become more scarce there is a tendency for managers to feel the need to be more in control of the methods used to attain the desired results. At the same time the task centred teams or groups will often be aware of this and become more concerned to compete with one another for a share of diminishing resources than with their primary tasks or overall objectives of the service.

If this happens the librarian will tend either to resort to rules and procedures to make decisions or use her or his position power. The abrupt change of management style from one supportive of task culture based on mutual respect and trust to a more formal one based on role or power can be demoralising and difficult to handle.

Writers on organisational design have suggested that different parts of the organisation engage in one of four different types of activity: steady state, innovation, crisis and policy. Each primary activity will have its own appropriate culture and associated structure. The steady state activities which usually consume the majority of staff time are best fitted to the role culture, whereas innovative activities are most successfully carried out in the task culture. Power cultures are held to be the optimal cultures for dealing with crises and the determination of policy issues such as the setting of priorities and standards, the direction and allocation of resources and the initiation of action. Most people would probably instinctively agree with these conclusions, although the individual's reaction to the appropriateness of the power culture for policy matters will depend upon their position within an organisation and their own belief system on how society should be organised.

Conclusion

Polytechnic libraries are complex organisations with complex structures to match. Some complexity appears to be inevitable but it can be costly. Problems of communication, staff morale, over-specialisation, inflexibility to internal changes and the developing needs of users are likely to occur. There is a danger that legitimate demands on the service will be perceived to be unrealistic at best or irrelevant at worst. These dangers become acute in a situation of rapidly declining resources with the associated freezing and/or deletion of posts. It is difficult to carry out the major restructuring that can be essential in this situation.

Reorganisation of staffing structures is always met by high levels of anxiety and often some resistance. This is understandable given that the major effects are usually to change the way individuals and groups formally relate to one another, and to alter the content or mix of individual jobs. In a time of retraction such reactions are likely to be far more acute and disruptive. Unions may have 'no cover for unfilled vacancies' and 'no co-operation with restructuring' policies. Management is likely to have particularly strong reasons for carrying out such restructuring if they have complex, differentiated and/or devolved structures.

The structure of the polytechnic library is affected by the culture of the host institution as well as influencing and being itself modified by the preferred culture of its staff. Some polytechnics are highly formal in their operational style and others much less so. The experience of this author is that this has had a perceptible impact on the atmosphere of their library services. The structures adopted play a large part in determining the prevalent culture, and the extent to which that culture is enhanced by the existence of other cultures in appropriate parts of the structure. This in turn affects the selection of staff. As Handy (1985, p.205) has said: 'You decide, in large part, on your culture when you decide on your people'.

The primary culture of most polytechnic libraries is a role one, reinforced by a hierarchical and differentiated structure. The majority of the staff tend to be low risk-takers with a high need for security. This is not the self-image that many staffs of polytechnic libraries would wish to own. They are certainly not the attributes that organisations facing the rapid changes in technology, markets and resourcing typical of many polytechnic libraries want or need in those of their staff occupying key positions. There appears to be a conflict here. Libraries need to consider all the means at their disposal to ensure that this is not the case. Recruiting new staff as agents of change is not an option for most. They urgently need to consider all the ways and means at their disposal to simplify their structures if they are to cope successfully with the problems that face them. The development of a team approach adopted by some public libraries, using non-professional teams to manage and deliver routine site or branch services supported by mobile task-centred professional teams, is one option, but not easy to implement in the smaller context of the average polytechnic library with its variable mix of sites and dispersed academic activity. Other options include the closure of some site libraries which are usually highly valued by their user communities and their staff who feel that they can provide a friendly and highly reactive service. Developments in remote access technology supported by appropriate systems of document delivery may be a further option worth considering.

Libraries that attempt to retain structures developed in a time of relative plenty, run the risk of having little left to restructure, but workable solutions are likely to involve a substantial amount of co-operation between the polytechnic as a whole and its library service. There are no easy answers in the present economic climate.

References

Beer, S. (1985), *Diagnosing the system for organisations*, Chichester, John Wiley.

Castens, M.E. (1983), *Grading of polytechnic library staffs: an investigation based on a case study at one polytechnic*. Submitted in partial fulfilment of the academic requirements for the Diploma of Management Studies (Education), London, North East London Polytechnic Anglian Regional Management Centre.

Conyers, A. (1985), 'The costs of a multi-site library service: a study of Brighton Polytechnic', *Aslib Proceedings*, vol.37, no.10 (October), pp.395–403.

Council of Polytechnic Librarians (1983), *Working papers on organizational charts* (British Library Research and Development Reports, no.5774), London, British Library.

Council of Polytechnic Librarians (1985), *COPOL staffing survey as at January 31st, 1985*, Oxford, Council of Polytechnic Librarians.

Council of Polytechnic Librarians (1986), *Statistics of polytechnic libraries 1984/85*, Coventry, Council of Polytechnic Librarians.

Handy, C.B. (1985), *Understanding organizations*, 3rd edn, Harmondsworth, Penguin.

House, D. (1985), 'Managing the multi-site system', in J. Cowley (ed), *The management of polytechnic libraries*, Aldershot, Gower, pp.135–56.

LAMSAC (1976), *The staffing of public libraries: a report of the research undertaken by the Local Authorities Management Services and Computer Committee for the Department of Education and Science*, London, HMSO, 3 vols.

Library Association (1982), *College libraries: guidelines for professional service and resource provision*, 3rd edn, London, Library Association.

McLean, N. (1982), 'Managing multi-site polytechnic library services', *Aslib Proceedings*, vol.34, no.5 (May), pp.237–48.

NATFHE (1982), *College libraries policy statement*, London, National Association of Teachers in Further and Higher Education.

National Board for Prices and Income (1969), *Salary structures* (Report no.132), London, HMSO.
Revill, D.H. (1977), 'Unit times in studies of academic library operations', *Aslib Proceedings*, vol.29, no.10 (October), pp.363–80.
Sidgreaves, I. (1985), 'Decision-making', in J. Cowley (ed), *The management of polytechnic libraries*, Aldershot, Gower, pp.59–83.
Thomason, G. (1981), *A textbook on personnel management*, 4th edn, Wimbledon, Institute of Personnel Management.
Turner, C.M. (1984), 'Staffing: policy and problems' in R. McElroy (ed), *College Librarianship*, London, Library Association, pp.203–20.

2 Recruitment and employment of staff

GRAHAM BULPITT

Decisions concerning the appointment of staff are among the most important to be made by librarians. Staff are a key resource, and poor decisions are not easily undone. All kinds of factors come into play when staffing decisions have to be made, and these often obscure the basic issues to be resolved. According to Drucker (1985, p.22), many promotion and staffing decisions made by managers turn out to be poor, yet 'what successful matching requires is a careful understanding of the most important capabilities that a given job requires and of the strengths and weaknesses of each candidate. No mystery here, just good management'.

New appointments and promotions in polytechnic libraries are becoming increasingly rare; around one professional post each week is advertised in the *Library Association Record*. For many librarians, such decisions are a small, though vital part of their work, and it is difficult at this rate to build up much specialist skill and experience. This chapter attempts to bring together a range of information and ideas to reduce the 'mystery' and increase the number of good decisions.

There are three sections. The first examines the labour market, and identifies trends that will affect the library and information workforce. The second section provides an overview of recruitment practice, and suggests alternatives to some procedures. The final section is concerned with conditions of service and other matters relating to the employment of staff. This part is not intended to be a legal treatise; colleagues should turn to specialists for advice here. The section does, however, deal with those areas that are relevant to librarians responsible for staff, and identifies key documents and sources of information.

The labour market

General characteristics of the UK labour market

The outlook for employers (and employees) has changed completely since the Institute of Personnel Management published *Recruitment and selection in a full employment economy* in 1968. The number of people out of work, which had been around 0.5 million in the late 1960s, increased steadily to reach 1.75 million by 1980. Unemployment has increased even more sharply during the 1980s, to a total of 3.3 million by the end of 1985, representing 13.3 per cent of the UK workforce.

These general statistics conceal a range of variations which mean that unemployment has affected different regions, age groups and types of worker to differing extents. The north/south divide here generally holds true. Unemployment is highest in Scotland, the north of England and Wales, with Northern Ireland being particularly badly hit. Central southern England and parts of East Anglia have the lowest unemployment rates, though it should be emphasised that rates will vary within regions: Humberside and Merseyside, for example, have particularly high numbers of people without work.

The evidence provided by UK Department of Employment statistics indicates that unemployment is highest among people aged twenty to twenty-nine. In October 1984 more than one person in three in this age group was out of work, twice the rate of the next most vulnerable group, those aged thirty to thirty-nine. Older workers, aged fifty to fifty-nine, are also likely to experience above average rates of unemployment. Particular types of employee have been badly affected by unemployment. Unskilled workers have suffered worst, and the rate of unemployment generally increases as the level of qualification falls.

School-leavers and graduates are important sources for library recruitment and a number of trends may be discerned here. Although the numbers of UK school-leavers will continue to decline until 1990, and then stabilise, the level of qualifications held is expected to rise. Currently, around 26 per cent of pupils leave school with the Certificate of Secondary Education, 20 per cent attain the General Certificate of Education at Ordinary level and 20 per cent reach Advanced level standard. At least 60 per cent of young people look for full-time work when they leave school.

The decline in the size of the eighteen-year-old population is the major reason for current government plans to reduce the number of university and polytechnic places in the 1990s. However, the unemployment rate for graduates is much lower than average (4 per cent in 1985), and there is some indication, from a recent Institute of Manpower Studies report (Pearson, 1986) of a shortfall in the number of graduates required by employers. Staff with qualifications in technology, particularly electronics and computing, have been in high demand for some years, but demand in other work, such as accountancy and management, is also high. Well-qualified graduates have been in high demand for some time, and the same is probably true of young people leaving school with good passes at GCE Ordinary or Advanced level. There are clearly implications here for employers who need to time their recruitment so that they can attract good quality candidates.

Three other factors may have longer-term effects on the supply of and demand for staff: general demographic changes, labour mobility and working hours.

The number of people entering and leaving the labour market is influenced by the birth rate and arrangements for retirement. According to the government's 'Labour force outlook for Great Britain' (1985), there will be substantial increases in the population of working age up to 1989, but it should remain roughly stable during the 1990s. However, the numbers of people available for work would be affected by changes similar to the increase in the numbers of working women, which characterised the seventies, or the recent entitlement for women to continue working beyond the age of sixty.

Labour mobility is affected primarily by employment prospects, environmental considerations and house prices. A study by Atkinson and Purkiss (1983) suggested that in the UK almost one-third of the labour force changes jobs over a period of one year. Younger people, particularly those under thirty, and highly educated people, were the most likely to move. There has been a gradual shift in population away from conurbations, such as Greater London and the West Midlands, and also sizeable increases in the number of people living in the south-east and south-west of England, and East Anglia (*Regional trends 20*, 1985). House prices both reflect this trend, and exacerbate it. Generally, prices are much higher in areas of high employment, and the difference in house prices between southern England and other parts of the UK may prove to be decisive for staff contemplating a move.

There has been a small reduction in the average working week over the past fifteen years. Men in non-manual occupations worked an average of 37.1 hours in 1983, and women worked for 36.1 hours. These figures compare with 39.1 and 37.1 hours respectively for 1970. A survey carried out on behalf of the European Association for Personnel Management (Cosijn, 1985) indicated that a number of organisations are developing new ways of organising working time to take account of reduced working hours and increased holiday entitlements. It is also noted that 20 per cent of UK employees work on a part-time basis, and this proportion is growing. There are implications here for librarians, who may wish to experiment with different working patterns in order to retain services over long opening hours.

The library and information workforce

The library profession has changed substantially over the past twenty years. There have been major shifts in the size and age structure of the workforce, in qualifications and in the job market.

The number of Library Association members grew from 10,800 in 1970 to 24,000 in 1985 of whom 14,000 were in employment. The exact size of the library and information profession is difficult to determine, since a number of people will not be members of professional bodies, but the latest census carried out by the Department of Education and Science in 1981 suggested that around 19,000 people were engaged in library and information work. An important study by Moore and Kempson (1985) has estimated that there were some 3,500 unemployed librarians in 1981, representing 15.4 per cent of the workforce. Allowing for new entrants and wastage from the workforce, the study suggested that by 1985 there was a pool of around 3,000 librarians who were unemployed and actively seeking work.

There has been a substantial change in the age structure of the qualified workforce. There was a large number of new entrants to the profession in the early 1970s, and a fairly high wastage rate, particularly among women. This meant that the largest cohort consisted of staff aged between twenty-two and thirty, and the cohorts of older staff at that time were much smaller.

During the 1980s, this age profile has changed. According to Moore and Kempson (1985), the combination of reduced wastage, a higher entry age for people joining the profession and the large cohort from the 1970s moving up the age range, means that the largest age group is between thirty and forty. This bulge of people working through the profession has major implications for the recruitment and deployment of staff. It is extremely unlikely that there will be sufficient middle and senior management posts to satisfy the aspirations of all the members of this cohort, so job satisfaction and career enhancement will prove to be major challenges for them.

Library and information work has moved, in common with other professions such as teaching, towards a graduate workforce. The practice which was common before 1970 of working and studying part-time for professional qualifications has largely changed, so that most new entrants study for a postgraduate qualification or undergraduate degree. Although enrolments are divided evenly between the two types of course, the differing course lengths and wastage rates means that library school-leavers are roughly 60 per cent postgraduates and 40 per cent undergraduates. The number of students completing courses in 1983, 1984 and 1985 remained constant at around 1,100 each year. The shortage of librarians with a technological background is emphasised by statistics giving the first destination and employment of *University graduates 1984* (1985). Only twelve graduates with an applied science degree entered library and information work, compared with ninety-seven with pure science degrees and 554 with humanities and social science degrees.

Approximately 70 per cent of library school-leavers find work within six months, according to Library Association surveys carried out in 1983, 1984 and 1985 (Library Association, 1985d). At least 7 per cent of the remainder, some eighty students each year, are unemployed and must be added to the pool of 3,000 librarians who are seeking work. Even allowing for job opportunities created by natural wastage, this means that the competition for junior professional jobs is very intense and is likely to remain so unless alternative job markets are opened up or the number of library school students is reduced.

In its evidence to the University Grants Committee/National Advisory Body Transbinary Group on Librarianship and Information Studies, which is considering demand and supply for staff, the Library Association (1985d) emphasised the importance of recruiting people with appropriate personal qualities. In addition to the traditional requirements for organisational and interpersonal skills, librarianship requires staff who are imaginative, highly motivated with

Table 2.1

Staff employed in UK polytechnic libraries at 31 January 1985

	Chief librarians	%	Other professional librarians	%	Non-professional staff	%	Total	%
Male	29	96.67	247.00	37.28	95.54	10.94	371.54	23.73
Female	1	3.33	415.52	62.72	777.76	89.06	1194.28	76.27
Totals	30	100.00	662.52	100.00	873.30	100.00	1565.82	100.00

Source: Council of Polytechnic Librarians (1985), *Staffing survey*, COPOL

good communication and management skills. A study by Armstrong and Large (1986) has suggested that these qualities are decisive in the selection of staff.

The workforce in polytechnic libraries

Some 1,566 people were employed in UK polytechnic libraries, according to the staffing survey carried out by the Council of Polytechnic Librarians on 31 January 1985 (Table 2.1). In order to gauge the scale of professional staff recruitment of this sector, a survey of advertised vacancies was carried out. A total of ninety-five posts were advertised over a two-year period in the major recruitment journal the *Library Asssociation Record Vacancies Supplement*. If an allowance is made for posts advertised locally, it is likely that between seventy and ninety professional staff are recruited each year. This suggests an annual turnover rate of between 10 and 13 per cent.

The ninety-five advertised posts reflected a range of library work, although experience in information technology or computer systems was sought for many posts. The majority of advertisements (80 per cent) specified that applicants should be qualified or chartered librarians, although a handful mentioned qualifications in information science as an alternative. About half of the posts required applicants to be graduates, and one or two libraries specified that candidates should hold good honours degrees. The advertised posts were evenly spread over junior and middle-range professional grades (up to NJC Senior Officer 1 or Burnham Lecturer II). Only thirteen senior management positions on higher scales were advertised over the two-year period that was surveyed.

The recruitment rate for non-professional staff is more difficult to gauge, but it is likely to be rather higher than that for qualified librarians. A turnover of 15 to 18 per cent per year, or 130 to 160 jobs per year is likely. An interesting perspective on staff turnover is given in a survey by Margaret Slater (1978) of some 1,770 libraries and information units. She found that half of the units had no turnover at all, whereas the other units experienced an average turnover each year of 45 per cent! A human explanation would be that staff leaving a workplace may have an unsettling effect on other staff, who in turn are motivated to leave. It may also suggest that high staff mobility in particular areas may be related to local work or environmental factors.

The increasing concern with equal opportunities has been taken up within the library profession. The implications for recruitment are considered in the next section, but it would be appropriate to note here the imbalance between men and women employed in polytechnic libraries. Pankhurst's survey (1981) found that although 60 per cent of professional posts were held by women, they held only 10 per cent of senior management positions. The 1985 staffing survey (Table 2.1) suggests that this situation has not altered.

The staff selection process

New staff recruitment and the alternatives

When a member of staff resigns, the natural response in most institutions is to recruit a replacement. This is often the appropriate solution, and it may be the easiest case to steer through polytechnic and local authority decision-making processes. Making a case for new staffing arrangements can be difficult at a time of financial constraint, when any difference may be seen as growth.

However, library services develop over a period of time and staffing needs will change too. A resignation from a member of staff, or more rarely a new staff post, provides an opportunity to reassign duties among other staff or recruit someone with different skills and experience. There are also several alternatives to full-time staff: part-time or casual staff, job-sharing, contract or consultancy work may all be better solutions, depending on the work involved and the potential labour market.

The reallocation of duties and responsibilities among existing staff may be an imposed solution if there is insufficient money available to cover replacements. However, this may also provide a means of giving staff new experience. Rogerson (1981) referred to a 'loosening of formality in respect of shared labour between Technical Services and Reader Services Divisions' as a consequence of local staff reductions. Since certain skills are at a premium, particularly those involving new technology, it may be appropriate to train existing staff in new areas of expertise and then redeploy them as opportunities arise. The problem of career stagnation, particularly for those librarians in the bulge, has already been referred to. New experience, even within the same organisation, will help to maintain their morale, particularly if it is accompanied by increased salary or status. This approach may also be appropriate with non-professional staff, who have very limited career progression in many libraries. Certain duties, such as the supervision of routine work, financial and record-keeping duties, dealing with simple and directional enquiries, may be most effectively carried out by senior non-professional staff, and may release professional librarians' time for other duties. The Library Association's *Professional and non-professional duties in libraries* (1974) may be useful here.

The alternatives to full-time appointments may be more attractive to employers and employees alike. Part-time working is well-established in libraries and is particularly suitable for staff who have other commitments, either at home, or with other work or studies. An example would be the audiovisual technician or designer who has freelance work for whom part-time work offers a secure basic income. Job-sharing, 'a form of part-time employment whereby two people voluntarily share the responsibility of one full-time position' (Equal Opportunities Commission), is still relatively rare in libraries. A report by Sorby and Pascoe (1983) has discussed the advantages and disadvantages of this arrangement, and has suggested types of work where job-sharing is particularly suitable. Work requiring a broad range of skills, subject to extreme fluctuations in pressure, or which is highly creative or very monotonous is considered to have job-sharing potential. Working with visual display units is an obvious candidate.

Contract and consultancy work has been a major growth area in recent years, in libraries and elsewhere. The negative side to this is the use of short-term and temporary contracts as an alternative to full-time employment. Manpower Services Commission projects, such as retrospective cataloguing work, have been funded as a response to unemployment, and many limited-term appointments are made because the employer does not wish to be committed to a permanent member of staff. Temporary contracts, which are particularly associated with secretarial work, can also be used to create additional job opportunities for librarians and may also be the best way of staffing specific projects. The HERTIS Information for Industry unit at the Hatfield Polytechnic Library, for example, appoints staff in this way to assist with large scale contracts undertaken for member firms. Consultancy work has proven to be an attractive career for many staff in library and information work, with its own particular challenge and satisfaction. Librarians faced with tasks requiring specialist expertise may find the use of consultants appropriate. The selection of a new automated system, for example, may justify a consultancy arrangement.

Documentation for staff recruitment

According to Drucker (1985), executives spend more time 'making people decisions than on anything else'. Also, 'no other decisions are so long in their consequences or so difficult to unmake'. Careful preparation and documentation provide the basis for good recruitment decisions.

Personnel management practice identifies three stages in job documentation: the job description, job specification and personnel specification. The whole activity is based on the process of job analysis. In practice, most polytechnic libraries tend to produce one document which combines all three elements, often used as the job details or further particulars sent to potential candidates. A single document sometimes serves for a number of similar posts, such as library assistants or subject librarians. Nevertheless, standard personnel practice has much to commend it, since the results are relevant for other personnel management activities such as staff appraisal and training. The elements are summarised below.

The process of job analysis is described by Plumbley (1985) as an attempt 'to measure the "hole" so that in turn we can measure possible "pegs"'. This involves producing an accurate description of the work which is to be done, and how it relates to other work carried out within the organisation. In order to gain a full picture of the work involved, it may be necessary to talk to staff doing the work and their supervisor, and it may even be appropriate to observe the work being carried out. A useful perspective on an individual's work might come from relating the purpose of the job to the objectives of the library and the section where the post is based. This is particularly important as libraries and work patterns develop. Although this process can be time-consuming, it is essential for the staff involved in recruitment to have a very clear idea of the requirements of the vacancy. Boydell's guide (1973) will help here.

The immediate result of job analysis is the job description, which should contain a general outline of the work, including the major duties and responsibilities involved. The following checklist illustrates the information which should be included:

1 *job title*: this should be as descriptive, accurate (and concise!), as possible;
2 *department, section or site*
3 *purpose of the job*: the main aim of the post should be summarised, for example, 'to deal in a prompt and intelligent manner with enquiries' or 'to ensure that library resources are fully exploited by art and design students';
4 *relationships to other staff*, that is, to whom the individual reports, and for whom they are directly responsible;
5 *principal duties and responsibilities*: the key activities should be listed, perhaps under six or eight headings. A subject librarian, for example, may be primarily concerned with stock selection, dealing with enquiries, user education, budgetary control, on-line searching and liaison with academic staff;
6 *working relationships*: in addition to listing the library and polytechnic staff whom the postholder will work with, it is necessary to indicate the level of other contacts, such as with academic staff, students, library suppliers and other external organisations.

A difficulty encountered with job descriptions is that they may be seen by members of staff as a full statement of their duties at work, and they may either be reluctant to carry out tasks which are not specified, or demand compensation for what they consider to be additional work. Frequently, a request from an established member of staff for a copy of their job description is a danger sign which requires investigation! Although it is important that safeguards should be adopted which ensure that increased responsibilities are rewarded, it may be appropriate to incorporate an agreed policy statement to ensure some flexibility in staffing. Middlesex Polytechnic, for example, includes a note in its conditions of service that an 'appointment is to the polytechnic as a whole rather than to an individual site'. More open-ended statements in job descriptions, such as 'other duties may be determined by the polytechnic librarian' may be acceptable to unions if accompanied by a qualifying phrase such as 'after appropriate consultation'. Guidance on the preparation of job descriptions is provided by Ungerson (1983), and the work of the former Office of Scientific and

Technical Information Manpower Project on the classification and description of library posts is described by Sergean (1976).

The job specification is the next stage of the analysis. This details the specific tasks involved in the post and identifies the knowledge and skills (including social skills) necessary to perform them. The final stage of this process is the production of the personnel specification, which determines the kind of person required to do the job. The Rodger's seven-point plan (1974) is a widely used system for classifying attributes:

1 *physical make-up* including appearance, manner, state of health;
2 *attainments* in terms of qualifications and experience;
3 *general intelligence*: the level required to perform the job;
4 *special aptitudes* such as numerical ability, technical knowledge, practical skills;
5 *interests* which may be helpful for a person doing the job, such as social or intellectual pursuits;
6 *disposition* such as the ability to work under pressure, ability to work unsocial hours, self-reliance, leadership qualities;
7 *circumstances* such as accommodation, travel and salary expectations.

Another widely used system is Fraser's five-point plan (1978), which uses the following headings: impact on other people; qualifications; innate abilities; motivation; and adjustment.

The personnel specification provides an important framework for the recruitment and selection process. Once the essential and desirable attributes are determined, the advertisements and information for candidates can be prepared. It should be noted, however, that the higher the level of personnel specification, the fewer candidates will be eligible. The ideal candidate is unlikely to exist, or if they do they will probably be working for another organisation on a much higher salary!

Attracting the candidates

Advertising for library staff is relatively straightforward. *The Library Association Record Vacancies Supplement* is firmly established as the major recruitment source for professional staff, and although some polytechnic posts are advertised in the national press, notably *The Guardian* and the *Times Higher Education Supplement*, this is unlikely to attract a wider field of candidates.

Library assistants and other non-professional staff are usually recruited through the local press and, since the free giveaways have established a large readership, they are often the most cost-effective medium. Two types of staff may present recruitment problems. Since junior professional staff are often paid on relatively low scales, personnel officers may prefer to advertise locally on the assumption that staff will not be prepared to move long distances for the salaries offered. The recruitment of graduates for non-professional posts may also be difficult. In order to attract a good field it will be best to advertise nationally in non-specialist publications such as the daily press. This, however, is very expensive and produces very large numbers of applications. *Current Vacancies*, published by the Central Services Unit for Graduate Careers and Appointments Services in Manchester, and distributed free, is a reasonable alternative, but advertising space is still expensive. There is potential here for a co-operative scheme to advertise and select staff, since many libraries regularly employ graduates for initial library experience, and there are many good potential applicants (although a shortage of candidates with a background in technology). Links with the Standing Conference of National and University Libraries (SCONUL) trainee scheme or the Library Association may offer a way forward.

There are several alternatives to advertising in the press, although it is generally standard practice to advertise in order to ensure fair and open competition. Local radio may offer free publicity to employers and may attract staff new to library work. Local Jobcentres and careers offices will advertise vacancies without charge and direct potential candidates to employers. It should be noted that job-seekers are not filtered, and some unsuitable people may be encouraged to apply. Links with local schools and careers offices may be profitable. Teachers and careers advisers usually welcome advice on employers' requirements and may be able to recommend suitable young people.

Many candidates send unsolicited applications to potential employers. Practice in dealing with these varies, but a minimum response might suggest alternative sources of job information, and at best these approaches may produce candidates for permanent or temporary work. Short-term contracts are also arranged by recruitment agencies active in the library and information field, such as the Department of Employment's Professional and Executive Register, Aslib Professional Recruitment Ltd and 'Task Force Pro Libra'. These agencies, which also arrange permanent employment, charge a fee to employers. Useful guidance on attracting candidates is provided in Ray (1980) and the Advisory, Conciliation and Arbitration Service series of advisory booklets (no.3, 1985; no.6, 1986).

The initial selection process

The ideal shortlist, according to Drucker (1985), should contain about five names. Reaching this point may not always be easy, but clear criteria, good information for candidates and well-designed application forms will provide a firm framework.

The essential and desirable attributes listed in the personnel specification should be made clear to potential applicants in advertising and job details. A self-selection process may take place at this stage, since candidates should make a personal judgement about whether they have the appropriate qualifications and experience to carry out the work. Recruitment is essentially a matching process, which implies that the candidate also needs to decide that the post is right for him. A full description of the organisation, the salary and conditions should be provided with the job description.

Although application forms have limitations, there is no doubt that a standardised arrangement of information is helpful in the initial sifting of candidates. Some information will be required from all applicants: personal details, education and employment histories, qualifications and the names of referees. Personal details should include a question relating to whether the applicant is registered disabled, but should exclude details of personal circumstances unless these are strictly relevant to the post. It is useful to ask for a note of duties in posts held, and to provide some space for information concerning hobbies and interests. This information will probably be sufficient for most non-professional posts. Indeed, long application forms may demoralise applicants who have relatively few qualifications and little work experience as they may have to leave large areas blank.

Professional appointments will require more information, and a different approach (certainly a different application form!) will be required. Employers will wish to know about the responsibilities and experience gained in previous posts, and details of professional activities, teaching, research and publications. There is a danger, here, of producing elaborate forms using a large number of questions. A more useful approach is to invite candidates to summarise their relevant experience under two or three broad headings, and allocate space on the application form for them. In addition to eliciting information, this approach also provides a useful test of the candidate's ability to select and communicate what they feel is relevant to the post. Alternative approaches would be to invite a letter of application to complement information given on an application form, or to rely on the preparation of a curriculum vitae. Any preference for typed information, or block capitals, should be made clear. Edwards (1983) has provided guidance on the use of application forms, and an Advisory, Conciliation and Arbitration Service advisory booklet (no.3, 1985) contains examples of designs.

Factual information from written applications should provide the basis for the initial selection, and an appropriate shortlist may be established on the basis of qualifications and experience. This process may be more difficult with school- or college-leavers, where a number of candidates may have very similar qualifications and little experience of work. It is probably worth arranging to see rather more than a conventional shortlist in order to provide an opportunity for as many candidates as possible to be considered. If necessary further sifting of candidates should be carried out to identify a suitable number for interview.

The importance of attributes other than qualifications has been emphasised by a British Library study carried out by Armstrong and Large (1986). Personal qualities relating to personality, attitude and drive are particularly valued by employers, and evidence about them may be obtained from application forms and through referees. Career progression may provide some clues here, but unusual moves or gaps without work may have quite reasonable explanations. These, and other areas, may be probed by talking to referees. Personal contacts are invaluable (Half, 1985), but it is essential to respect confidentiality. The usual method of assessing personal qualities, and making the final selection, is by interviewing.

Table 2.2

The Institute of Personnel Management Recruitment Code

Recruiters' obligations

1 Job advertisements should state clearly the form of reply desired, in particular, whether this should be a formal application form or by curriculum vitae. Preferences should also be stated if handwritten replies are required.
2 An acknowledgement or reply should be made promptly to each applicant by the employing organisation or its agent.
3 Applicants should be informed of the progress of the selection procedures, what these will be (for example, group selection, aptitude tests), the steps and time involved and the policy regarding expenses.
4 Detailed personal information (for example, religion, medical history, place of birth, family background) should not be called for unless it is relevant to the selection process.
5 Before applying for references, potential employers must secure the permission of the applicant.
6 Applications must be treated as confidential.

Applicant's obligations

1 Advertisements should be answered in the way requested (for example, telephone for application form, provide brief details, send curriculum vitae).
2 Appointments and other arrangements must be kept, or the recruiter be informed promptly if the candidate discovers an agreed meeting cannot take place.
3 The recruiter should be informed as soon as a candidate decides not to proceed with the application.
4 Only accurate information should be given in applications and in reply to recruiters' questions.
5 Information given by a prospective employer must be treated as confidential, if so requested.

Interviewing

Although formal interviews are often the focus of the selection process, it is common practice to arrange for candidates and existing library staff to meet informally. A library tour and an introduction to the work involved with the post will provide an opportunity for library staff and candidates to exchange information. This will help candidates to relax and should help both employer and job-seekers make good decisions. In the appointment of professional staff, it may be necessary to allow a full day for an introductory programme and interviews.

The IPM recruitment code (Table 2.2) emphasises the importance of keeping candidates informed of the progress of their applications. It is particularly useful for people being invited for interview to have full information concerning the arrangements for the day, including the names of staff who they will meet, particularly those on the interview panel. It is also helpful to forewarn candidates about when and how the final result will be communicated to them.

Given that interviewing is an imperfect method of selecting staff (some alternatives are noted later), it is probably also true that the effectiveness of interview panels diminishes as their size increases! The chief librarian or a senior colleague will be present, together with the immediate supervisor of the person to be appointed, and the head of the department or section where the post is based. Staff from outside the polytechnic library – such as representatives of the directorate, academic board or personnel department – may also be involved in appointments for senior staff and subject librarians. It may also be appropriate to involve an advisor from outside the institution, such as another polytechnic librarian, where specialist staff or internal candidates are involved. Normally, the most senior member of staff chairs the proceedings.

A full treatment of interviewing technique is beyond the scope of this chapter, but guidance in this area has been provided by an Advisory, Conciliation and Arbitration Service advisory booklet (no.6, 1986), Plumbley (1981, 1985) and Goodworth (1983). It may, however, be appropriate to summarise the main elements of good practice.

The objectives of interviewing should be kept clearly in mind: to establish whether the candidate is suitable for the job, to ensure that the candidate has a clear idea of the work involved, and to make the candidate feel that he has had a fair hearing.

Careful planning is essential. Interviewers should brief themselves thoroughly on the job and personal specifications, and on the candidates (a chronological chart showing educational and career progression for each person may help here). A checklist of areas to be covered should be agreed by the panel and allocated to each interviewer. Rodger's seven-point plan (1974) will ensure that all the ground will be covered. The interview room should be free of distractions and arranged with the appropriate degree of formality consistent with the level of appointment. Non-professional staff, particularly school-leavers, will probably respond best to an informal setting; with more senior staff, the formality of a panel interview might be softened by the interviewers and candidate sitting around a table, rather than on either side.

Some care should be taken to put candidates at ease. The interviewers should be carefully introduced, and the format of the interview explained. The candidate should be encouraged to talk by asking about matters which will be familiar and expected, such as his education and work experience.

A conversational style will stimulate the candidate to talk and will thus provide more information about his qualities to the interviewers. The use of open questions will encourage the candidate to express ideas and attitudes and are a useful way of revealing strengths and weaknesses. It is best if interviewers attempt to keep a dialogue going by moving easily between topics and questions. The candidate will be inhibited by interviewers expressing opinions or using leading questions, and these should be avoided.

Practical considerations should be checked at the end of the interview. Matters such as salary, hours of work, leave, accommodation and travel should be raised to ensure that they are clear to the candidate. This may cover some of the candidate's own points, but quickly checking through these items will provide an opportunity for him to prepare his own questions. These should then be answered, and it is worth checking with the candidate at the end of the interview that he feels that nothing relevant has been omitted.

A final question should be to ask whether the candidate would accept the post if it were offered. Any hesitation here should be explored, since the candidate should by now have had enough information about the post and the organisation to make a decision. The candidate should leave the interview with a clear indication of how and when the result will be notified.

The choice of candidate should be based on an objective evaluation of the whole range of information available. Personal prejudice, based on appearance or manner, should be eliminated, and the candidates should be measured against the personnel specification for the post. Brief interview notes on each candidate, using the agreed criteria, should allow comparisons to be made. Comments from staff who have met candidates informally should be requested by interviewers, though they should be discouraged from making a specific choice since this may cause conflict with the interviewers' decision.

It is essential to let candidates know the outcome of their interviews as soon as possible. If all candidates can wait until an interview session is finished, this allows the matter to be cleared up quickly and eliminates the uncertainty. However, this is not always practicable, and it may be necessary to telephone candidates on the following day. Any further delay should be avoided if at all possible.

Alternatives to interviewing

Although interviewing is used universally as a selection method, it has a number of weaknesses. It is particularly susceptible to the distortions that arise from any interpersonal contact. The interview situation is unique, and brings its own pressure which may affect the behaviour of both interviewer and candidate. Hannabuss (1982) and Arvey and Campion (1983) contain useful commentaries on the limitations of interviewing. The careful planning and conduct of interviews will reduce the distortions, and this is an area where staff training can help.

There are a number of methods that can act as alternatives to interviewing. Perhaps, more accurately, they will provide information that will supplement what can be assessed in a formal interview. These are sometimes used in polytechnic libraries.

Job sample tests, which assess the candidate's ability to perform the tasks associated with the post, are particularly suitable where skills can be measured simply. For example, applicants for secretarial work can be asked to carry out a number of keyboarding tasks that are typical of the job, and potential casual staff may be asked to sort one or two piles of books ready for reshelving. Care must be taken to ensure that the tests are representative of the work and are administered equally to all candidates. Job samples are more difficult to use in assessment of professional staff, since local knowledge of systems and people is so important in library work, and time considerations may rule out any thorough investigation. Nevertheless, it may be appropriate to test professional skills and problem-solving abilities by asking candidates to comment on real or potential issues at work. For example, applicants for an information technology post might be asked to comment on existing provision and suggest how this might be developed with a specified sum of money, or potential subject librarians might be asked to say what criteria they would use for book selection or the allocation of money. This approach may be particularly useful where internal candidates are involved where an alternative to judgements based on personal knowledge of the applicants is required.

There are examples of other techniques being used in libraries to help with selection. Feedback from informal contact with library staff has been noted earlier, though this may perhaps be best used as a safety net to ensure that no shortcomings have been missed at interview. It may be considered appropriate to involve library staff formally in the appointment of senior posts. One way would be to include a representative on the interview panel, but an alternative used by at least one institution has been to invite candidates to address a staff meeting.

Group selection procedures, which involve an assessment of candidates' behaviour in group activity, can provide information about interpersonal skills, powers of expression and leadership qualities, but need to be administered by skilled observers. This is also true of psychological and personality tests, which must be administered by trained staff. These techniques are rarely used in libraries. Pendlebury (1983) has a useful summary and guide to further reading.

The employment of staff

Appointment and conditions of service

The arrangements relating to the appointment of staff will normally be the responsibility of a specialist department within the institution or local authority. Normally, standard letters offering appointment will be used, accompanied by particulars of the conditions of service that apply to the post. However, it should be noted that an oral contract of employment will be established if a job offer is made and accepted following an interview, so it is important that statements made at this time are carefully phrased since they will be considered to be part of the contract. Similarly, job descriptions and information given at interview should be accurate, and qualified where necessary such as by indicating that a quoted salary would be confirmed by the staffing office.

Written statements containing the main terms of employment must be supplied to all staff (except certain part-time staff) and should include the job title, salary scale, payment times, hours of work, holiday and sick leave arrangements, pension schemes and the period of notice required, together with a note of discipline and grievance procedures. In practice, polytechnic library staff are employed under one of three schemes covering further education teachers: Burnham; Local Authorities' Administrative, Professional, Technical and Clerical Services (NJC); and the Inner London Education Authority (ILEA).

According to the 1985 staffing survey (Table 2.1, p.30) there were almost 700 professional librarians employed in polytechnic libraries. Of these, 380 were employed on NJC scales, and 110 were employed on ILEA scales. The remaining 200 staff were employed on Burnham grades, although seventy-seven of these had modified conditions of service.

There has been a continuing professional debate about the most appropriate salary scales for professional staff working in college and polytechnic libraries; this is also referred to elsewhere in the book. Hertfordshire pioneered the concept of the tutor librarian in the 1950s, when librarians with a teaching responsibility were appointed to colleges. Many librarians feel strongly that they have an educational role which should be recognised by appointments on Burham salaries and conditions (Revill, 1981). This view is supported by trends in educational practice towards resource-based work, which directly involves librarians in the design and management of student learning. Both the Library Association (1985c) and the National Association of Teachers in Further and Higher Education (1982) have advocated that senior library staff and those with teaching responsibilities should have Burnham appointments. It is also true, however, that it is often difficult to explain the educational role of librarians to people outside an academic library environment, and there remains a varied pattern of grading and conditions of service across different institutions.

The main focus of concern is on the salaries, and hours of work and leave entitlement which are associated with Burnham and NJC contracts. Burnham salary scales are longer and generally better paid than the NJC equivalents, and have teachers' working hours and holiday entitlements. Most library staff with Burnham appointments, in common with other senior academic staff, do not normally take the full entitlement of time off. In many institutions 'modified' Burnham contracts are used which give librarians a similar working week and holiday entitlement to that enjoyed by NJC staff. In some cases 'hybrid' appointments are made, where librarians are appointed on NJC contracts, but Burnham salaries are used as 'convenience' scales. The Library Association and trade unions are opposed to 'hybrid' appointments, but many senior polytechnic library staff feel that a 'modified' Burnham arrangement may provide a basis for ending the present uncertainties. It should perhaps be noted that ILEA staff have their own salary scales and conditions of service which are similar to, though generally more generous than, those for NJC staff.

Conditions of service documents

The detailed arrangements covering conditions of service for polytechnic library staff (and others) are given in published schemes. Burnham appointments are covered by the *Scheme of conditions of service* for further education teachers in England and Wales (National Joint Council for Teachers in England and Wales, 1981), also known as the 'silver book' from the colour of its cover. The 'purple book' covers NJC appointments and is also published as the *Scheme of conditions of service* by the National Joint Council for Local Authorities' Administrative, Professional, Technical and Clerical Services (1975). Both schemes are updated by loose-leaf amendments. Inner London Education Authority staff are covered by the ILEA Staff Code agreed at the Whitley Council and issued from the ILEA Establishment Branch. There may in addition be policy statements and agreements covering individual local authorities and institutions.

Conduct at work

Senior library staff who have responsibility for other employees should be aware of the legislative framework which affects people at work. Indeed, many Acts of Parliament place responsibilities on employees too, and it is essential that these should be clear to all concerned. It must be emphasised that this brief outline of areas covered by legislation and agreements is not intended to be comprehensive, nor is any interpretation of the law intended. Such matters should be referred to legal experts for advice.

The conditions of service documents described in the preceding section are produced by joint councils which are representative of both employers and trade unions. Many of the issues that arise at work will be covered by these documents, together with local agreements. Salary scales for teachers are discussed in the Burnham Further Education Committee, and published in a separate document, *Scales of salaries for teachers in further education, England and Wales* (Department of Education and Science, 1983). Conduct at work is also regulated by legislation, and a number of major changes have taken place in the UK since 1970 covering matters such as equal opportunities, health and safety and relationships between employers and employees.

Many potential difficulties at work will be overcome by good working practice, following advice given elsewhere in this book on such matters as clearly defined responsibilities, proper supervision and training, and good communications. The Advisory, Conciliation and Arbitration Service *Code of practice* (1980) has provided useful guidelines on maintaining good relations between employers and staff. Professional staff will generally be bound by the Library Association 'Code of professional conduct' (Library Association, 1985a) and the 'purple book' has noted that 'the public is entitled to demand of the local government officer conduct of the highest standard' (National Joint Council for Local Authorities' Administrative, Professional, Technical and Clerical Services, 1975, p.67).

Absence from work has been studied by the Industrial Society (1985), and their survey suggested that an average of eleven days are lost each year per employee owing to sickness, giving an annual rate of 4.6 per cent. It was found that the absence rate increased in larger organisations. Careful records of sick leave should be kept, both in order to comply with Department of Health and Social Security regulations, and also to ensure that members of staff receive attention for any difficulties that may be responsible for absence.

Working conditions are the concern of the Health and Safety at Work Act 1974, which imposes a duty on 'every employer to ensure, so far as is reasonably practicable, the health, safety and welfare at work of all his employees'. The Act also requires employees 'to take reasonable care and safety of himself and of other persons who may be affected by his acts or omissions at work'. In addition to ensuring that staff are familiar with emergency procedures and local policy documents, good preventative measures should be adopted. It should be noted that most accidents in libraries are associated with falls, ladders and steps, lifting and handling and people striking against fixed objects. The health and safety practice of a successful British store group is described by Burling (1985) and many of the points raised are relevant to libraries. The Health and Safety Executive and the Health Education Council publish a large number of booklets which provide practical advice.

The employment of disabled persons is one area which is included in most equal opportunities policies adopted by polytechnics and local authorities. The Disabled Persons (Employment) Act 1944 established a voluntary register of disabled people and imposed a requirement for employers of twenty people or more to employ a quota of registered disabled staff. The normal quota is 3 per cent of the total number of employees, although there are not enough registered disabled people for all organisations to reach their quota and most local authorities fall some way below this target. It is not an offence to be below quota, and an arrangement exists whereby such employers may obtain a permit to allow them to recruit staff who are not disabled. A study of Sheffield employers (Jones and Pedler, 1985) found that most had prejudices against employing disabled people that were proved to be unjustified. For example, disabled staff tend to have lower rates of sickness and turnover than the average for all workers. The same article argued that employers should look for the same attributes and performance levels in disabled staff that they would require in others and that these staff should be fully integrated into the organisation. A survey carried out in the United States (Warren, 1979) found that most disabled people in libraries were employed in cataloguing and similar work. The Manpower Services Commission has produced a *Code of good practice on the employment of disabled people* (1984) and can provide advice on grants for equipment to mitigate the effects of disabilities.

Discrimination at work is also outlawed by the Race Relations Act 1976 and the Sex Discrimination Act 1975. This legislation makes it illegal to discriminate directly or indirectly on the basis of colour, race, nationality, ethnic or national origins or sex. Since the survey of polytechnic libraries referred to earlier (Pankhurst, 1981) showed that there was evidence of discrimination against women, it is likely that employers will need to adopt a more positive approach with all groups who are likely to be affected.

Employees' rights, disciplinary procedures and the dismissal of staff are covered by a number of statutes, including the Employment Protection (Consolidation) Act 1978 and the Employment Act 1980, in addition to the arrangements contained in the conditions of service documents. The Advisory, Conciliation and Arbitration Service *Code of practice 1* (1980) deals with disciplinary procedures, and codes of local practice will specify the manner in which formal proceedings are to be handled. It is clear that formal disciplinary action needs to be carefully handled, but most difficulties will be resolved on an informal basis. It should be emphasised that open and regular communication should allow potential problems to be resolved at an early stage.

Conclusion

The 'mystery' that Drucker suggested is associated with good staff appointments can be solved by careful planning and research, and sound procedures, as in all good management practice. Librarians are likely to have many of the professional skills that are highly relevant to the recruitment and employment process, for library work involves constant contact with people and knowledge of sources of information. Advice is available from colleagues with responsibilities in the area of personnel, and there are many good publications on this area, many of which are produced by government departments concerned to encourage good industrial relations. The most important additional help, however, will come from training. Courses on interviewing techniques and inter-personal skills work are widely available and are likely to prove a sound investment.

References

Advisory, Conciliation and Arbitration Service (1980), *Code of practice 1: disciplinary practice and procedures in employment*, London, HMSO.

Advisory, Conciliation and Arbitration Service advisory booklets: no.3 (1985), *Personnel records*; no.5 (1985), *Absence*; no.6 (1986), *Recruitment and selection*; no.10 (1986), *Employment policies*, London, Advisory, Conciliation and Arbitration Service.

Armstrong, C.J. and Large, J.A. (1986), 'Employment criteria in the library and information sector', *Education for Information*, vol.4, no.3 (September).

Arvey, R.D. and Campion, J.E. (1983), excerpts from 'The employment interview: A summary and review of recent research', *Journal of Library Administration*, vol.4, no.3 (Fall), pp.61–90.

Atkinson, G. and Purkiss, C. (1983), 'Recruitment and mobility of labour' in B. Ungerson (ed), *Recruitment handbook*, 3rd edn, Aldershot, Gower.

Boydell, T.H. (1973), *A guide to job analysis*, London, British Association for Commercial and Industrial Education.

Burling, P. (1985), 'Top marks', *Occupational Safety and Health*, November, pp.36–9.

Cosijn, E. (1985), 'European patterns in working time', *Personnel Management*, September, pp.33–6.

Department of Education and Science (1983), *Scale of salaries for teachers in further education, England and Wales, 1983*, London, HMSO.

Drucker, P.E. (1985), 'Getting things done: how to make people decisions', *Harvard Business Review*, July/August, pp.22–6.

Edwards, B.J. (1983), 'Application forms' in B. Ungerson (ed), *Recruitment handbook*, 3rd edn, Aldershot, Gower, pp.64–82.

Fraser, J.M. (1978), *Employment interviewing*, 5th edn, London, Macdonald and Evans.

Goodworth, C.T. (1983), *Effective interviewing for employment selection*, London, Business Books.

Half, R. (1985), 'How to really check an applicant's references', *The Office*, November, p.90.

Hannabuss, S. (1982), 'Interviews are here to stay', *An Leabharlann The Irish Library*, vol.11, no.4 (Winter), pp.118–27.

Industrial Society (1985), 'Absence from work', *Industrial Society*, December, pp.41–2.
Jones, J. and Pedler, M. (1985), 'A positive approach to the employment of disabled workers', *Personnel Management*, July, pp.21–2.
'Labour force outlook for Great Britain' (1985), *Employment Gazette*, vol.93, no.7 (July), pp.255–64.
Library Association (1974), *Professional and non-professional duties in libraries*, London, Library Association.
Library Association (1985a), 'Code of professional conduct' in *Library Association yearbook, 1985*, London, Library Association, pp.A88–89.
Library Association (1985b), *Evidence submitted to the UGC/NAB transbinary group on librarianship and information studies*, London, Library Association.
Library Association (1985c), *Recommended salaries and conditions of service for library staff in colleges and polytechnics*, London, Library Association.
Library Association (1985d), *Student employment 1984 – seven out of ten again* (report to the Manpower and Conditions of Service Committee), London, Library Association.
Manpower Services Commission (1984), *Code of good practice on the employment of disabled people*, Sheffield, Manpower Services Commission.
Moore, N. and Kempson, E. (1985), 'The size and structure of the library and information workforce in the United Kingdom', *Journal of Librarianship*, vol.17, no.1 (January), pp.1–16.
National Association of Teachers in Further and Higher Education (1982), *College libraries: policy statement*, London, National Association of Teachers in Further and Higher Education.
National Joint Council for Local Authorities' Administrative, Professional, Technical and Clerical Services (1975), *Scheme of conditions of service*, London, The Council.
National Joint Council for Teachers in England and Wales (1981), *Scheme of conditions of service*, London, The Council.
Pankhurst, R. (1981), 'Women and libraries, Part 1, Women in polytechnic libraries: a preliminary report on their representation at various levels', *Information and Library Manager*, vol.1, no.3 (December), p.88.
Pearson, R. (1986), *Graduate supply and availability to 1987 and beyond* (Institute of Manpower Studies Report,

no.114), Brighton, Institute of Manpower Studies.
Pendlebury, A.C. (1983), 'Testing intelligence and aptitude' in B. Ungerson (ed), *Recruitment handbook*, 3rd edn, Aldershot, Gower.
Plumbley, R. (1981), *The person for the job*, 2nd edn, London, Kogan Page.
Plumbley, P. (1985), *Recruitment and selection*, 4th edn, London, Institute of Personnel Management.
Ray, M. (1980), *Recruitment advertising*, London, Institute of Personnel Management.
Regional trends 20 (1985), London, HMSO, tables 2.5 and 2.6.
Revill, D.H. (1981), 'Academic librarians in colleges of further and higher education', *Journal of Librarianship*, vol.13, no.2 (April), pp.104–18.
Rodger, A. (1974), *The seven-point plan*, new edn, London, National Institute of Industrial Psychology.
Rogerson, I. (1981), 'Resource management in scarcity-staffing', *Library Association University College and Research Section Newsletter*, no.4 (June), pp.8–10.
Sergean, R. (1976), *Librarianship and information work: job characteristics and staffing needs* (British Library Research and Development Reports, no.5321 HC), London, British Library.
Slater, M. (1978), 'Career patterns and mobility in the library/information field', *Aslib Proceedings*, vol.30, no.10/11 (October/November), pp.344–51.
Sorby, B. and Pascoe, M. (1983), *Job sharing: the great divide?*, Leeds, Leeds Polytechnic School of Librarianship.
Ungerson, B. (ed) (1983), *Recruitment handbook*, 3rd edn, Aldershot, Gower.
University graduates 1984: Summary of first destination and employment (1985), Manchester, Central Services Unit for Graduate Careers and Appointments Services.
Warren, G.G. (1979), *The handicapped librarian*, Metuchen, NJ, Scarecrow Press.

3 Staff training and effectiveness

ANGELA CONYERS

The library's role in training and development

The training and development of staff is a key responsibility for the library manager. Continuing education has become of major importance to librarians with the rapid developments within the profession and changes in the social, political, technological and economic environment in which it operates. Polytechnic libraries have seen their fair share of these changes; institutional mergers, uncertainty about the future, declining budgets, staff cuts, lack of job mobility, poor promotion prospects – all are familiar features. This chapter looks at aspects of staff training in the polytechnic library and aims to show how training and development can contribute to the effective running of the library service. For, as economic constraints make it more difficult to find either time or money, staff training and development become even more crucial, not only as a means of coping with technological advances, but also for maintaining the level of job satisfaction and morale on which an efficient library service will depend.

At policy level, the library will aim to ensure that staff are well trained in order to carry out their work efficiently and are encouraged also in their personal development for the benefit both of the individual and of the library service itself. Some polytechnic libraries have a written policy that sets out how these broad aims are to be achieved in terms of the organisation of the training function. At Brighton Polytechnic this policy states:

> Learning Resources takes a responsibility as a management structure for ensuring that all staff have the best possible staff training and development opportunities: it also takes the responsibility for ensuring that staff are actively encouraged to make use of them.

Implicit in such a policy is the need to create an atmosphere of 'training awareness' in which individuals are encouraged to take advantage of opportunities available. Whether or not the policy is written down, a commitment to training and development will be demonstrated by the way that the function is organised and by the level of support it receives.

The organisation of training

All librarians with a management or supervisory role will have some responsibility for staff training, but it is common in polytechnic libraries to designate one person with a specific responsibility for organising or co-ordinating training and development activities. This may be the deputy librarian or another member of the senior management team. The varied aspects of this role are summarised by Jones and Jordan (1982, p.179):

> The job of the training officer is to operate as a 'fulcrum of training activity' and the 'catalyst for training change and development' and in this role has to create a training atmosphere in the library and an acceptance by line managers of their training responsibilities.

An important function is to enhance the profile of training within the library, as it is an aspect of work that can easily be overlooked among the many day-to-day problems with which managers have to contend. Co-operation between the training librarian and the other library managers is essential if the training programme is to be an integral part of the structure and be relevant to real needs. As any training librarian will be aware, it is not sufficient to set up an organisation for running training events and wait for the ideas to flow in. It will be necessary first to identify training needs from personal observations and from discussions with managers and other library staff and then to organise appropriate activities.

In the work of seeking out and developing ideas, it is common for the training librarian to work with a training group of representatives from all departments and different staff levels. This ensures that views are represented and that the load of planning events is shared, an important point with training usually only a subsidiary role among other duties for the training librarian. The structure of such a group generally includes a mechanism for regular changes of membership to allow a continuous flow of fresh ideas. At the same time, encouraging more people to join the group in itself provides a staff development opportunity which will eventually ensure that the library service has a large pool of training expertise on which to draw.

Having launched a successful programme, it is not possible to let it run each year without considering how far it continues to meet the library's present and future training needs. The organisation of training activities should regularly be preceded by an analysis of needs; as Pepper (1984, p.4) has stated: 'the question that must be asked of the training manager is "what *should* you be doing?" as well as "what *are* you doing?"' This requires that the training librarian as a member of the management team keeps alert to training aspects of any new developments. At the same time, the management team itself will wish to build in a feedback system with regular reviews of the training programme.

Financial and time constraints

The library with a commitment to training will try to ensure wherever possible that time and money do not act as deterrents:

> Training of staff must be accepted as part and parcel of the library routine. It should never be regarded as an optional extra which is vulnerable to be cut back in times of economic stringencies or when the workload is particularly heavy (Casteleyn, 1981, p.18).

Lack of money and lack of time for training were problems commonly cited by professional library staff in academic libraries in a survey conducted by Elliott (1983). With rising costs of conferences and travel, budgets rarely appear adequate to meet all needs and some fine judgements have to be made, with relevance to the actual job taking precedence over personal development.

The size of the training budget and its method of allocation vary: the library may have its own budget based on staff numbers or a set fixed sum each year, or put in bids to a central training pool. Sometimes the training group has a role in co-ordinating attendance at outside courses. Funds cover day release, short courses and conferences and, with funding intended primarily for external activities, the amount available for internal training is generally small. Some libraries put a ceiling on the amount they will normally spend on a course or conference and all will watch budgets carefully to ensure an equitable distribution.

Attempts have been made to quantify the amount of time an individual can or should spend in training. Some libraries set a maximum time for attendance at outside courses and conferences. At Brighton a target of 5 per cent of the working year (or eleven and a half days) is suggested. In practice, time spent varies according to individual needs and interests, but the target provides a useful yardstick and a reminder of the need to set aside some time for training on a regular basis.

Taking time off for training can in itself cause tension. Managers and other library staff may resent time taken as an unnecessary interruption from a busy workload. Those undertaking the training may be equally conscious of the work left behind to await their return. Even in polytechnics where vacation periods provide a 'natural break' for training events, there will be conflicts with other work to be done, requiring a commitment to the value of training and development activities.

Identification of training needs

Training is a continuous process and needs will vary for different groups of staff at different stages in their careers. Effective training must be given in the knowledge, skills and attitudes needed to run the library service. The first step is to identify what the training needs are. For new staff or pre-licentiates, libraries have been able to devise special programmes. For established staff, interests will be more diverse and much of the work will be on an individual basis.

In addition to the continuing need for professional development, there are two specific areas of training that have assumed a high priority for all groups of staff in recent years. One of these is information technology and the second is the area of management and inter-personal skills.

Induction of new staff

The objectives of an induction programme will be to enable the new member of staff to be absorbed as quickly as possible into the work environment, to understand the specific jobs assigned to them and to see how these fit into the broader aims of the library service and the polytechnic itself. A typical induction programme will cover the following stages:

1. introduction to the site or section; physical layout of the library, meeting immediate colleagues, domestic arrangements;
2. phased introduction to the particular job;
3. introduction to other areas of the library service;
4. introduction to the polytechnic as a whole.

Induction programmes of this type are used by most polytechnic libraries and it is common to include a checklist to ensure that all areas are covered. While much of the actual job of training will devolve on the immediate supervisor, a senior member of staff will usually be available to spend a brief time talking with the new member of staff. It is generally recognised that the first day is not the right occasion for the librarian to discourse at length on the polytechnic committee structure or the finer details of the library budget. Time is generally set aside later for such details. Similarly, visits to other areas are carefully timed so as to be of most benefit.

Attempting to cover too much too soon is a danger with any induction programme and visits arranged during the first few weeks or even months will be far more meaningful than a hasty tour in the first couple of days. Where the number of new staff warrants it, joint programmes of talks and visits have the added advantage that staff working in different sections get to know one another.

Pre-licentiate training

Polytechnic libraries have now gained experience of the pre-licentiate scheme and have general programmes approved by the Library Association for introducing the newly qualified professional to the work environment. These programmes will ensure coverage of a number of aspects of library work and will often include a special project and a planned system of job rotation and job exchange. Regular contact with the supervising librarian is built into the programme. At Middlesex, a rolling programme for pre-licentiates ensures that all necessary aspects are covered by visits, talks or practical work at some point of the year. This brings together those pre-licentiates who join at different dates.

Those libraries that already had established training programmes have worked into them the special requirements for pre-licentiates. The ideal arrangement is to view provision for pre-licentiates as part of the library's overall training responsibility for its staff. Within libraries that have only a small number of pre-licentiates, there is an inherent danger in singling them out for special treatment while neglecting equally valid training needs of other groups. As much of the programme as possible should therefore be open to all, though the library may wish to make certain elements compulsory for pre-licentiates.

Encouraging interest in professional developments

An important part of the training librarian's job will be to maintain interest and awareness of professional developments. At the pre-licentiate and licentiate stages, keeping up professional contacts will help in the compilation of the log-book and the presentation of the report. For more established staff, the incentives may be less obvious, but the need to maintain contact with other professionals is no less vital, particularly in a period of low job mobility where opportunities to meet new people at work are more limited.

The library can keep people in touch with new developments through its programme of seminars and visits and through publicising details of external courses and relevant book and journal articles. Several libraries have their own newsletter which can be used to publicise training information.

It is not known how much professional reading librarians actually do, but this can certainly be encouraged by circulating current contents lists and making articles available. Where polytechnics themselves have departments of librarianship, such lists are probably being produced within the library already and can be made available more widely.

The Library Association with its system of local branches and groups and the other professional bodies provide many polytechnic library staff with the experience of taking an active role in professional activities at national or local level. Experience of committee work and course organisation provides an opportunity for individual development which the library service would wish to support.

As external courses and conferences are an important part of the process of keeping in touch with developments and meeting colleagues, attendance is encouraged as far as time and funds allow. Asking those who have attended such courses to present a short written or verbal report helps the individual and the library manager to assess its value and also enables more people to benefit from the knowledge gained. In some libraries there is an actual requirement to write such reports included in the training policy.

Information technology

In a period of rapid technological growth, librarians have seen their jobs change radically, first with computerised cataloguing and then with automated issue systems, while the whole area of subject enquiry work has been affected by the growth in online databases. At the same time, increasing use is being made of software packages on mainframe and microcomputers for management purposes. Many libraries are now including software as library materials and having computer terminals available for student use. With all these developments affecting both library staff and users, the librarian has in a comparatively short space of time had to acquire a high degree of computer literacy.

Most polytechnic libraries have devoted attention in the past few years to ensuring that staff are familiar with computer hardware and software. At Brighton, members of the department of computing have run training courses in 'computer literacy' and 'computer applications' specifically for library staff, and there are many other similar examples from other polytechnics. To be really effective, staff need to be encouraged to follow up such courses with tasks involving use of the skills acquired. Time set aside for individual practice will help to increase confidence and ensure that the training is put to good use. This has been recognised at the Polytechnic of Central London, where microcomputers have been made available for staff use and time allocated each term for work on a specific project following training.

A variety of external courses run by database suppliers are available for subject librarians to train in online information retrieval. Staff trained in this way can pass on their expertise at internal seminars.

The introduction of automated issue systems has involved a major in-house training effort to ensure that all library staff are confident in the use of the new system. Much informal co-operation has taken place with visits to other libraries where similar systems are already installed. Training has been recognised from the start as very much part of the process of introducing a new system and the experience has highlighted the importance of concise, straightforward oral and written instructions and plenty of 'hands-on' experience.

Inter-personal skills

Introducing computer technology is as much about changing attitudes as about teaching technical skills, whether in relation to encouraging more use of online searching or in reviewing the effect on people's jobs of the change from a manual to an automated issue system. This point has been made by Jones and Jordan (1982, p.25):

> Staff development and training that is confined to learning new technical skills alone does not solve the problems of inter-personal conflicts, since the introduction of new ideas and changes is ultimately dependent on the people who will operate them.

In parallel with the major training effort in information technology has been a growing realisation of the importance of inter-personal skills. This has arisen not only from the recognition of the effect of technology on jobs, but also from management research evidence of the importance of personal motivation and job satisfaction. Changing work patterns and expectations have contributed to the growth in interest in transactional analysis, assertiveness training, team building and similar inter-personal skills. Courses introducing these techniques have benefited many library staff in relationships with work colleagues and library users.

In polytechnic libraries, the emphasis that has always been placed on services to users carries with it the responsibility for training subject librarians in teaching techniques for user education programmes and for equipping all staff with the necessary skills to handle any potentially difficult situations with confidence.

Management training is of particular importance as librarians move into more senior posts, generally without formal management qualifications. Courses dealing with general issues such as motivation, delegation, decision-making and staff supervision are all of relevance to the personal development of the individual and the more effective working of the library service. Specific items for a library training programme include budgeting and planning, and committee work.

Training programmes

There are a number of different ways of organising the training programme; some libraries hold annual or bi-annual day conferences with a particular theme involving all staff, while others have regular weekly or monthly training sessions at the local level. Both these approaches demand much in the way of organisation and the continual development of fresh themes for discussion, but both have the merit of providing a framework that ensures a regular training pattern. Events may be planned for a year ahead or arranged on a more *ad hoc* basis in response to demand. Some form of advance planning is obviously vital for a well organised programme. On the other hand, too rigid a structure may be difficult to maintain and to keep responsive to new developments. Libraries in fact often choose to vary their training pattern to avoid events becoming mere routine and losing impact.

On-the-job training

The most common form of training, which is practised every day in libraries, is on-the-job training. This is cheap, quick and causes little interference with day-to-day work. An induction programme will include some on-the-job training at an early stage, to give the new member of staff some practical work experience as soon as possible.

This time-honoured approach to training will work very well if the trainer is as experienced at explaining the job as he or she is at carrying it out. Training the trainer is an important element of the staff training programme that is easy to overlook. With a new member of staff or a change of duties, it may also be helpful to look afresh at the requirements of a particular task to ensure that it is still being carried out in the most efficient way. There is a risk otherwise of perpetuating out-dated or inefficient ways of working which are passed on unquestioningly from one person to another.

On-the-job training need not be confined to the explanation of practical tasks to new recruits or those taking over new duties. There are other means of developing staff within the work environment; for example, the coaching of individuals by managers in a particular area of work, or the encouragement of staff to develop skills by working on a special project of value to the department. Coaching is particularly appropriate as follow up from a management or inter-personal skills course, to ease the transition back from theory to the realities of the work situation and to provide continued encouragement in the development of new skills. Similarly, working on a special project either individually or as part of a group, will provide insight into different ways of working and experience of seeing a piece of work through from planning stage to completion.

It often appears easier to take time out for a three-day course than to spare time within the busy working day to learn new techniques or develop new skills. It is important to try and free staff for these types of activity, an exercise itself in time management and the assessment of priorities. It requires a recognition that, in some circumstances, this form of training is of equal if not greater importance than attendance at outside courses or conferences.

Internal courses

Organising internal courses is a cost-effective way of ensuring that staff are trained in a way that suits the particular library. Off-the-job training takes people away from work pressures to turn their attention wholly to the issue at hand. Ideas for courses may arise either from management requests for training in specific skills, or from suggestions by members of the training group reflecting staff interests. Training courses run by polytechnic libraries range from sessions dealing with reference materials to general discussions on wider issues of professional concern, from talks on library policy to workshops in inter-personal skills. Exchange of experience seminars are especially valuable in multi-site libraries where opportunities for getting staff together on an informal basis to discuss matters of common interest are more limited.

The training skills necessary to run an internal training programme have been described by Rae (1983). While some courses demand a level of expertise that may not be present among the library staff, many internal training sessions can be run successfully without any outside support. Courses and training materials covering public speaking, presentation techniques and use of audiovisual aids are readily available.

The training librarian will have neither the range of skills nor the time to conduct many training sessions single handed. Members of the training group can be invited to help with the organisation, and staff who have attended conferences or have developed a particular professional interest can be asked to give papers. Such sessions provide valuable experience for those taking part, as well as sharing knowledge among a wider group.

To add variety to the programme and introduce a fresh perspective, it is desirable, where funds permit, to invite the occasional external speaker to provide a keynote address or lead a discussion. Knowledge gained at external courses and conferences and through professional contacts is helpful here in identifying suitable speakers.

The expertise that the polytechnic library can call on within its own institution is considerable. There are examples of assistance given to libraries with training events from departments of computing, education and management and from counselling and personnel staff. Most local authorities have training units running regular programmes of courses in public speaking, report writing, and management and supervisory skills, which are appropriate for many library staff. Attendance at these gives the opportunity to meet with other professional groups outside librarianship and to identify common problems. As an alternative, members of the local authority training unit may be willing to run courses specifically for library staff. The Local Government Training Board also provides a range of courses and offers advice. Library schools are another source of speakers, or will assist in arranging courses.

To help with the actual running of an in-house course, many training materials are available, either produced commercially or by educational institutions. Details can be obtained from catalogues or from informal contact with other librarians who may be able to recommend particular packages. Videotapes provide a means of introducing a topic for discussion, and many general training programmes are relevant to the library service. Some libraries produce and sell their own training materials; from Hatfield, for example, a trigger video is available which uses specific library incidents as a basis for discussion in inter-personal skills courses (Dolphin, 1986).

Training materials can be used by individuals as well as in group situations; the development of computer-assisted learning and inter-active video suggest that these might become significant influences on staff training in the future, allowing people to work at their own pace and to choose from a range of options for further study.

Visits

Visits to other libraries or similar establishments are popular and easily arranged events which will feature in all polytechnic library training programmes. A survey of attitudes to continuing education among university and polytechnic library staff by Konn and Roberts (1984) found that 'visiting libraries was seen by all grades as a useful means of broadening horizons and obtaining new ideas'. Visits can be arranged to large national libraries, local libraries, academic, public or special, and to book suppliers, binders, publishers or printers. A specially arranged visit with a particular focus is on the whole more valuable than a general guided tour.

Such visits have to them an element of the 'staff outing', but few would begrudge library staff a day out if they return refreshed with some idea of how another library operates, bringing suggestions for improvements in their own services or a realisation that the situation in their own library is not so bad after all.

External courses

External courses provide a level of expertise that is unlikely to be available in-house and also give the opportunity for contact with other professionals. The range of courses available is wide and, with the growing importance attached to continuing education within the profession, it is likely that many individual and library training needs will be covered. Both the Library Association and ASLIB run varied continuing education programmes, with groups and branches catering for special interests. Using regional centres outside

London is making courses more widely accessible. For polytechnic libraries in particular, COPOL regularly organises seminars on topics of interest where staff can exchange views and compare experiences.

Keeping track of courses coming from a number of different sources may be difficult. The training librarian can help by circulating a regular calendar of events and holding a central stock of course leaflets. Asking staff who have been to courses or conferences to report back can not only share the knowledge more widely but can also act as a guide to the course's usefulness for future reference.

With money for external courses and conferences limited, those responsible for the training budget will want to be sure that a course selected represents good value for money and is of relevance to the individual. This will entail a look at the course objectives and how these fit in with the needs of the library service and with personal objectives. If the training policy allows for personal development as well as specific job-related training, the range of relevant courses can be wide. Libraries vary in the extent to which they will direct people to particular courses rather than rely on individual applications, but all will recognise the importance of individual motivation in gaining benefit from a course.

Co-operative training

Mid-way between internal and external courses are the activities of the various co-operative groups. Training is one obvious activity for local library co-operation. Hatfield is unique in having a formal link through Hertfordshire Technical Information Service (HERTIS) with other libraries in the area, and this includes close liaison on training matters. Most polytechnic libraries, however, belong to some form of regional grouping that offers co-operative training events. Best known of these schemes is the Sheffield Libraries Co-ordinating Committee (SLCC), which has a long tradition of running joint sessions through its Training and Education Working Party. Joint seminars and visits are also a feature of Birmingham Libraries in Co-operation (BCOP) as described by Hadcroft (1985). These are all groupings of different types of libraries within a limited area. For polytechnics, training librarians in polytechnics in London and the south-east region have formed the South East Training Group

(SETG). This organises a biennial conference and regular seminars, has 'open days' at member libraries and provides a forum at its regular meetings for the exchange of information about courses and training activities.

Evaluation

An important but often neglected aspect of training is the evaluation or assessment of how effective it has been both for the individual and for the library service as a whole.

Many libraries ask members of staff returning from courses to present a short written or oral report. This gives the individual a chance to reflect on how well the course has met his or her own objectives and gives the immediate manager or training librarian an idea of what the course has been like. If the report is presented at an informal staff seminar, the experience can be shared with a wider group.

For internal courses, the organisers will start with setting course objectives and should be aware of how they will afterwards evaluate how well these have been met. Replies to a reactions questionnaire will show how successful the course has been in terms of content, relevance, presentation and general atmosphere. Most libraries use an evaluation form or reactions questionnaire for their own courses and, although formats vary, these generally include a form of ranking from 'excellent' to 'poor' for each aspect of a course, and leave space for general comments.

Evaluation at the reactions level immediately after the course is the easiest to deal with and the most commonly found. Depending on objectives set for the course, the organiser may also wish to build in some form of evaluation to see how well the learning has been grasped. This can be done by a test of knowledge learning, a practical demonstration of a new skill, or a 'role play' exercise to look at attitude change. For some courses, informal feedback sessions at the end will be more appropriate than elaborate testing techniques.

Far more complex is the evaluation of the effect of training on job behaviour. Several research studies have looked at ways of evaluating job performance, using work study or observation techniques, or asking trainees to keep diaries over a specified period. To be really effective, it is also necessary to have a control group which has not received the training, but this is hardly feasible in a work situation.

Many courses, particularly in the management or interpersonal skills area, end with agreement on an action plan which the trainee will put into operation back at work, focusing perhaps on some particular area of difficulty. With or without an action plan, trainees will return to work after a good course full of ideas and enthusiasm, which will be short lived if they are met with blank indifference or even hostility. Elliott's survey (1983) found this a common cause of concern.

Some courses will have follow-up evaluation built in, either in the form of a return session to check on progress or by the use of questionnaires or interviews. Where this is not arranged, it is an advantage to check regularly on how far good intentions have been put into practice. Most evaluation is best done on this individual type of basis. Such interviews need to go beyond the 'how did the course go?' level of general enquiry. Anyone going on a course starts with some expectations of what will be gained from it. These can be discussed beforehand in relation to training needs and followed up afterwards to see how far expectations have been met and training put to practical use. This will especially be the case where specific training needs have been identified.

As well as following up progress on individual courses, the manager will wish to have regular sessions with each member of staff at which training needs are identified and future plans discussed. Training records for each person will provide a framework for action.

Evaluation also encompasses the organisation of training itself. Questions need to be asked on how far the training provided is meeting the objectives of the library service and how good it is at identifying needs and meeting them with relevant, well-supported courses. Attempts to apply any form of cost-benefit analysis to assess the effectiveness of training in relation to the time and cost involved are unlikely to be successful. Feedback from full reports from the training librarian or training group should provide the basis for informed debate on the part of a committed management team.

Motivation and effectiveness

The primary purpose of staff training is to make the library staff more effective in order to improve the service to users. This can operate at a number of levels. Staff must be trained to work the equipment and carry out the necessary routines, but must also have the motivation to ensure the smooth running of the service. Few would disagree with Cowley (1982, p.8) that:

> Efficient use of personnel and their job satisfaction are crucially important to the individuals involved, to the users of the service and to the needs of the organisation. An efficiently organised service manned by well-trained, highly motivated staff should guarantee good results even in working conditions which may not be ideal.

The human relations school of management theory has demonstrated the importance of a well motivated and satisfied staff to the effective running of the organisation. Maslow's hierarchy of needs and Herzberg's 'satisfiers' draw attention to the importance of motivation and the individual's need for recognition and self-esteem. In Herzberg's terms, it is the 'satisfiers' relating to achievement and recognition that are important as motivators, and not the 'dissatisfiers' that relate to the working environment, which, while it may cause grumbles, in fact has little effect on job performance.

The development of polytechnic libraries with their predominantly multi-site structures has encouraged the growth of 'organic' rather than 'mechanistic' management systems, with a high degree of participation and local decision-making, rather than an autocratic leadership with a number of hierarchical levels. This type of organisation is the ideal of McGregor's Theory Y management, allowing individuals to reach their potential by being given responsibility and decision-making powers. If polytechnic libraries aim fully to achieve this participative management style, then ensuring that staff have the qualities to contribute to this aim is a high priority.

The training programme must therefore take into account both the practical needs of the service and the individual's needs for personal motivation and self-esteem. Training schemes can be devised for the induction of new staff or the introduction of a new system, but, in dealing with the individual personalities who make up the library staff, needs and aspirations will be far more diffuse and can really only be tackled on a one-to-one basis.

Staff appraisal

Many organisations in both the public and the private sectors have introduced schemes of staff appraisal as a means of evaluating performance and identifying training needs. The techniques of appraisal and appraisal interviewing are discussed by Scott and Edwards (1982) and their application to libraries is considered by Jones and Jordan (1982).

At first sight, appraisal interviews may be seen as a threat, with the manager sitting in judgement over the weaknesses of the staff. At the other extreme, a concerned manager may feel that he or she knows the staff too well to bother with formal systems. In reality, an appraisal system is designed for the benefit of staff as an aid to the identification of training needs with the aim of improving performance and at the same time increasing job satisfaction. To be truly effective, it demands skilled handling by the appraiser and plenty of advance preparation on both sides.

Inherent in any appraisal scheme is the search for an objective measure or standard by which to judge performance. Schemes may incorporate merit ratings using five-point scales, but there is always the danger of managers selecting the safe middle point and such ratings may reveal little more than the 'what sort of person are you?' quiz in popular magazines. Written comments to a series of points are to be preferred to scale ratings or a line of ticks. It has to be recognised that any such comments must be subjective; for true objectivity, an appraisal scheme needs some form of measurable target for assessment. In the commercial world it is easy to set financial or productivity targets for an individual or a department, but in libraries the choice of suitable targets is more problematic and a system of 'reward appraisal', which relates salary level to job performance, hardly fits with the polytechnic pay structure. Several libraries have tried the system of Management by Objectives (MbO) to provide measures of performance for the library service (Revill, 1985), but neither MbO nor appraisal systems as such appear to have gained wide acceptance within polytechnic libraries.

Training interviews

In spite of these difficulties, the link between appraisal and training is a strong one, as, before staff can be helped to improve performance, training needs must be identified.

Even where formal appraisal schemes cannot be operated or are not considered appropriate, some form of structure for the regular review of an individual's training activities and plans is important, as otherwise reviews of progress will depend very much on the attitudes and interests of individual managers.

The approach adopted at Brighton is for all staff to have an annual training interview with their departmental head. This takes the form of a review of training undertaken in the past year and an assessment of training needs and plans for the future. Such a system helps to maintain the atmosphere of 'training awareness' by reminding managers regularly of their responsibilities in this area and allowing both sides time away from work pressures to concentrate on the effects of training already received and any future needs or plans. Like the formal appraisal system, it demands advance preparation and a commitment on both sides to follow up the ideas discussed.

Professional stagnation

Identifying training needs and sending people on courses is not just a convenient way of ticking that training has been done and putting an end to the matter. Middle managers in the survey by Konn and Roberts (1984) reported concern at taking more and more courses and not seeming to get anywhere. This is not of course a problem unique to libraries, but a generally recognised danger of any staff development scheme in a period of contraction. Training people and giving them nowhere to go can be counter-productive, as Pepper (1984, p.199) has pointed out in relation to the running of training schemes within commercial companies: 'running a development scheme which has an "output" far in excess of the company's promotion requirement can magnify the disappointment and frustration felt in the company'.

Within libraries, this problem has been defined as professional stagnation:

> The problem is essentially one of no growth and low mobility and the ensuing danger of stagnation, both for individuals who will run out of intellectual stimulus and the organization which will be deprived of new blood and new ideas (Hall, 1982, p.3).

Polytechnic library staff have suffered at least as much as other groups from these effects. As jobs disappear, more emphasis has to be on routine work and it is perhaps this aspect that contributed to the findings in a Centre for Library and Information Management (CLAIM) survey that polytechnic library staff were more dissatisfied with their jobs than their colleagues in public and university libraries, with 82 per cent of respondents in the two polytechnics surveyed reporting that 'some or quite a bit of their work could be handled by someone with less experience than themselves' (Stewart, 1982, p.11).

It has always been an accepted part of the library profession that no one library service can provide promotion opportunities for all its staff and that encouraging personal development will often lead to people seeking promotion elsewhere. In the current climate, opportunities for promotion both internally and externally are severely limited and any professional post advertised will receive many high quality applicants. Librarians who in better times could have expected promotion elsewhere now have to accept the frequent failure of job applications or the alternative of staying put and making the most of it.

The profession as a whole has a low age structure and in polytechnics the early retirement of ex-college staff after mergers, coupled with heavy recruitment in the expansion days of the seventies, has meant that many libraries have a middle band of professional staff of roughly similar age who have been in post for some time. The prospect of such a group growing old together without the impetus of fresh ideas is a daunting one and a challenge to the library manager. Some people will be content to 'jog along' and to make up for lack of continuing job satisfaction with outside interests, while others will grow increasingly dissatisfied and disenchanted. Neither attitude is good for the library service. Practical training activities which are of interest to less experienced staff are unlikely to be considered appropriate by those who have been in post for some time. Alternative training strategies must be adopted and ways be found to instil fresh ideas and re-motivate existing staff in the absence of new appointments.

Staff development

Staff development is seen as a key factor in solving the problem of professional stagnation or librarian burn-out as it is known in the United States. In a situation where this development is less likely to lead to promotion and may just accentuate dissatisfaction, management needs to take positive action to see that individuals can make practical use of the training and development opportunities available. Classic management answers to lack of motivation and job satisfaction are job enlargement, job enrichment, job rotation and job exchange, all of which have relevance to the library situation.

Job enlargement

Job enlargement is perhaps seen as an undesirable feature of life in many polytechnic libraries as posts have been cut or frozen. Merely giving people 'more of the same' does not necessarily lead to job satisfaction and adding one boring job to another hardly produces a fresh challenge. Even where at first the enlarged job appears to offer some variety, the effect may be short-lived:

> Job enlargement is not a once-for-all process. It needs constant self-renewal. We humans are often stimulated by variety. We seek to reduce it to order and system; having done so, we get bored by the routine (Handy, 1985, p.323).

Job enrichment

To be effective as a 'satisfier' in Herzberg's terms, the enlarged job needs to include some added responsibility. The ideal is 'job enrichment' rather than 'job enlargement'. There are several examples of how this has been achieved within polytechnic libraries. Added management responsibilities such as staff training, information technology or research and development have given wider roles to a number of staff at senior or middle management levels. At the pre-licentiate stage, newly qualified librarians often have the opportunity to work on a special project, allowing them to explore an area in detail and input new ideas to the discussions of more experienced managers.

Finding ways of enriching the jobs of staff at all levels is a particular responsibility for library managers and an exercise in establishing true democratic decision-making. Involving individuals or groups of staff in special projects or in participation at regular management and planning meetings gives valuable new experience, adds fresh ideas and produces a truly participative management style.

Job rotation

Job rotation is extensively used in polytechnic libraries among the teams of library assistants. To give experience of a number of areas of work to all members of staff increases job interest, decreases boredom and brings flexibility to the team. A new member of staff often provides the impetus for change, but, where the staff have been in post for some time, regular review and change of responsibilities can introduce the necessary element of variety.

Job rotation is also particularly suited to the pre-licentiate stage, giving the new professional an idea of a number of different areas of work from which to select future specialisms and at the same time offering a rounded introduction to library work. This pattern is more difficult for established professional staff, whose subject specialist work makes moving into different areas within the same library service more difficult to arrange.

Job exchanges

Professional and non-professional staff can benefit from job exchanges and job swaps with colleagues doing similar work elsewhere. There are specialised agencies to deal with international exchanges and there are examples of successful swaps, particularly with North America. Indeed the cynic might observe that it is easier to get a librarian to go to California than to work at another site a few miles down the road, for exchanges within institutions and between neighbouring libraries have not always met with much enthusiasm. This is one area where co-operative schemes can be of help. Hadcroft (1985) has described some of the initial problems in setting up a staff exchange programme within Birmingham libraries which after an initial lack of enthusiasm is now running successfully.

Personal development

While it may be hoped that these measures will increase job satisfaction and lead to the development of the individual for the benefit of the library service, it is unrealistic to assume that all personal development can be so closely related to the work environment. Many library staff have chosen to take further qualifications or pursue research interests for career advancement or personal interest, often taking advantage of the opportunities for part-time study within the polytechnics themselves. In some cases, financial support and day release are wholly appropriate, but, where the area of interest is not so directly related to work responsibilities, funding is less likely. Even in the absence of financial support, encouragement and interest from library managers for any form of personal development is an important element in maintaining job satisfaction in circumstances where the job itself is not always able to offer the individual sufficient scope.

Conclusion

An investigation of the approach to training and development in individual polytechnics would reveal a number of differences in detail but also many broad features in common. The extent to which libraries are running internal training programmes for new and established staff and encouraging attendance at outside events points to a generally high level of awareness of the importance of training and development. The interest in co-operative schemes and in opportunities for professional exchange of information show how much can be learned in this area from the experience of others.

Underlying any approach to training must be the need to look beyond the narrow concept of job-related training towards a recognition of the importance of personal job satisfaction. Both management theories and library surveys point to this as an area of concern, particularly in a period of reduced promotion prospects and low job mobility. By identifying and providing for specific training needs and at the same time looking for ways of improving the jobs of individuals and encouraging their personal development, a well organised and well supported staff training programme can make a significant contribution to the effectiveness of the library service.

References

Casteleyn, M. (1981), *Planning library training programmes*, London, Deutsch.

Cowley, J. (1982), *Personnel management in libraries*, London, Bingley.

Dolphin, P. (1986), 'Interpersonal skills training for library staff', *Library Association Record*, vol.88, no.3 (March), p.134.

Elliott, L. (1983), 'Professional staff development in academic libraries', *Journal of Librarianship*, vol.15, no.4 (October), pp.237–53.

Hadcroft, M. (1985), 'Library co-operation within a city', in J. Cowley (ed), *The management of polytechnic libraries*, Aldershot, Gower in association with COPOL.

Hall, J. (ed), (1982), *Fighting professional stagnation: staff development in a period of low mobility*, Leeds, Leeds Polytechnic, School of Librarianship.

Handy, C.B. (1985), *Understanding organizations*, 3rd edn, Harmondsworth, Penguin.

Jones, N. and Jordan, P. (1982), *Staff management in library and information work*, Aldershot, Gower.

Konn, T. and Roberts, N. (1984), 'Academic librarians and continuing education: a study of personal attitudes and opinions', *Journal of Librarianship*, vol.16, no.4 (October), pp.262–80.

Pepper, A.D. (1984), *Managing the training and development function*, Aldershot, Gower.

Rae, L. (1983), *The skills of training*, Aldershot, Gower.

Revill, D.H. (1985), 'The measurement of performance' in J. Cowley (ed), *The management of polytechnic libraries*, Aldershot, Gower in association with COPOL.

Scott, B. and Edwards, B. (1982), *Appraisal and appraisal interviewing*, rev edn, London, Industrial Society.

Stewart, L. (1982), *What do UK librarians dislike about their jobs?*, Loughborough, Centre for Library and Information Management.

4 Staff management and communication

C. BARRY WEST

In a television programme on war, a US marines sergeant summed up the problem of motivating his new recruits this way: 'At the end of recruitment training, we can motivate them to do anything we want.' The programme then went on to show how this was achieved: the arrival of the recruits at training camp was timed for 2 am, when their resistance to their treatment was at its lowest, their heads were shaved so that outward signs of individuality were removed, they were isolated from the outside world, and then subjected to a rigorous code of discipline from which even a minor deviation brought immediate and harsh retribution.

Such methods of man management are probably essential in a profession where the physical survival of its members may depend upon each individual responding immediately and unquestioningly to a given order. To a greater or lesser extent, such discipline is also required in the police, in hospitals and in the fire service. In these professions, the objectives are of such paramount importance that the individual has perforce to be subservient to the group, and the lines of authority must be clear and unquestioned. The hierarchy of command is of central importance, and there are usually clear boundaries laid down between each level of responsibility. Uniformity of action is reinforced by the requirement to wear a specified uniform.

Theories of motivation

Individual needs and organisational objectives do not necessarily coalesce so readily in other types of organisation. The factors behind an individual's motivation to work and those that act as disincentives have been closely studied in the management literature ever since Maslow (1943) identified five levels of human need. Maslow emphasised that only when the 'lower order' needs of hunger and safety were taken care of could an individual progress towards the satisfaction of 'higher order' needs of friendship, status and self-actualisation.

Maslow's theories were developed and extended by others in the 1950s and 1960s, notably McGregor (1957a, 1957b) and Herzberg (1966) in what came to be known as the Human Relations school. McGregor in particular tried to show that people work best by directing their own efforts towards organisational objectives, rather than by requiring to be driven and constantly directed. McGregor identified the traditional managerial style, which he labelled Theory X, as making negative assumptions concerning man's motivation to work: that he is lazy, lacks ambition and is resistant to change. McGregor contrasted these assumptions with an alternative view of man's motivation, which he labelled Theory Y, which postulated that, given the right kind of leadership and encouragement, people will realise their innate capacity for responsibility. The task of management is to create the organisational conditions to bring this about.

Herzberg took a rather different perspective, in trying to elicit what are the positive and negative factors in the workplace which determine how well employees perform. His 'two factor' theory (motivation/hygiene) purported to show that the hygiene factors (within which he included less obvious elements such as company policy and administration as well as physical working conditions) can act only as *dis*-incentives to perform well. Once they have been put right, they cease to have any effect upon subsequent performance. It is at this point that managers must pay more conscious attention to the motivating elements, such as responsibility, challenge, the job itself.

Incentives

How are these theories useful within what many outsiders still believe to be the relatively cushioned environment of academia, and the academic library in particular? It was in American librarianship that human relations theories first made their impact, notably in the work by Plate and Stone (1974) and the subsequent rise of participative as opposed to authoritarian styles of management. Plate and Stone's results largely verified the theories of McGregor and Herzberg, showing that the two biggest motivators were recognition and achievement, and the biggest dissatisfier was institutional policy and administration.

> Respondents attacked rigid policies, the tenure system, staff cutbacks, inadequate budgets, misguided priorities and the lack of information necessary to make rational decisions. Some expressed a general feeling of helplessness in the face of institutional policy and administration (p.107).

In the UK, it was not until the late 1970s that the professional literature began to pay much attention to such human managerial issues. This may in part stem from the fact that library managers work within extremely tight constraints, so that incentives to better performance, which exist, for example, in commercial organisations, are effectively denied them. Pay is regarded in management literature as only a short-term motivator. Nevertheless, even if one accepts that it is only of over-riding importance when below subsistence levels, the fact remains that better pay is rarely a bargaining power within the library manager's direct gift. This has not prevented chief librarians from devoting a great deal of energy to obtaining better grades or different grades for their staff, both professional and non-professional. In terms of encouraging individual performance towards corporate goals, however, the commercial firm has a clutch of incentives ranging from share ownership to company cars, season ticket loans and luncheon vouchers, which are likely to be for ever out of bounds to the public servant except in exceptional circumstances. Likewise, the obverse applies. Just as it is difficult to reward staff directly through fringe benefits, so it is frequently difficult to exercise control upon the 'sleeper' who, once embarked on a long pay-scale, is content to time serve without the need to over-exert himself. This used to be particularly marked in the university sector, where long pay scales linked to academic scales meant that the career grade professional member of staff had little incentive to move.

Interestingly enough, there is a sharp division in the findings of Stewart (1982b) between academic and public librarians on the question of pay. In public libraries, where pay scales have traditionally lagged behind those of some of their academic counterparts in university libraries, the primary dissatisfaction was found to be pay. In academic libraries (Stewart did not distinguish between the different types of academic library in this connection), the primary dissatisfaction was lack of recognition. Perhaps a rider needs adding here, however. On an admittedly fairly small sample of four polytechnic libraries, of which two were Inner London Educational Authority ones, Stewart found that a worryingly large 29 per cent of respondents were dissatisfied with the efficiency with which the organisation was run, and nearly half anticipated that their length of stay would be less than two years. This is in sharp contrast with the replies from university librarians, where 44 per cent *expected to stay* until retirement. It is tempting to speculate that either the perceived disparity in pay between polytechnic library staff and their university colleagues for doing similar work or the disparities that exist within polytechnic libraries themselves, where some staff (usually the subject or tutor librarians) are paid on Burnham (that is, teachers') scales and some on National Joint Council (NJC) scales are at least partly to blame for this apparent dissatisfaction.

Most people entering the profession of librarianship probably realise that it is not well paid. Other aspects of the work must therefore make it appear attractive as a career in order to draw increasingly well-qualified recruits into its ranks. Margaret Slater (1979) looked at these factors in some detail, and found indeed that a number of Maslow's higher order factors were at the top of the list of things that librarians liked most about their jobs. These included 'feeling useful', 'intellectual challenge' and 'freedom, responsibility'. Factors that caused most dissatisfaction included, at the very top of the list, non-professional element and chores (27 per cent of respondents), monotony and low status. As the problem of lack of resources grows ever more acute, these findings seem bound to increase the polytechnic library manager's problems in retaining a good, well-motivated library staff. The apparent desire of some professional staff to move is being frustrated by the drying up of new professional posts, and at the same time the posts that do become vacant are usually non-professional and are at the greatest risk of being frozen. This in turn means that professional staff find themselves loaded with a greater proportion of non-professional duties, since bread and butter problems of keeping small site libraries open the requisite number of hours, or ensuring that material gets put back on the shelves and stays in the right order, do not go away. Library managers in academic libraries find themselves in a classic 'double bind', since they must continue to find ways of encouraging more effective user exploitation of library materials in order to be able to justify even retaining their existing allocation of resources, meagre as this may be, but in doing so they are exacerbating the problem of keeping the library running efficiently. An indication of how far out of line the professional:non-professional split has become may be seen from the fact that a normal library ratio is reckoned to be about 40:60, whereas at Coventry (Lanchester) the ratio is now 50:50 and the ratio for all polytechnic libraries in 1984/85 was 45:55.

In these circumstances, it might seem that the outlook for professional library staff in polytechnic libraries is gloomy. However, ways now exist to utilise professional staff in more professionally stretching ways than formerly. By increasing the proportion of staff devoted to reader services at the expense of technical services, which the development of co-operatives for bibliographic data has encouraged, library managers are now able to give middle management professional staff the kind of role that best matches the Maslow highest order need of self-actualisation. The growth of online services, the skills needed to interrogate them, and now the introduction of online catalogues, have all contributed to making academic librarianship, particularly subject librarianship, a much more exciting and creative career than twenty or even ten years ago. In an increasingly information hungry society, library and information work has risen notably in status. Likewise, to be in the forefront of new technology can have a dramatic effect upon the status of the library within its community. If, as is frequently the case in polytechnic libraries, the library service can be seen to be taking an active role in leading new initiatives and innovations in the teaching-learning process, rather than following them, its central role is underlined and more highly valued.

The library manager must be aware, however, of the danger of stagnation, a problem that has received a great deal of attention lately. As Hall (1985) has pointed out: 'For many in the thirty to fifty age range, professional stagnation is a real problem which may have serious personal consequences'. He maintained that after six or seven years 'even such potentially interesting activities as user education and the provision of computer based information services can lose their glitter'. Among the solutions that Hall has suggested to the turned-off professional is to assess how far his or her needs are being satisfied at work, and 'increase, maintain or scale down your commitment to work accordingly'.

Although scaling down one's commitment to work and only coming alive outside work might have the advantage to the individual of preventing ulcers, it is hardly a strategy that will commend itself to the majority of hard-pressed polytechnic librarians who are constantly being exhorted to 'get more from less'. Nevertheless the danger of a falling off of commitment at a time when there are so few opportunities to move is very real.

How should a library manager react when faced with a loss of enthusiasm, or worse, a crisis in the morale of the staff? Several strategies present themselves. One is to look very hard at the organisation chart and see if it is really giving the staff, both professional and non-professional, the opportunities to develop, at least within the organisation. Does the organisation chart have the rigidly hierarchical structure which suits a Theory X style of management, or does it encourage the kind of participatory style, with opportunities for staff to discuss common problems together? At Coventry (Lanchester) Polytechnic, the move to a structure that strongly emphasised a team approach took place in 1978/79 and was modelled on the structure already obtaining at Newcastle Polytechnic. The original purpose was to reflect the faculty structure of the polytechnic by creating subject teams headed by faculty librarians for science, engineering, art and design, and social sciences. These new teams were set beside the already existing reader services teams. The head of each team, together with the polytechnic librarian and deputy librarian, formed a new senior management team. The unanticipated bonus of the new structure is that the team approach itself has developed into a positive, motivating force.

Teams quite naturally develop a competitive spirit, which of course could equally become a destructive force if the balance is not carefully nurtured at the highest level. The chief librarian has a vital role to play in ensuring that no one team becomes regarded, justifiably or otherwise, as 'top dog', since this is clearly likely to breed a reaction of jealousy amongst other groups not so favoured. An example might be the technical services team versus the subject teams, where the former might become envious of both the 'higher status' which subject librarians may be thought to have, and of the greater control they are able to exercise over their work, its intellectual challenge, and so on, all strong motivators in Herzberg's terms. If these perceived differences are reinforced by dramatically different pay scales, as has been pointed out is the case in some polytechnic libraries, then one has a recipe for strong dissatisfaction amongst the 'out group'. At Coventry, the effects of group envy were minimised by giving a subject role (albeit a fairly limited one) to the major heads of sections in technical services, that is, to the acquisitions and periodicals librarians. This has had the doubly beneficial effect of giving the staff concerned an opportunity to exercise their subject skills and to act as bridge between the subject teams and technical services, whilst not diminishing the team approach. There is evidence that the team approach is beginning to become favoured amongst polytechnic libraries where circumstances permit its adoption – for instance at Kingston Polytechnic (Kingston Polytechnic Learning Resources, 1986) – since in addition to its group dynamic effects, it also helps promote better communication, both upwards and downwards within the library, as well as within the polytechnic at large. This is a theme that will be taken up later in the chapter.

It would be a mistake to think that a participatory style of management implies that decision-making is a completely democratic process. The polytechnic librarian takes the ultimate responsibility for the management of the library, and there will be many occasions when he or she will be obliged to over-rule what may be the wishes of the majority of the staff, simply on the grounds that their wishes cannot for economic or political reasons be implemented. Consultation should not be considered by either side as a substitute for effective management control. Likewise, it is the library manager's responsibility to determine how best to relate the human skills at his or her command with the objectives of the library. A wise manager will recognise that different staff have different needs as well as differing abilities. As Hannabus has pointed out (1983), motivational theories are apt to over-simplify reality. 'What is job satisfaction for one person might be job dissatisfaction for another.' Some staff are and will remain temperamentally more suited to a job away from the public. Others would find loss of contact with readers would take away much of their job satisfaction.

The participative style of management, in which emphasis is placed upon consultation and positive encouragement of ideas from all levels of the organisation, is sometimes mistaken for a 'soft' attitude to getting work done. This charge tends to be levelled at non-profit organisations. There is a common belief that, where the profit motive is absent, the only objective that management will pursue will be of keeping a contented workforce which is not pushed too hard. This is at the basis of the criticisms of the Civil Service made by Leslie Chapman (1978). He asked (p.109) that there should be a: 'diminishing. . . emphasis. . . placed. . . on the ability of a civil servant to get on with other people', on the grounds that no manager who is concerned with cutting costs, especially through reductions in staff expenditure, is going to be very popular. Blake and Mouton (1964) showed this dichotomy, the concern for production and the concern for people, as a grid, from one (low) to nine (high). At the bottom of the grid, a one,one manager was unconcerned for either people or production. A one,nine manager showed a low concern for production but a high concern for people. This is the 'country club' style of management, which many outsiders might say is typical of libraries. A nine,one manager was the old-style authoritarian manager who did not care what his workforce thought, as long as they obeyed orders and did the job. The trick was to be a nine,nine manager with an equal concern for both. Some managers attempt to achieve this through a form of management by objectives, which is the approach favoured at the City of London Polytechnic Library (Pankhurst, 1985).

Non-professional staff

In academic libraries, problems of motivation for non-professional staff can be much more difficult to combat than for professional staff. Few non-professional jobs in academic libraries give much scope for the individual to exercise his or her creative skills, and promotion prospects are usually poor. There is a now well-documented divide between professional and non-professional staff, which presents a challenge to the academic library manager. The problem has grown with the rise in the educational level of recruits, particularly in London, where many library assistant posts are occupied by graduates. Russell's survey (1985) showed a deep resentment of the attitudes that some professional staff exhibit towards their non-professional colleagues. The main substance of the criticisms levelled by non-professionals in academic libraries, as shown in Russell's survey, concerns the condescending manner in which they are treated. The belittling term 'junior', used by someone fresh out of library school to a non-professional with sixteen years' experience, is a typical example of the lack of concern for a library assistant's feelings and for the development of a 'them and us' attitude. Stewart (1982a) similarly commented that: 'the greatest conflict in libraries lies not between managers and employees but between professionals and non-professionals'.

If this is so, the blame must to some extent be laid at the door of the prevailing management style within libraries. It is not difficult to make a conscious effort to involve *all* staff who wish to be involved in expressing their opinions upon aspects of library policy, even if for operational reasons these are not always acted upon. It is also important, when considering programmes of staff development, to ensure that the needs of non-professional staff are not overlooked. Here there are refreshing signs that things are changing for the better. Telford College of Further Education has recently extended its Distance Learning Course for the City and Guilds Library and Information Assistants Certificate. Its chief attraction to hard-pressed managers is that it involves no necessity for time off in the form of day release. Clearly, any library assistant who embarks upon it is showing considerable commitment to the job, and deserves proper recognition both in terms of increased pay and status. Awareness of the valuable contribution that non-professional staff can make is shown in a number of polytechnic libraries where posts of senior library assistant are now common. (In polytechnic libraries, senior library assistant usually means senior non-professional and not, as in university libraries, the designation for the first professional post.) At Trent Polytechnic, a total of fourteen posts help to support what is a federal structure of libraries serving eight schools together with central services on other sites. At Coventry, senior library assistants support the subject teams, the technical services team and the reader services team. The post of counter supervisor is an 'either/or' post, that is, a middle management professional or a very experienced non-professional can hold the post.

Delegation and supervision

'Delegation is another of those "good" words; one cannot it is generally felt have enough of it; managers, when questioned, feel they ought to do more of it and wish they got more of it from their supervisors' (Handy, 1976).

Delegation is generally thought to be one of the hardest management arts to practise, because it brings with it the twin threats of losing touch and of having to take the blame from one's own supervisor if the subordinate to whom one has delegated an area of responsibility fails to do the work properly and makes mistakes. Not that delegation should imply a complete lack of supervision, or, more helpfully, a lack of support. This is particularly important in the early stages, and when for example a member of staff has been recently promoted to a more senior position, carrying greater responsibility for supervision. The extent to which managers at all levels, in libraries as elsewhere, are able to exercise positive but not intrusive supervision, whilst allowing the subordinate a degree of freedom within which to organise his or her work, brings us back to McGregor's Theory X/ Theory Y style of management. Although most supervisors would prefer to see themselves as Theory Y followers in their expectations of their subordinates, in practice resisting the desire to interfere under the guise of helping out can be difficult. This might manifest itself, for instance, at the issue desk, where going in to reduce the length of the queue of borrowers might be viewed as an implicit comment on the length of time a library assistant is taking to sort out a registration problem. This might be seen in a particularly unfavourable light if it is the 'supervisor of the supervisor' who steps in, which in this instance would probably be the reader services librarian, since this implies a double distrust of both the library assistant and the counter supervisor. It is these sorts of pitfalls that the newly promoted supervisor must try hard to avoid. The lessons can only be assimilated, however, if a sense of trust exists between supervisor and supervised, so that such misunderstandings can be fully discussed without defensive responses on either side.

Job performance

Standards of job performance are a matter for legitimate concern for management. Methods of supervision will vary according to the type of managerial style that prevails and whether the appraisal of performance is formal or informal.

Little appears to be written in the management literature about the problem of below par performance, although of course informal performance appraisal takes place in every organisation, including libraries, all the time. There are signs that appraisal is now becoming a feature of staff development exercises, for instance at Brighton Polytechnic Library and Learning Resources (1984). In the United States, performance appraisal has been standard for many years and is often directly linked to salary increases, as well as promotion. Some libraries are now even experimenting with upward appraisal, that is, formal appraisal of senior managers by their subordinates. See, for example, the article by Peterson (1985).

However, a formal system of performance appraisal for all staff is not something that a library manager would readily wish to take on, because, as McGregor (1957b) has said, there are problems 'playing God'. Cowley (1982) has pointed out:

> Performance appraisal carries with it a high potential for disruption and decline in performance. The assessment of the individual's contribution to library operations and comments on ability and potential are highly charged subjects. Appraisal systems can seriously undermine morale despite the good intentions behind their introduction.

Jones and Jordan (1982) have devoted a chapter to the subject of staff appraisal, with examples from public libraries, but only by implication cover what to do about the consistently poor performer, and the reasons why the poor performance has developed in the first place. Stewart and Stewart (1982) have tackled the problem head on, from detection through causes to remedies.

Detecting the signs of poor performance is obviously the important first step. These may be in the form of a pattern of consistent lateness or frequent non-certificated sickness. Not many librarians indicate the number of days lost each year through sickness, but these in themselves can involve a considerable loss in productivity to the library. Liverpool Polytechnic Library lost an average of ten days per member of staff in 1985 (Revill, 1985), and a check on Coventry's absence records produced a similar result. Stress and depression are modern diseases, with multiple causes. Part of the problem may be the physical working conditions, part might be lack of motivation, because the job no longer holds any interest. Or these days the cause might well be simply the stress of having to take on too much work because of frozen posts. Much literature now exists in the United States on the rather fashionable concept of burn-out as it applies to librarians; for example Haack *et al.* (1984) and Smith and

Nelson (1983). Smith and Nelson found little evidence of burn-out amongst academic reference librarians, but Haack *et al.*, using a different method of measurement, found that 42 per cent of their sample had symptoms of chronic or severe chronic psychological stress. They found that progressive stages of burn-out identified in previous studies – enthusiasm, stagnation, frustration, apathy – were strongly featured in their results.

> Librarians with high scores indicated that they feel fatigued at work; that they experience headaches on the job or are absent because of other illnesses . . . that they avoid their supervisor; that they have trouble getting along with fellow employees.

So far, not much attention has been given to the problem as it exists in British libraries. Indeed, an article in the *Sunday Times* (Rayment, 1985) put librarians at the bottom of the stress league. Subsequent enquiries by the present author, however, elicited the fact that the six stress researchers who had been consulted were merely recording their subjective impressions, an interesting comment upon the image of library work even amongst professional psychologists. Professor Cary Cooper, who carried out the original survey, thought that academic librarians are now likely to be under considerable pressure because of the problems posed by frozen posts.

Whatever the causes, the results of poor performance can have devastating results for the organisation. Sensitive counselling can have a beneficial effect if the problem is not too deep-seated. The deputy librarian has a key role to play in such circumstances, standing as he or she does as a link between the library staff and librarian, and also, in most cases, being responsible for staff training. It is important to keep the lines of communication open, both to detect problems early and to give the member of staff concerned the opportunity to improve on performance. In handling such matters, Stewart and Stewart have given much sound practical advice. In particular, it is important to '*handle the problem, not the person*' (p.102. Original italics). In this way, a manager avoids letting personal dislikes cloud the judgement and has a better chance of avoiding hostile or defensive responses.

The library manager must have the ability to empathise with the real problems that individual members of staff have which may be acting as a negative influence on their work performance, and be in a position to give positive assistance and advice where possible. If the personal problem is work related – for instance, the inability because of a personality clash to work harmoniously with a colleague or colleagues – the answer can sometimes be a simple move in the timetable, or a transfer to a different site library. If on the other hand stress is being caused because of problems in their private life, these too must be handled sensitively. The more skilled a senior library manager becomes in these situations, the more likely he/she is to be able to handle awkward problems which may arise between library staff and the library users. This theme will be further developed in the section on communication.

Dismissal is fortunately a very rare phenomenon in academic libraries. Although incapacity to do the job one was employed to do is counted as grounds for justified dismissal in the 1980 Employment Act, it would take a strong nerve, particularly in today's unhappy employment market, to dismiss a member of staff for not doing his or her new job properly. The normal period of probation in local authorities is six months, during which time poor performance has not only to be detected, but the employee has to be given every opportunity to improve. The library manager would be well advised to seek the assistance of the personnel officer at an early stage to ensure that the letter of the law is being followed. The appropriate trade union representative also needs to be involved at an early stage if dismissal seems likely.

Relations with trade unions

In a polytechnic library, the chief librarian may find himself or herself dealing with as many as five different trade unions, namely the National Association of Teachers in Further and Higher Education (NATFHE), the Association of Polytechnic Teachers (APT), the National Association of Local Government Officers (NALGO), the Transport and General Workers Union (TGWU) and the National Union of Public Employees (NUPE). NATFHE mainly represents library staff on Burnham pay scales and/or conditions of service, NALGO represents the majority of library staff who are on NJC pay scales and conditions of service, APT represents some library staff who do not see their interests being represented by either union. The TGWU and NUPE represent manual staff, who may be on the library's staff establishment as porters, cleaners or possibly shelvers. Most local authorities encourage new employees to join the appropriate trade union, and some will even pay the employee's union dues up to a certain level. Clearly it behoves the librarian to keep good relations with the officers of the trade unions and to meet departmental representatives within the library in any matter of common concern. Most notably in recent years this has concerned occasional industrial action against cuts in government expenditure on higher education. However, circumstances can occur where the librarian unwittingly finds himself in the midst of a dispute which is not of his own making, but on which he may nevertheless be bound, by his terms of contract, to take a different position from, perhaps, that taken by the majority of his staff. Such a case occurred at North London Polytechnic, during the Harrington case, extensively reported in the *Times Higher Education Supplement* and elsewhere.

Most contacts with the trade unions will be more routine than this. Many concern health and safety matters, for which every employer has specific responsibilities under the 1974 Health and Safety at Work Act. Libraries might to the outsider be considered among the safer places in which to work, but with the inheritance of old buildings this is by no means always the case. There are at least two examples in polytechnics in recent years where site libraries have had to be temporarily closed in order to effect the removal of dangerous asbestos. In these circumstances, the safety and hygiene factors of Maslow and Herzberg become very obvious. Nor are health hazards confined to old buildings. It can sometimes appear that there are more natural and man-made hazards in the library workplace than the average back street factory. In the current climate of severe curbs on public expenditure, problems of heating, lighting, air conditioning or even having sufficient cleaners to keep the library reasonably hygienic, can prove very costly in terms of staff morale.

The actual and potential hazards of prolonged exposure to visual display units (VDUs) have frequently been documented. These range from very mild radiation to headaches, eye strain and pain and discomfort in the neck, shoulders and arms. Library managers have to be aware of these potential problems when installing new technology and be willing to try to create an ergonomically sound environment in which the staff can work. Coventry City Council has a policy that all employees must undergo a standard eye test before being asked to work on a VDU.

Much of a library manager's contact with trade union representatives will concern matters relating to pay scales and conditions of service. These are likely to be concerned with such matters as additional increments or other special payments for taking on new responsibilities, or because of other changes in their working conditions. One example where special payments might be claimed is in the use of new technology equipment.

Communication

> Clearly, if the systems or organizations are to work well, the information must not only be well developed, but it must be well communicated. If there is one general law of communication it is that we never communicate as well as we think we do (Handy, 1976, p.353).

Considering the importance of good communication within an organisation, in libraries as elsewhere, it is saddening to note that Handy's assertions are backed by solid research evidence. The explanation lies partly in the fact that sometimes, however well-expressed the original message, the receiver is not in the appropriate receptive frame of mind. This is particularly the case with written communication. Although face to face communication can take a great deal longer, and may therefore seem a poor use of a busy manager's time, it is frequently much more effective because, being a two-way process, immediate positive or negative feedback is received.

Good communication techniques can be learnt but it remains true that communication in organisations is a complex process, which requires many different factors to be working well in combination for it to be truly effective. Adair (1973) has pictured communication in the shape of a five-pointed star, the five points being the sender, the receiver, the method, the content and the situation. In the middle of the star is the *aim* of the message. He then demonstrates that effectiveness is required in each part of the process for the whole transaction to be effective. The sender must be a good communicator, choose the right method, at the right time and the receiver must be able to decode the message correctly. All kinds of barriers can obstruct the understanding of the message, as Kossen (1983, p.71) has made clear – and he is considering only verbal communication:

> differing perceptions;
> faulty translations;
> emotions;
> distrust;
> poor listening habits;
> poor questioning techniques.

Good communication in organisations usually goes hand in hand with a democratic management style. If participation in decision-making is encouraged, there is more likelihood that there will be a commitment on the part of a large number of staff to convey the results of decisions, since there will be a form of emotional investment in them. There is also likely to be a greater sense of trust, particularly if upward communication is actively encouraged. Here the manager faces a dilemma, however, since there is plenty of evidence to show that a good deal of 'filtering' occurs in upward communication. This amounts to telling the boss only what you think he wants to hear, or that you may think it good for him to hear. O'Reilly and Roberts (1974) showed in a series of experiments that material favourable to the sender is likely to move upwards, especially if favourable and important. If however the material is important but unfavourable to the sender, it is likely to be blocked. There is obviously a relationship between communication and trust. The less trust a subordinate has for his superior the less information is likely to be passed on. Their results also supported the contention that staff in the lower echelons of the organisation often fail to receive information from above.

Distance is another factor that can act as a communication barrier, and it is one that has received a great deal of attention in the literature on polytechnic libraries, because of the problem of multi-sites. As Jackson (1959) has pointed out:

> Other things being equal, people will communicate most frequently to those geographically closest to them, even within a relatively small organization. Spatial distance itself can thus be a barrier to communication.

House (1985) thought that some of the 'sense of deprivation' that staff at outlying sites feel is exaggerated, but did acknowledge that there can exist a sense of isolation amongst staff in such situations. Equally, it is easy for mutual distrust to grow between staff at the sites furthest out and staff in the centre. Misunderstandings can grow into a sense of 'us and them' if active steps are not taken to control the problem. This does not mean that the power in the centre site should be used as a control mechanism – far from it, since this is only likely to deepen the resentment felt at the site. Ashworth (1980) has recommended an 'organic' approach, with each site able to operate under a broad umbrella in the best interests of the users of a particular site. This is perhaps best illustrated in an example where the library is serving a specialised client group, for instance in art and design.

Library managers can adopt various strategies to overcome the communication problem within the library. One method is to ensure that particular problems are assigned to working parties which draw their membership from across the spectrum of the staff. This has the double benefit of ensuring a cross-fertilisation of ideas within the group and the representation of the many different interests that exist. The installation of a new automated system helps illustrate this. Modern integrated standalone systems require a complete re-think of a library's methods of work. Such changes require not only that staff are kept fully informed, but that key personnel can get together to examine their implications and point out any difficulties that may be foreseen in adopting particular solutions. Other working parties might be assigned to look at staff training programmes, or induction programmes for new students. All give excellent opportunities to staff at many different levels of the organisation to initiate new strategies and at the same time come to appreciate the value of the contribution that each member is able to make. Perhaps the most useful spin-off of *ad hoc* working parties that cut across the normal teams is the breaking of the stereotype of the job holder by the job he or she currently holds. As Pinder (1985) put it in a slightly different context: 'I am a periodicals librarian, therefore I look after the periodicals collection', and by implication can have no views, nor be expected to contribute to discussions of any policies not directly concerned with the running of the periodicals collection.

Effective communication in whatever form – verbal, non-verbal, written – and of whatever character – upward, downward or lateral – requires the sender to encode the message in a form that it will be understood without ambiguity, and for the recipient either by direct response or some behavioural change to indicate that the message has indeed been assimilated. In this respect, effective communication between colleagues within a library has a direct bearing upon the success or otherwise of the library's effectiveness with its clients, and in fact there is an intimate relationship between the two, as Mathews (1983) has pointed out. Social skills are increasingly expected in the effective librarian. Cronin and Martin (1983) put the problem thus: 'A single rude or socially inept librarian can make a mockery of the most carefully conceived marketing strategy.' Polytechnic libraries are characterised generally by their absence of 'stuffiness', and a general informality of manner that has not always been the hallmark of academic libraries, and this partly stems from the tone of polytechnics as institutions.

Of course, informality should not imply absence of control. The organisation chart may give only a partial view of the pattern of communication within an organisation, but it does indicate who has the responsibility for communicating policy decisions to which group of people. Perhaps even more important, the formal communication channels are the manager's only defence against ill-informed rumour. As Emery (1975) emphasised, the grapevine has its positive aspect, and the information conveyed is usually very accurate; one could add that negative information is only likely to thrive where there is already an atmosphere of distrust. However, the only sure method of keeping 'the library gossip monger' (Emery's words) at bay is to keep the formal systems of communication functioning regularly and effectively. The effect of a good formal communications system will, as Emery noted, remove the basis of the gossip monger's activity, since people will come to rely upon receiving undistorted official communication. Formal channels do not imply regular meetings of all the staff, which in most organisations would be quite impractical. They do require written statements which can be conveyed via the heads of sections to their staff, via noticeboards or through updates to staff manuals of procedure.

Non-verbal communication

Spoken communication is far and away the most practised and many would say most useful form of communication in organisations, because of the value of instant positive or negative feedback. The manager needs, however, to become skilled at interpreting non-verbal cues and signals. These may often be the only true indication of whether, or how, the information has been received. Argyle (1978) has made a study over several years of the importance of non-verbal communication, particularly in such areas as gaze. Eye contact is usually very important in face to face communication, although, if the contact is continuous for more than a few seconds, it can be as equally disturbing to the communicator or receiver as no eye contact at all. The speaker will usually tacitly expect reaction to his words in the form of nods, and sub-vocalised 'hm hm's as indications of agreement and/or understanding.

Other strong non-verbal clues are provided by facial expression and gesture, which may often be quite unconsciously made. Tension may be revealed by such mannerisms as twisting the fingers or looking at the floor. Embarrassment or anger might be overtly controlled in the voice, but reveal themselves through blushing, flushing or tightening of the mouth corners. Tone of voice in a reply is a good indicator of how a particular message has been received.

Informal communication

Mention has already been made of the speed and effectiveness of the grapevine. Information is passed informally between individuals and groups in a variety of situations, and research evidence shows that in each organisation there will be key individuals whose knowledge or expertise in a particular area will mean that information which they convey in that area is more likely to be accepted by individuals or groups. There may, for example, be an information technology 'expert' or an office ergonomics 'expert' and so on, whose opinions are more likely to be accepted in those areas, whether or not they have any formal responsibility in the organisation for them.

Inter-personal communication, particularly between colleagues at work, is a sensitive subject. As Mathews (1983) put it:

> The interaction with a client is relatively short and uncomplicated. Interactions with . . . (colleagues) are far more complex, as we must work closely with the same people day after day. And, along with our professional self, each of us brings with us to our work environment our needs, frustrations, fears, insecurities, subconscious thoughts about others, stereotypes of others, our past experiences, assumptions, our expectations, and our need to be understood and appreciated.

In academic libraries, there is now an increasing awareness that training in the area of inter-personal communication is as vital as, for instance, on-the-job training. Philippa Dolphin (1986), at Hatfield Polytechnic Library, has described how she uses a 'trigger video' for training sessions in communication both between library staff and customers, and between library staff. It uses the effective device of a single direct statement to the camera, such as 'It's all right for you. You can sit in your office all day. We're the ones to suffer when there are staff cuts', and leaves the trainer to lead a discussion with the training group to work out how the situation should be handled. Role play is another training device which can be used to good effect, provided that the trainer is sensitive enough to avoid a situation that may prove too close to home for some participants, or that gives others the opportunity to pay off old scores. If it can be afforded, it is a good idea to employ an outside trainer, who will be seen by all participants as being neutral. The College of Librarianship Wales offers this facility, on a consultancy basis. The Library Association now has an increasing number of courses in the area of communication at work. Leeds Polytechnic School of Librarianship has run a number of highly effective seminars on communication skills and interpersonal competence.

Communication within the polytechnic

Polytechnic libraries do not operate in isolation. They are responsible to the institution that they serve, and the health and well-being of the host community has a direct bearing upon the health and well-being of the library. Chief librarians have always, of course, been involved in the political infighting within the community in the constant battle to obtain more resources. In recent years, this has become much more a matter of common concern for all professional staff, and the success or otherwise in even maintaining the existing share of the diminishing cake can sometimes be attributed to how effectively the library is able to make its voice heard in the labryrinthine network of course committees, faculty boards, user groups and so on. It is now commonplace for the library to have representatives on all relevant course and course planning committees, faculty boards and the librarian himself on the academic board, but in addition it can be highly useful for there to be a library staff member on advisory committees, if they exist, in such areas as health and safety and relevant *ad hoc* working parties, such as data protection and copyright. Naturally, if there is a library committee (as in most polytechnics) the librarian and deputy will be ex-officio members with probably an elected member of the library staff in addition.

The value of wide representation of senior library staff on such committees can hardly be over-stated. In addition to acting as a two-way communication link between the library and faculty, subject and site or faculty librarians in particular are able to report on changes in curriculum and brief the librarian on resource implications. However, perhaps even more important is the cementing of formal and informal contact with members of the teaching staff outside the confines of the library. Without doubt one of the greatest benefits of a departmental or faculty library (to be set against the disadvantage in economic terms) is the regular casual contacts made over coffee between library and teaching staff. With a large central library, such contacts have to be consciously sought.

Conclusion

In such a brief survey of motivation and communication, much has necessarily been omitted or treated superficially. The main objective has been to show that a library that strives to construct a healthy organisational climate, in which there is trust, in which opportunities are given for staff to contribute and to grow and develop as professionals and non-professionals, is less likely to have communication problems and is likely to be in a better position to survive the hard times. It is also likely to become well regarded within its parent institution, whatever may be the apparent deficiencies in library stock, or however physically cramped the building appears to be, since a keen and well-motivated staff will irradiate a healthy spirit in their daily transactions with the users.

References

Adair, J. (1973), *Training for communication*, London, Macdonald.

Argyle, M. (1978), *The psychology of interpersonal behaviour*, 3rd edn, Harmondsworth, Penguin.

Ashworth, W. (1980), 'The multi-site dilemma', *Journal of Librarianship*, vol.12, no.1 (January), pp.1–13.

Biscoe, E.L. and Stone, E.W. (1980), 'Motivation and staff development', *Journal of Library Administration*, vol.1, no.1 (Spring), pp.55–72.

Blake, R.R. and Mouton, J.S. (1964), *The managerial grid*, Houston, Texas, Gulf Publishing Co.

Brighton Polytechnic Library and Learning Resources (1984), 'Staff training and development' in *Council of Polytechnic Librarians*, working papers on staff training, Oxford, Council of Polytechnic Librarians, pp.18–27.

Chapman, L. (1978), *Your disobedient servant*, London, Chatto and Windus.

Cowley, J. (1982), *Personnel management in libraries*, London, Clive Bingley.

Cronin, B. and Martin, I. (1983), 'Social skills training in librarianship', *Journal of Librarianship*, vol.15, no.2 (April), pp.105–22.

Dolphin, P. (1986), 'Interpersonal skills training for library staff', *Library Association Record*, vol.88, no.3 (March), p.134.

Emery, R. (1975), *Staff communication in libraries*, London, Clive Bingley.

Haack, M., Jones, J.W., Roose, T. (1984), 'Occupational burnout among librarians', *Drexel Library Quarterly*, vol.20, no.2 (Spring), pp.46–72.

Hall, J. (ed) (1982), *Fighting professional stagnation: staff development in a period of low mobility*, Leeds, Leeds Polytechnic School of Librarianship.

Hall, J. (1985), 'Professional stagnation: the solution' in *Professional stagnation*, proceedings of a seminar held in Bath University Library, 27 March 1985, Bristol, Library Associa-

tion, University College and Research Section, Southwestern Group, pp.15–27.
Handy, C.B. (1976), *Understanding organizations*, Harmondsworth, Penguin.
Hannabuss, S. (1983), 'Motivational theories and managerial questions', *Information and Library Manager*, vol.2, no.4 (June), pp.98–101, 111.
Harrington, J. (1981), 'Human relations in management during periods of economic uncertainty', *Drexel Library Quarterly*, vol.17, no.2 (Spring), pp.16–26.
Herzberg, F. (1966), *Work and the nature of man*, London, Staples Press.
House, D. (1985), 'Managing the multi-site system' in J. Cowley (ed), *The management of polytechnic libraries*, Aldershot, Gower in association with COPOL, pp.135–56.
Jackson, J.M. (1959), 'The organization and its communication problems', *Journal of Communication*, vol.9, pp.158–67.
Jones, N. and Jordan, P. (1982), *Staff management in library and information work*, Aldershot, Gower.
Kingston Polytechnic Learning Resources (1986), *2nd annual report of the Head of Learning Resources (for the year 1984/85)*, Kingston, Kingston Polytechnic Learning Resources.
Kossen, S. (1983), *The human side of organizations*, 3rd edn, New York, Harper and Row.
McGregor, D. (1957a), 'The human side of enterprise', *Management Review*, vol.45, no.11, pp.22–8.
McGregor, D. (1957b), 'An uneasy look at performance appraisal', *Harvard Business Review*, vol.35, no.3 (May/June), pp.89–94.
Maslow, A. (1943), 'A theory of human motivation', *Psychological Review*, vol.50, pp.370–96.
Mathews, A.J. (1983), *Communicate!: a librarian's guide to interpersonal relations*, Chicago, American Library Association.
O'Reilly, C.A. and Roberts, K.H. (1974), 'Information filtration in organizations: three experiments', *Organizational Behavior and Human Performance*, vol.11, pp.253–65.
Pankhurst, R. (1985), 'Short term planning' in J. Cowley (ed), *The management of polytechnic libraries*, Aldershot, Gower in association with COPOL, pp.17–58.
Peterson, L. (1985), 'The pecking order reversed: a description of administrative review at the William Robert Parks and Ellen Sorg Parks Library', *Journal of Education Media and*

Library Sciences, vol.22, no.3 (Spring), pp.231–49.
Pinder, C. (1985), 'Professional stagnation: the problem' in *Professional stagnation*, proceedings of a seminar held in Bath University Library, 27 March 1985, Bristol, Library Association, University College and Research Section, Southwestern Group.
Plate, K.H. and Stone, E.W. (1974), 'Factors affecting librarians' job satisfaction: a report of two studies', *Library Quarterly*, vol.44, no.2 (April), pp.97–110.
Professional stagnation (1985), proceedings of a seminar held in Bath University Library, 27 March 1985, speakers: Chris Pinder and John Hall, Bristol, Library Association, University College and Research Section, Southwestern Group.
Rayment, T. (1985), 'Working can be a health hazard', *Sunday Times*, 24 February 1985, p.17.
Read, W. (1962), 'Upward communication in industrial hierarchies', *Human Relations*, vol.15, pp.3–16. (Reprinted in Lyman W. Porter and Karlene H. Roberts (1977), *Communication in organizations*, Harmondsworth, Penguin.
Revill, D.H. (1985), *Annual report of the Polytechnic Librarian for the period 1 October 1984 to 30 September 1985*, Liverpool, Liverpool Polytechnic Library Service.
Russell, N.J. (1985), 'Professional and nonprofessional in libraries: the need for a new relationship', *Journal of Librarianship*, vol.17, no.4 (October), pp.293–310.
Rutledge, D.B. (1981), 'Job permanency: the academic librarian's dilemma is the administrator's challenge', *Journal of Academic Librarianship*, March, pp.29, 41.
Slater, M. (1979), *Career patterns and the occupational image: a study of the library/information field*, London, Aslib.
Smith, N.M. and Nelson, V.C. (1983), 'Burnout: a survey of academic reference librarians', *College and Research Libraries*, vol.44, no.3 (May), pp.245–50.
Stewart, L. (1982a), 'Relationships', *Information and Library Manager*, vol.1, no.4 (March), pp.122, 127.
Stewart, L. (1982b), *What do UK librarians dislike about their jobs?* (Centre for Library and Information Management Reports, no.18), Loughborough, Loughborough University.
Stewart, V. and Stewart, A. (1982), *Managing the poor performer*, Aldershot, Gower.

5 Staff in mergers

JOHN COWLEY

Library mergers became a reality, and a management problem, in the mid-sixties when the new London boroughs were created. At that time scores of librarians who had held senior posts in smaller authorities suddenly found themselves challenging for places within the new, larger systems. Competition was fierce and political influences became enmeshed with professional concerns. The successful were elevated to new levels of salary and status to match the greater span of responsibilities, while the unsuccessful looked apprehensively at early retirement or acceptance of posts well down the extended hierarchy. Protected salaries and involvement in new areas of responsibility did little to soothe the hurt of relegation for those who had been used to controlling affairs before the boundary changes were introduced. The same pattern of change was imposed on the country at large as the metropolitan areas came into being in the mid-seventies, and mergers became the order of the day in education as the comprehensive schools replaced the smaller secondary units. The 1966 White Paper introduced a new approach to higher education and by 1970 the polytechnics, commonly formed by merger, were being created. Even after initial designation, additional units were added to the polytechnics as central government policies placed pressure on the smaller independent colleges. The process continues to this day both in the UK and overseas. Ulster Polytechnic and the University of Coleraine merged across the binary line, Kings and Chelsea Colleges came together in London and Bedford College left its central London location to merge with Royal Holloway College.

Bundy (1981, p.10) has described the recent creation of new, large but scattered institutions in Australia, and in 1986 the amalgamation took place of the famous John Crerar Library with the University of Chicago, a project involving the construction of a $22 million building housing two science collections totalling 900,000 volumes and 6,000 serial titles. Recent pronouncements from the DES suggest that mergers are to continue, with pressure on the smaller colleges either to merge with each other or, more likely, to become new departments of existing polytechnics or universities, as illustrated by the recent merger of Thames Polytechnic and Avery Hill College.

Before computer systems became commonplace, the library merger was often seen as a development raising questions mainly of systems standardisation, recataloguing and stock editing and amalgamation. Librarians tended to defend one manual system against another, argue about the physical form of the catalogue and stock and spending priorities. Behind all such problems could be detected human concerns and clashes of personality, but frequently the debate centred on systems rather than people. In days when there was public money available to do so, personnel problems were looked at by administrators as matters to be solved by golden handshakes or inflated salaries. Little attempt was made to assess and develop individual skills, interests and enthusiasms against the true needs of the new organisation. More commonly, the politicians and administrators sought to buy off dissidents and to accommodate the remainder in a pre-defined structure often born of political concerns rather than professional analysis. However the problems of human stress involved in mergers were substantial and gradually began to be recorded and analysed in management literature. Systems integration, though not an insignificant question, became that much simpler with the development of computerisation and machine modification of stock records. Furthermore, as salary funding came under increased pressure, buying off staffing problems became less viable and there developed a new emphasis on re-training and a more dynamic approach to staff management. It was recognised that the 'bringing together of two or more previously independent systems to form a single larger institution carried a high potential for stress and difficulty' (Cowley, 1982, p.83). Increases in size required the extension of the bureaucratic system, the creation of a new range of specialist posts and much longer lines of communication. In dismantling the old systems and creating new, there ensued a period of organisational shock and disruption.

Background to merger

It is useful to differentiate between the main types of

merger seen in higher education in the last decade. The first is exemplified by the mergers which took place in the 1969/73 period when the polytechnics were first designated. In this instance, the new institutions were formed by bringing together a number of colleges of roughly equal standing. The old North-Western Polytechnic and the Northern Polytechnic came together to form the Polytechnic of North London, while Middlesex Polytechnic had within it the Hendon College of Technology and the Enfield College of Technology, both successful institutions of similar coverage and academic standing.

The coming together of previously successful and independent units with their own management styles and leadership presented great difficulties for those holding senior positions in the constituent colleges. Naturally, each aspired to dominance or at least parity within the new institution. Substantial battles were fought in interim Steering Committees with much jockeying for position. Exactly the same processes were discernible in the college libraries involved. The impression was gained of a great deal of eloquent self-defence, reports made to unreceptive committees and interminable discussions involving staff about to be merged, but the level of emphatic decision-making needed to drive the new institutions along was frequently not forthcoming until new managements were drafted in. The process of resolution began at the top with the appointment of a director to replace the numerous principals, many of whom became members of the directorate team on the strength of their experience and local knowledge but significantly deprived of their final authority. There was a parallel development in the libraries as new heads were appointed from outside to bring a fresh outlook to bear on future library development. Even when one of the existing, competing college librarians was seen to be a cut above the rest, it was decided advisable to seek an outside appointment in the hope that such a move would be more unifying and provide a means of breaking out of the bonds of parochialism. Once the polytechnics were established and their management and libraries operating successfully, there came the second type of merger which required a somewhat different approach.

Around the country, the large polytechnics were asked to take into the fold small, independent colleges which had escaped the earlier amalgamation process. They tended to be specialist institutions, not infrequently colleges of education.

They could not compete in terms of size and academic range with the polytechnics and this type of merger took on the quality of an enveloping cloak, the imposition of a new culture and gradual erosion of the old identity. The well-established polytechnics with their powerful management teams took aboard the smaller partner. It was politely done, with proper academic restraint, but nevertheless often led to drastic change. The smaller college library entered the larger environment attempting to cling to its expertise and self-respect but without trying to challenge the management style of the parent organisation.

Within these two main types of merger could be detected specific problems. To return to the Middlesex example, repeated around the country in such places as Brighton and Preston, it could be seen that the strains of the merger were present when either (i) two almost identical colleges were brought together, for example Hendon and Enfield, or (ii) a small specialist college such as Hornsey was forced to merge with larger groupings of academic disciplines perceived to be at odds with the specialist college and its unique traditions. There is no doubt that art and design and education were areas of study which did not wish to merge with engineering, science and the other major disciplines. Their view of educational needs, management style and organisation of courses did not fit easily into desired patterns. It was to take years for the full spirit of amalgamation and common purpose to become a reality. The special nature of art and design libraries demanded particular care in the context of library mergers. The problems persisted over the first fifteen years of polytechnic existence and have been exacerbated by the overall resource problems now afflicting public sector higher education. Equally, enlightened management has been able to absorb the problem of specialist interests by accepting a measure of local autonomy and acknowledging the value and stimulation of departments or faculties having something unique to offer the larger organisation.

The problem of like colleges coming together on the other hand presented difficulties of duplication of stock and effort, made worse in some instances by a fierce sense of uncompromising competitiveness. This problem has tended to be solved by the rationalisation of courses, the relocation of book stocks and a gradual achieving of common purpose as new management has made its impact. Duplicate courses and surplus staff resulting from the enforced merger of like institutions presented polytechnic managements with problems of inflated student/staff ratios (SSRs) and excessive salary bills which took more than a decade to sort out. It was ironic that polytechnics were criticised in the eighties for carrying excessive staff and not meeting SSR targets when enforced mergers had created the problem in the first place. Local authority adherence to policies of no redundancy and limited voluntary severance guaranteed that the process of adjustment to a leaner model would take time. What was true for the polytechnics in general also applied to their libraries. The bringing together of similar teams created the inevitable duplication of skills and functions. Surplus of staffing tended to occur at senior level, as had happened in the public libraries in 1965, with the resultant pressure on salary costs. There followed a gradual thinning-out process, encouraged by enhanced pension arrangements, but remaining senior staff had to be redeployed and newly motivated. In some cases the transition into posts carrying system-wide responsibilities was successfully accomplished whilst for others the change from college librarian to site or faculty librarian was not too painful where local autonomy was legitimised and supported.

Organisational change

The individual and the group operate in the context of an organisational structure which becomes familiar. The familiarity is comforting despite the fact that the organisation and its bureaucracy may on occasions frustrate and defeat the aims of the group and ambitions of the individual. The organisation represents continuity and its protocols are understood. Change, though frequently emanating from the individual, is processed through the organisation. The initiators of new developments have as points of reference precedents in terms of practices and responses. The location of power within the organisation is understood and the individual is also familiar with the centres of informal influence. The Library Development Plan tracked its way from the librarian's office to the library committee, on to the resources committee and up to the final academic board debate, the outcome of which was often predictable in that careful informal preparation in the privacy of offices had guaranteed its ultimate success. These known structures and practices are frequently damaged or modified in the merger situation. The previously powerful are rendered powerless; the line of command is changed and lengthened; supportive individuals are replaced by those with new standards and preferences; the patient cultivation of contacts has to begin afresh. Mergers dramatically change the organisational structure and the sources of real power and authority. The individual who is not adaptable or whose face does not fit can be left floundering in the reorganisation process.

To those involved in the merger of two or more partners of equal stature, the changes brought about will be disruptive but perhaps not overwhelming. The new, enlarged structure may not depart radically from that known earlier and, in any case, the creation of a multi-site organisation may leave considerable power devolved at site level thus easing the shock of the loss of independence. However for the small unit absorbed into the larger body, the organisational and culture shock can be profound. The degree of influence residing in the former will be drastically eroded as it is expected to fit into the larger existing structure. The individual of some importance and influence in the small setting will tend to become almost invisible in the larger context. The detached observer may be able to discuss practicalities and justifications on both sides of the merger. The larger organisation, if it is to avoid being nothing more than a loose federation, must establish a working structure and appoint to key posts those who seem to be capable of furthering the goals of the new entity. When this process involves disappointing others and dismantling existing structures, this is seen as a necessary development. On the other hand, the defender of what had been, the protector of known standards, the preserver of earlier practices and traditions, can be seen to be acting legitimately in the early period of change. It is not unreasonable for someone who has provided good service to a known community to wish to preserve methods and attitudes that have worked well in the past. This might lead to the point where the parties involved in the merger accept the existence of genuine differences of opinion which can be brought to some sort of synthesis given time, understanding and proper planning. The merger will make it necessary to redefine the purpose and role of the new organisation and to re-assess the structure and systems needed to conduct efficient operations. Attention will have to be paid to changes in external controls, not least those concerned with resource provision. The structure and technology of internal systems will require detailed attention, and it will be essential to create agreed organisational aims and objectives.

Communication and participation

The communication system and the act of communicating take on a particular importance during the time of mergers. 'Communication between members is more likely to become distorted than at any other time' (Mangham, 1979, p.189). Reporting relationships are thrown into disarray, and key people in the long-established communication system suddenly find themselves involved in a chain of ambiguity and uncertainty. In the organisation at large, key figures in financing, resourcing and management depart or are given new functions so that the library's contacts with the wider environment are changed. Within the new, enlarged library system parallel changes take place involving altered status, new functions and modified structures. As lines of communication lengthen, local matters which earlier had prompt attention now move out along the extended system, perhaps to be actually lost in a mass of paperwork or judged to be of low priority. In this extended system there is a tendency to ignore the significance of local detail and to modify local objectives and priorities by reducing them to fit the wider view of the grand plan. There is the danger that local needs will be misunderstood or misrepresented and that central responses will be bland, delayed and not entirely relevant.

It is therefore essential to establish quickly a new and understood communication system covering the whole of the library-in-merger. Any new library must be briefed on formal communication practices, must have explained to it the functions of committees, working groups and individuals holding special responsibilities. It will have to be clear how decisions are reached on finances, resources, staff training, the introduction of new technology and so on. Local representation will have to be explained and acted upon by the introduction of new staff from the merged unit. Crucially, expertise within the new team must be identified and drafted in on working parties or standing committees so that it can be applied to system-wide problems. The involvement of new staff in the wider decision-making processes will convince them of management's desire to use and value their talents.

The whole library system could be modified by the impact of the merger. Even if the merger involves a large host library and a relatively small newcomer, the potential for change throughout should not be ignored. Even if the new unit has little to offer in terms of personnel or ideas, it is essential for it to benefit from the communication process and to be encouraged to contribute to the input of information and points of view. Crucially in the very early stages, the merger-manager will have a large part to play in assessing the levels of local expertise, encouraging the new library's participation in forward planning and explaining ways in which to make use of existing communication networks.

Local flavour is particularly pronounced in academic libraries where the nature of courses, the approaches to study and the use of library materials can vary significantly according to the demands of the discipline served. It is important, therefore, that site views are provided with an outlet through an understood communication system. Whatever the configuration of the enlarged library, the full expression of ideas must be facilitated. Those responsible for the final executive function will rely heavily on the advice and specialist knowledge communicated through the various committees and working groups. The merger-manager must spend a good deal of time ensuring that the views expressed by the recently acquired unit are understood and fairly interpreted. The care taken with transitory, developmental problems will indicate to those under new management the likely quality and nature of the executive style to be experienced in the future. The manager must not only set objectives but also clearly communicate how they are to be attained. The staff's ability and willingness to respond will be influenced by their understanding of the ideas and instructions communicated to them. The complexities prevailing within the merger require that information and attitudes be freely transmitted around a network that allows for comment and feedback from all points within the system. Messages and instructions will be mediated by groups of receivers, who will send back responses that will range from the critical to the supportive. It is likely that staff-in-merger will have a set of standards initially at variance with the aims of the system as a whole. The first stage in the modification of views is concerned with the establishing of a communication system that allows the diversity of opinion to surface and be subject to debate and analysis. When it is understood that even strong, centralist leadership is willing to receive and consider messages from within the system, then there is a real chance of collaboration and adjustment on all sides. However this process of analysis and synthesis will initially depend on the quality of the communication on offer.

Cultural change

It is acknowledged that an organisation is not only made up of a formal structure backed by a system of communication but also possesses a character or culture unique to that organisation. Time, with the concomitant arrival and departure of individuals and the introduction of new systems and technology, modifies any organisation so that evolutionary cultural change is always present and acceptable to the majority. There is stimulation in a modicum of change, as witnessed by staff reaction to the introduction of the first automated circulation control, but this kind and level of change does not challenge the underlying, deep-rooted cultural ethos. Even the arrival of new senior staff, though speeding change, is to some extent absorbed into the network of tradition and influences at work within the institution. The newcomer modifies and is modified by the institutional ethos. Those intent on change have to understand that every team within the organisation has created for itself a unique way of doing things and sees itself far enough away from the centres of power to resist change when it is seen to be too drastic or threatening. Prevailing attitudes colour the habits and style of local management; the workforce has its own broad understanding of conventions and precedent. The culture of the small sub-organisation may be likened to that of a large family operating informally, with little difficulty over communication and a willingness to accept leadership that is within reach and known to them. The trickle of new staff moving into the system is smoothly absorbed and rapidly indoctrinated into the cultural climate. The traditional approach to operations and training is maintained over periods of time, with only slight modification and adjustment. Such tranquillity and conservatism is swept aside by the act of merger. Organisational change of this magnitude causes great stress for the staff concerned. All parties to a merger undergo a period of anxiety and uncertainty.

Staff in the smaller merged unit in particular will be subject to great pressure. The small independent institution will have operated informally and often in a paternalistic atmosphere. Students will know the staff and will tend to solve problems by making use of the informal system of pastoral care. It is likely that there will be a large measure of trust and a matching low level of politicisation. Staff and students will join together in cultural and leisure pursuits and rarely will serious conflicts arise. This tranquil state of affairs will probably be damaged or even destroyed in the merger period. Students will find it more difficult to make contact with staff, new rules will be laid down from afar, library personnel and systems will be changed, courses re-located, paternalism and pastoral care replaced by a greater degree of conflict and politicisation. Initially, at least, cultural deprivation will dominate everyone's thinking and the merged staff and students will tend to resent this new state of affairs.

Individual reaction to merger

First news of a pending merger will trigger off a state of uncertainty in the minds of individuals involved. Everyone will be concerned about his or her place in the new organisation. As Gill (1978, p.15) has put it: 'Personnel at all levels . . . are likely to begin thinking about consequences of the merger for their careers. Tension, role conflict, ambiguity and distrust are an inevitable consequence.' Close links with the old leadership will disappear and well-established practices will be replaced by new methods that may not easily be understood. Psychological preparedness for these changes might be insufficient and the disturbance of the working equilibrium achieved through long familiarity with a known environment can have serious consequences for the individual. The previous internalisation of modes of behaviour, which allowed for near automatic responses, can be completely destroyed during a merger. The outcome of change of this magnitude will depend on the individual's capacity to absorb changed circumstances and the quality of managerial skills employed in making the transition more acceptable. The individual's personality and attitudes will play a significant part as will the manager's ability to reduce tension and create a climate for change which is at least acceptable to the majority of those involved.

The psychological preparedness for merger will be insufficient in many cases. Some concerns will be expressed and alleviated during the preparatory period but real psychological distress may only surface some time after the merger takes place. This is likely to happen when individuals cannot believe that significant change is impending and initially hope that the impact on them will be slight. This delayed realisation of significant change may result in major problems surfacing after the merger has taken place, in individuals who had shown little sign of concern in the early stages. It may take as long as two to three years to absorb and respond to this kind of reaction.

How staff react to merger will depend to a certain extent on the personality and attitudes of the individuals involved. Some will display antagonism and will vigorously defend the values of the old system. Those who have lost status and power may well take every opportunity to impede the introduction of new methods. Others will take refuge in withdrawal and non-involvement and will attempt to remain at a distance from the new organisation. They will do the minimum necessary to satisfy superiors but will fail to inject any enthusiasm into their work. They will be the source of little difficulty but will equally lack a sense of commitment and are not likely to be creative or productive. Fortunately there will be others who perceive the merger as an opportunity for career extension. The more ambitious will welcome the merger as a means of gaining new experience. They will be the types to benefit from retraining and redeployment. Their enthusiasm will be vital in overcoming the doubts of others and injecting positive thinking into committees and working groups. The manager can expect to deal with responses ranging from the substantially enthusiastic to the openly rebellious and will need to give considerable time to the study of individuals caught up in the merger.

Management initiatives

Searby (1969, p.4) has stated that:

> Change is certain after a merger – not evolutionary change, but sudden, often traumatic change. This is most apparent when the new partner is being fully integrated into a centralised enterprise. But even if the

acquired company is to be an autonomous subsidiary, new reporting relationships are created, new corporate goals and obligations are assumed and the changes affecting both the acquired company and the acquirer are inevitable.

Thus the problems inherent in sudden change can never be under-estimated by management. Staff need to be prepared by information transmission, training, persuasion or indoctrination. The problems are exaggerated when changes are initiated by new management whose every move is viewed with apprehension and suspicion after the merger. At least when businesses merge, the workforce can be persuaded that the marrying of interests, wider utilisation of skills and access to an enlarged market will bring a new level of prosperity to the merged companies. Furthermore, if such action is seen to be necessary, the new management can demand acceptance of change if necessary by removing dissident elements or superfluous staff. Managers of mergers in the public sector may have ambitions to introduce change as fundamental as any in commerce or industry without having the power to achieve these aims, particularly with regard to the redeployment or dismissal of staff. The merger has to be achieved having regard to the prevailing rules. In the public sector this will mean reliance on persuasion and gradual adjustment rather than dramatic action. The only solution to the problem of superfluous staff is that of voluntary severance, which is not without its attractions for the minority as long as the terms are reasonably advantageous, but which cannot be forced on the unwilling.

Immediately after the merger there is high potential for confusion and misunderstandings. Management must be prepared to expend much time and effort on the associated problems. Reporting relationships and lines of communication must be established. All involved in the merger must feel they have a point of contact with the decision-makers and have access to a manager or convenor of a working party in order to feed in concerns, ideas or responses. Experience suggests that when a library initiates change, such as the introduction of new technology or the mass transfer of book stock, there is considerable advantage in appointing one person to manage the operation. Given that mergers pose such major problems, it is essential that an experienced manager be given a leadership role. The ideal person will combine a good command of systems with a deep understanding of personnel matters. He or she must be assigned responsibility for planning and overseeing the post-merger activity by 'identifying needed action, sequencing steps and monitoring the pace of change' (Searby, 1969, p.8). The merger-manager should be a continuous presence among the merged, should be able to represent their views, moderate them in the light of desired institutional objectives and act as a feeder of information back to top management. The alternative of a small steering committee could be used, particularly if representation of conflicting interests is a major concern. In this case the chairman of the committee might take on the role of merger-manager, albeit with less power to make quick decisions. Whatever line is taken immediately following the merger, there is a need for a clear and immediate point of leadership.

Timing of change

Circumstances will influence the timing of changes which inevitably flow from the merger. Some managers will take the view that not too much initial disturbance is the best tactic to employ. This might convince the merged library that the new management is considerate and restrained and will introduce only necessary change in a measured way. It might even be agreed that changes will not be made until a full review of objectives has been carried out with all parties to the merger fully involved. It is possible however that such an approach carries fundamental weaknesses. After a merger most staff expect change and will see no action as a sign of indifference or weakness on the part of management. A slow beginning might encourage the opponents of change to man the barricades with greater vigour. It is more appropriate therefore to introduce significant change as soon as possible and to use the period before the actual merger date to carry out reviews of the constituent parts and their future working together.

It is crucial to make key staff appointments from the beginning. If the merger demands the appointment of new staff or the redeployment of existing personnel, this should be at the forefront of the action. Ideally the newly merged groups should have key personnel in post and a merger-manager nominated from the first day of the coming together. The resultant injection of new thinking and decisive leadership should pave the way for rapid results. As long as the correct choices are made, new appointments can help to raise morale in the merger period. Staff will witness the departure of those who have ceased to make an effective contribution and the arrival or promotion of individuals who will bring new ideas and enthusiasm to bear. Nothing engenders staff interest more than the arrival of new managers; the healthy disrespect of those down the line for their bosses, whose term of office can appear to be interminable, is assuaged for a time at least when new managerial appointments are made. Internal promotion of high quality staff has the added advantage of knock-on effects so that even a couple of senior promotions can lead to other staff movements as teams are reorganised. Previously stagnant staffing positions can be translated into fluidity and opportunity as a result of the merger. Management must stress these advantages to counteract the more destructive aspects of merger which, if allowed, can begin to dominate staff thinking.

All mergers will provide career opportunities for some, and managers must capitalise on this fact. For those eased out of a job or who gain nothing in the way of personal advancement, the merger will seem to be threatening, but there is little point in management allowing negative attitudes to dominate. Where personnel changes are required, as many as possible should be made quickly just as soon as key positions have been identified and suitable people found to fill them. Conversely those who have been resistant to the whole process of merger and give no indication of being able to adapt to the new régime should be encouraged to look elsewhere for employment. All staff must be informed of the changes and opportunities ahead and allowed to feed their reactions into the discussions in the planning period. They must be made aware of posts to be filled and the opportunities for retraining. They must be given every chance to discuss their own position in the merged organisation. Once the merger has taken place, however, individuals continuing to adopt an antagonistic stance should be treated correctly but firmly. Those in the right age-group can be offered financial incentive to retire early while the younger librarian, given ample recognition of past services and all the help that it is practical to give, should be encouraged to seek other employment. It is highly likely that the numbers involved will be very small if the management is of a high standard but it will be to everyone's advantage to see the back of dissident elements.

Motivation and synergy

A key factor in successful integration is the maintenance of motivation among employees where it already exists and the introduction of fresh motivation where it is lacking:

> Employees at all levels have a set of expectations, or psychological contract, for their work which embraces what they are asked to do, how they are organised, controlled and rewarded. Motivation occurs when the psychological contract, as viewed both by the individual and the organisation, coincide . . . if congruence is not achieved . . . then he or she will work less well and may even decide to leave the organisation because psychological discomfort or stress is being experienced (Jones, 1986, p.41).

First news of the merger may shift the emphasis in the individual's mind away from good performance and self-fulfilment towards an obsession with security and status. Passive management will allow this crucial change of attitude to take place. Positive steps taken to inform, discuss and encourage the individual may successfully restore the right attitudes. Managers of post-merger change should aim to restore equilibrium and seek ways of enhancing factors that motivate; promotion, redeployment, retraining, participation in introducing change, recognition of skills and expertise, involvement in problem-solving and exposure to new systems and technology. The latter element has been important in libraries in the past decade. Most large academic libraries have established sophisticated real-time, online systems whereas the smaller institutions have not been able to find the resources to do this. A merger provides the opportunity for the technologically frustrated librarian to move into the eighties and solve problems associated with the use of old manual systems which at best had been limping along.

When businesses merge it is expected that there will follow the creation of synergy which can be described as 'the gain that is said to arise when two firms merge; it is normally described as the 2 + 2 = 5 concept' (Newbould, 1970, p.162). This can be achieved by a maintained level of output from reduced resources or by using the combined resources to produce greater output. Management of merged firms are said to be synergy-creating when they use a combination of reduced resources to achieve higher productivity and a greater share of the market. Synergic outcomes might include improved market penetration by improved products, economies arising from the integration of administrations and the redirecting of human expertise into innovative sectors. This concept of synergy can usefully be translated into a library merger. In the simplest terms it implies decisive management responses aimed at tackling tasks either more economically or more effectively. The elimination of duplicate posts and the retirement of those who elect to go will provide both economies in salary and the opportunity to redirect effort into crucial development areas. It might be felt, for instance, that the new enlarged team would benefit from a full-time training librarian, and that this post is now justifiable in the context of staff requirements and numbers. The newly-merged smaller unit might benefit from spare capacity in the larger library's computer systems which can be introduced at costs easily absorbed into the joint budgets. New reader services, such as library publications and online searching, could be extended to the new unit, while the specialist resources of the smaller library can be made available to all users. However if the approach to merger is well managed, the most beneficial element will be that involving the promotion and redeployment of staff who can be given new career development within the enlarged library. Every opportunity should be taken to remove superfluous effort in over-staffed areas and re-direct resources into more productive areas.

Conclusion

Mergers will inevitably have their casualties. The most caring, experienced management will not be able to solve all the problems associated with dramatic change. There will be some predisposed to resist change to the point of overt rebellion or disgruntled departure. Others will be quieter victims of change, frustrated within the new system and longing for the return of earlier times. It is likely that early retirement will be a wise choice for the minority in the right age group, particularly those who feel unable to respond to the opportunities provided through staff development programmes. Fortunately, experience suggests that these negative responses are in the minority as long as new management operates effectively. Skilled management can guide staff through the first shock of merger and create in them a mood of positive response to change. Over a period of about two years it should be possible to restore equilibrium and attain new levels of performance.

To achieve this, good management will need to be decisive and responsive. The period from the first announcement of merger to the date of implementation must be used fruitfully. The merger-manager, or equivalent, should be nominated at the beginning and given time and support to carry out the work efficiently. He or she must be a presence in the unit to be merged and should have the confidence of the staff and other senior colleagues.

The library merger should be carried out in a manner consistent with wider academic policies, and it is here that the head of library services would have a major part to play in interpreting for his colleagues the recommendations of the academic board and the executive. Key new appointments must be made quickly and new policies and objectives generated after proper debate and staff participation.

The problems of longer lines of communication must be overcome so that individuals at all points in the system feel able to express their views and feel involved in decision-making. Programmes of staff training and development must be linked to planned redeployments and the introduction of new systems. The merged unit should benefit from the range of resources and new technology previously unavailable, and the skills and expertise of the new staff should be made available to the system at large. A sense of involvement and participation should be generated. The manager must work through the period of initial anxiety and low morale and lead the staff into a new era of confidence taking care to enhance those factors that motivate and encourage. It will not go unnoticed if, at the same time, the newly merged library reaches a state of synergy by providing improved services and more efficient use of resources. Essentially the manager should view the operation as an opportunity to achieve enhanced performance and the remotivation of staff from both sides of the merger.

References

Bundy, A.L. (1981), *Amalgamations and libraries* (Occasional Publications, no.3), Footscray, Footscray Institute of Technology.

Cowley, J. (1982), *Personnel management in libraries*, London, Clive Bingley.
Gill, J. (1978), 'Managing a merger: the acquisition and the aftermath', *Personnel Management*, vol.10, no.5 (January), pp.14–17.
Jones, C.S. (1986), 'Change and motivation following a takeover', *Management Accounting*, vol.64, no.2, pp.40–2.
Mangham, I. (1979), *The politics of organisational change*, London, Associated Business Press.
Newbould, G.D. (1970), *Management and merger activity*, Liverpool, Guthstead.
Searby, F.W. (1969), 'Control postmerger change', *Harvard Business Review*, vol.4, no.5, pp.4–12, 154–5.

6 Staffing in contraction

CHRISTINE E. MOON

Staffing reductions: an overview

The 1970s were years of enormous growth for the thirty[1] polytechnics which had been designated at the beginning of the decade. Most were formed initially from the merging of institutions; some continued to grow later in the seventies through further mergers in the wake of government policy on teacher education. The libraries in the polytechnics followed the pattern of growth set by their parent institutions and merged library systems and multiple-site libraries became the norm. Total library staff increased from just over 1,000 in the mid 1970s to an all-time high of 1,661 by 1980.

The first half of the 1980s had a very different feel, being dominated by reductions in public expenditure as a major plank of government policy. The Advanced Further Education (AFE) pool was capped in the financial year 1980/81, and since then public sector higher education has been moved steadily year-by-year toward unit funding. In its review of 1984/85, the Committee of Directors of Polytechnics recorded its grave concern about the continued fall in the real value of the unit of resource and stated that:

> Over the period from 1979/80 to 1983/84, DES figures showed that there has been a fall in unit costs in real terms of 18.4 per cent. The combination of increasing student numbers and the capping of the AFE quantum resulted in a further decline in the real value of the unit resource of over 4 per cent in 1984/85 (Committee of Directors of Polytechnics, 1986, p.2).

Naturally, the polytechnic libraries have not remained unaffected in this financial climate. Having peaked at 1,661 staff in 1980, library staff numbers had fallen back to 1,582 by 1985.

Reductions were therefore at their peak in the years between 1980 and 1985. Figure 6.1 shows the fluctuation in staff numbers for the thirty polytechnics during that period. The majority of polytechnics lost some staff, though four managed to maintain their staffing and eight achieved

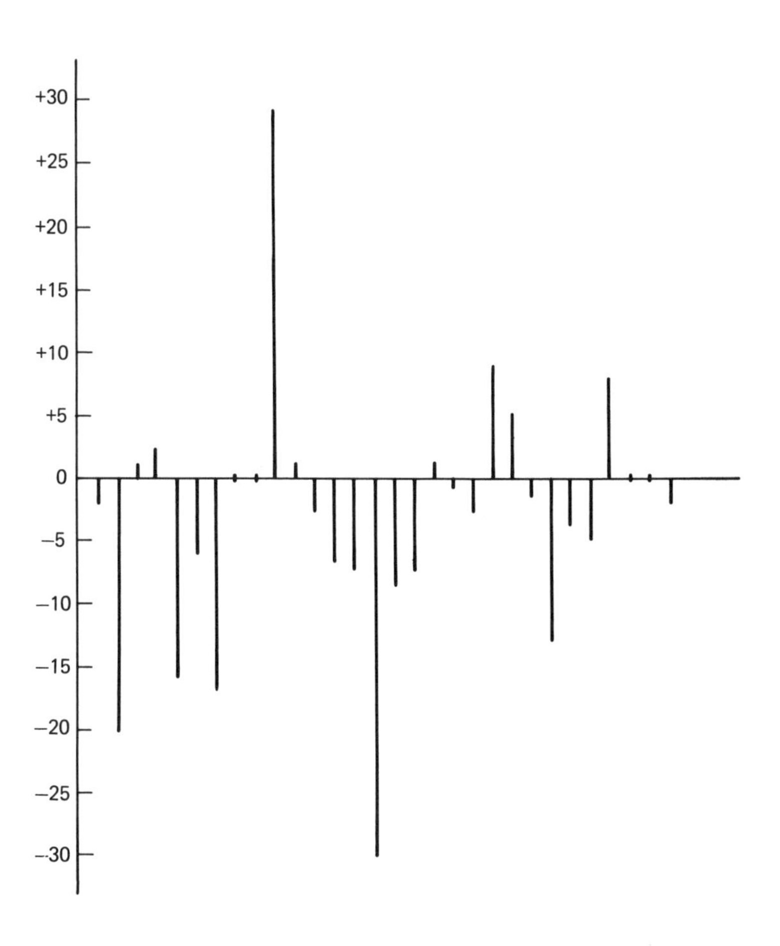

Figure 6.1 Changes in staff numbers in the thirty polytechnic libraries 1980 to 1985

increases, one or two of the latter through mergers rather than real growth. Although there is no absolute correlation between overall unit costs per FTE in individual institutions at the start of the financial cutback and the fate of their library staffing, some patterns do emerge. It is scarcely surprising, for example, that of the five polytechnic libraries that lost more than ten posts, three (Brighton, Kingston and North East London) were institutions with notably high unit costs at the start of the exercise. Brighton and North East London also had particularly high non-teaching staff costs when compared with the rest of the polytechnics. Hatfield and Lancashire, the other two whose staffing dropped by more than ten posts, were exceptions in that their unit costs were fairly near the average. Lancashire had, however, closed a number of sites which enabled it to make reductions without difficulty. Those that suffered no cuts or that grew tended to be close to the average or low on unit costs. Interestingly, even the two institutions with the lowest unit costs (Manchester and City of London) lost some library posts. Although the staffing reductions sustained have been hard felt in many cases, it is perhaps surprising that, though institutions have typically lost around 20 per cent of their funding, library staff have been reduced by a little less than 5 per cent.

Library staff:student ratios

In monetarist terms, the years from 1980 to 1985 could be characterised as ones of high 'productivity'. There has been an overall increase of 31 per cent in polytechnic student numbers whilst funding has dropped by around 20 per cent in real terms. Although library staffing has declined by less than 5 per cent, putting this together with the vastly increased student numbers brings about a dramatic worsening of the library staff-to-student ratio. Table 6.1 shows the relationship between these factors and the decline in the average staff:student ratio (SSR) which results.

In the optimistic atmosphere of the mid 1970s, COPOL (Council of Polytechnic Librarians) devised a target SSR of one member of library staff to every seventy to eighty full time equivalent (FTE) students (Revill, 1985). This was never achieved overall and even in the best years only eight polytechnic libraries managed to get within this range. Curiously, as recently as 1982, the National Association of Teachers in Further and Higher Education (NATFHE) produced a policy statement (NATFHE, 1982) on college libraries recommending a ratio of 1:80 for single-site libraries with an unspecified addition for extra sites. Since the mean had risen to 1:118 by 1984/85 these targets must now be seen as the products of a different era.

Table 6.1

Library staff and student numbers 1980 and 1985

	1980	1985	percentage change
Library staff	1,661	1,582	–4.75
Students (full time equivalent)	141,921	185,891	+31.00
Staff:student ratio (mean)	1:85	1:118	+39.00

Source: Council of Polytechnic Librarians statistical and staffing surveys and Polytechnic Finance Officers' Group annual reports

Since much can be concealed by broad brush-strokes and the statement of averages, it is worth looking in more detail at the effects on SSRs. Table 6.2 shows the extremes of the range for the two years under scrutiny.

Table 6.2

Library staff:student ratios 1980 and 1985

	1980	1985	percentage change
Highest SSR	1:140	1:164	+17
Lowest SSR	1:47	1:71	+51
Mean SSR	1:85	1:118	+39

So marked has been the worsening of the SSR that what in 1980 was clearly the worst SSR (1:140) had by 1985 become quite common. In fact, a ratio that would have been regarded as the poor relation in 1980 had been forced upon a fifth of the polytechnics by 1985. Twenty-nine polytechnic libraries have seen their SSR worsen; one (Oxford) has just managed to hold on to its SSR at 1:103; none has improved its SSR despite staff increases in some polytechnics.

There has inevitably been considerable variety in the severity of the experience. Thirteen polytechnics have stabilised this worsening of SSRs at 30 per cent or less. However, another fourteen show a range of degradation between 30 per cent and 100 per cent whilst two cases exceed 100 per cent. Table 6.3 shows the shift in the number of polytechnic libraries working within a range of SSR bands between 1980 and 1985.

Table 6.3

Shift in staff:student ratios 1980 to 1985

SSR band	Number of polytechnic libraries 1980	1985
1:47–70	7	0
1:71–90	9	1
1:91–110	12	11
1:111–140	2	12
1:141–164	0	6

Changes in staff balances

The gross numbers of staff and students quoted above are clearly of interest in any consideration of library contraction, but they are basically only a starting point. More interesting, possibly, is a consideration of the kinds of changes which have taken place in the balance of staff during this time of retrenchment. One indicator is the breakdown of staff between Burnham graded posts (with or without Burnham conditions of service), and NJC (including ILEA) professional and non-professional posts. Table 6.4 shows this breakdown for the two years in question, 1980 and 1985.

Table 6.4

Burnham and NJC library staffing 1980 and 1985

Year	Burnham	NJC professional	Non-professional	Total
1980	258	493	910	1,661
1985	214	489	879	1,582

Source: Council of Polytechnic Librarians annual staffing surveys

It would appear from Table 6.4 that most of the pruning has been carried out at the extremes of the staff structure. Out of a total reduction of seventy-nine posts, forty-four were Burnham posts and thirty-one were non-professional NJC posts. A number of the Burnham posts were retirements of senior staff from merged colleges taking advantage of the Crombie scheme in its later stages. At the non-professional end of the spectrum the loss of posts is more likely to reflect high turnover at this level combined with the random axing of vacancies. Although the closure of sites would have enabled *some* libraries to reduce their junior staff with little difficulty, most have had to cope with such large increases in students that substantial cuts at this level would have been avoided if at all possible.

At first sight, it is easy to see why the expensive Burnham posts were sacrificed. Even at junior levels of the Burnham range the scales are extremely long and become expensive at the top end. Many libraries had financial rather than head-count targets and, when combined with a relentlessly increasing demand for basic services, one can well appreciate the *immediate* attraction of retaining two-and-a-half library assistants in place of one senior lecturer librarian. Indeed, the situation at the non-professional end would have been far worse had this approach not been taken. In the longer term, however, one might well doubt the wisdom of this strategy since it will always be harder to reinstate high-cost posts at a later date, and the loss of invigorating leadership even in the short-term is scarcely to be recommended. In a period of constraint, creative leadership is probably even more vital than at other times.

Focusing in on levels in more detail, however, reveals a slightly more complex picture. Although *exact* comparability across grading schemes (Burnham, NJC, ILEA) is not possible, Table 6.5 attempts a grouping into five categories of staff. From this it can be seen that both in percentage terms and in actual numbers it is the junior professional group which has sustained the most severe loss. Promotion and 'grade-creep' into the 'senior professional' band will have contributed to some of the reduction at this level, particularly as older staff at more senior levels retired or left for other posts. However, at such constrained times and with natural wastage the preferred means of reducing staff establishments, it is interesting to see that there has been sufficient mobility to enable forty-one posts to be abolished.

Table 6.5

Structural changes 1980 to 1985

	1980	1985	Difference	
			no. posts	percentage change
Clerical staff (Scale 1–3)	910	879	–31	–3.4
Junior professional (Scale 3–5; LI)	369	328	–41	–11.11
Senior professional (Scale 6–SO2; LII)	227	229	+2	+0.88
Managerial (PO; SL; PL; HOD)	125	116	–9	–7.25
Head of service	30	30	0	–
Total	1,661	1,582	–79	–4.75

Note: Includes ILEA grades distributed according to salary level.

Source: Council of Polytechnic Librarians annual staffing surveys.

Throughout the professional bands the Burnham posts have been very thoroughly pruned. Eight lecturer I, seventeen lecturer II/senior lecturer, thirteen senior lecturer and seven principal lecturer posts have gone. In the senior professional band the loss of seventeen lecturer II/senior lecturer posts has, however, been matched by increases at scale 6/senior officer, which is why the numbers overall have been maintained. In the junior professional group it has been the posts up to scale 4 which have been lost. Forty-five in all went from this level.

It would appear, then, that libraries have endeavoured to keep the core of their academic support by retaining site librarians, faculty librarians and senior subject staff at the expense of some management posts and a lot of junior professional and non-professional posts. This is hardly surprising. In most systems the subject librarians have a high public profile, have built up extensive subject expertise and are, in large part, the most obvious deliverers of the service from the users' point of view. Their loss has always to be publicly acknowledged and tends to cause the loudest outcry in the academic arena – a factor that may well have been used to good advantage by some. Posts have undoubtedly been lost from this area of reader services, but, for the most part, libraries have tried to shield their users from the worst effects of staffing loss and have endeavoured to maintain strong faculty support.

Staff costs and other expenditure

The major sources of statistical and financial information on polytechnic libraries are COPOL and the Polytechnic Finance Officers' Group (PFOG) – organisations that have become increasingly sophisticated in their data-gathering in recent years. The most recent year for which complete financial data is available at the time of writing (1986) is 1984/85. The comparisons that follow will therefore be made between that financial year and 1979/80 when public expenditure cuts began to be seriously felt.

The total bill for the 1,661 polytechnic library staff in 1979/80 was £8.84 million. By 1984/85, with seventy-nine fewer staff, the bill was £14.29 million. In that period the average cost of each member of library staff (salaries and employment costs) rose by 70 per cent from £5,327 pa to £9,035 pa.

In considering staff reductions and the financial implications of library staffing generally, it is worth setting staff costs alongside those for the other elements of the library service. Table 6.6 shows average spending in the polytechnics on library staff, materials and services (inter-library lending, information services and automation, stationery and supplies and so on) in 1979/80 and 1984/85.

Table 6.6

Materials: services: salaries – average costs 1979/80 and 1984/85

	1979/80 £	Percentage of total	1984/85 £	Percentage of total
Materials	218,000	40	284,000	34
Services	40,000	7	83,000	10
Staff	295,000	53	476,000	56
Total	553,000	100	843,000	100

Source: Council of Polytechnic Librarians statistical surveys and Polytechnic Finance Officers' Group annual reports

At first sight it looks as though the shift in the proportion of the budget spent on staffing has not been enormous. At a quick glance, a shift from 53 per cent to 56 per cent is not dramatic. However, 3 per cent of a large sum will involve a significant cash difference. Hence the actual sum for staffing has risen by an amazing 61 per cent, whilst that for materials has risen by only half that amount.

Automation accounts for the major part of the increase in 'services' costs, which have risen by over 100 per cent. There is clear evidence of this growth in Ellard (1986) where one can see, for example, that in the period since 1982 almost every polytechnic library now uses computers for some administrative and management-related tasks, whereas only twelve were doing so four years ago. Current awareness services using computers are now the norm in more than twenty polytechnics, whereas only five were working in this way in 1982. Ten polytechnics have automated inter-lending, where none had done so four years ago; and even circulation, which caught on early, has spread to a further seven libraries, leaving just three manual systems.

Few librarians would claim to have been able to make staff savings from the automation of procedures. However, it is fairly apparent that in the recent climate of financial cut-back and growing demand, it would not have been possible to maintain the existing range of services and develop others without having done so. Jackson (1985, p.1) put it succinctly: 'Automation is mitigating some of the effects of this (staff shortage), and without the systems now operating the library would need a dozen extra staff to maintain the same levels of output and productivity.'

Conclusion

The 1980s have been decidedly lean years for the polytechnics with the loss in real terms of about 20 per cent of their previous funding and a growth in their student population of around 30 per cent. Their libraries have faced increasing demands from a growing user population and library staff numbers have dropped a little. The downward shift in library staff:student ratios has been almost universal. For the most part, reductions have been made in two broad areas: at the junior professional/non-professional end of the structure; and in the academically-related Burnham posts. Despite reductions in staffing numbers, the proportion of the library budget spent on staffing has risen at twice the rate of the budget for materials. Considered against the scale of cuts overall and set alongside the rate of salary inflation, it is perhaps remarkable that polytechnic libraries haven't lost more posts; it is, however, hard to conceive of the kind of service they would now be providing had they done so.

The handling of contraction

Contraction has been a dominant feature of the British economy since the mid 1970s. The coal, steel and shipbuilding industries are, for example, known almost more for their job losses and their manner of handling them than for anything else. With contraction so commonplace, it might not be unreasonable to expect common approaches to its management, but this is not the way it appears to happen in real life. Even in the relatively small world of polytechnics, there has been no common approach to the handling of cutbacks. Some have sought to maintain teaching staff numbers at the cost of materials and support services, others have taken the opposite view; some have engaged in open debate about cuts whilst others have used more autocratic approaches. Some polytechnic librarians have been given a significant amount of freedom to plan and manage cut-backs; some have had almost no power to influence the process at all. In some institutions the librarian has participated at the earliest stages where decisions were made in policy and resources committees about the scale of cuts and where they should fall across the institution. Others have been omitted from participation at this stage and have merely received the wisdom of their financial and academic planners. Yet others have been forced to work almost totally in the dark with no clear target, financial or otherwise. Librarians in this latter situation have been subject to the gradual and random removal of posts as they became vacant, with power over which posts may or may not be filled, residing in an often remote and inaccessible directorate. In this situation librarians have had to cope with the wholesale freezing of vacant posts for lengthy periods, the stop-go effect on services which result and an erosion of confidence in the service and its place in the institution.

For all organisations it is periodically necessary to review objectives and goals and to plan in the light of them. It can be argued that, in periods of contraction, explicit priority setting in the allocation of scarce resources is more important than at other times. Paradoxically, though, economic conditions have substantially shortened the time-scale on which it is possible to plan.

Jones (1984) has stated that in times of cut-back managers tend to 'satisfice' rather than 'optimise' and that decision-making is 'reactive, piecemeal and short-term'. He quoted Lindblom (1968), who coined the term 'disjointed incrementalism', to describe the situation where policy-making is 'a never-ending process of successive steps in which continuous nibbling is a substitute for a good bite'. The result is that:

> Each year, in response to another budget squeeze, cuts are made across the board, staff extemporize as well as they can, and after some years of such incremental distortion a different kind of library service begins to take shape and is one day recognised almost with hindsight (Jones, 1984, p.231).

Roper (1981) in an article on contingency theory for polytechnic libraries also noted that librarians are, more often than not, presented with budget cut-backs in a piecemeal fashion since this is the way the system has tended to operate at higher levels. In such circumstances it is difficult to take a long-term and radical approach to decision-making. Some polytechnic libraries faced relatively gentle incremental cut-backs in the early 1980s and year by year it was possible to absorb the workload of the one or two posts that disappeared. It is only with hindsight that one is able to see the effect of this process. Some, of course, who sustained large cut-backs had relatively generous levels of staffing at the outset which enabled them to cushion the effect of 'across-the-board' cuts.

In Brighton, where substantial financial savings had been required in the Department of Learning Resources throughout 1979 and 1980, a further 15 per cent reduction in salaries costs was required over a three-year period starting in 1981/82. The department was therefore given scope to plan across a reasonable, though not excessive, time period. Interestingly, it chose to take one 'big bite' at its Educational Development Unit whilst library cuts were made 'across the board'. Having established the long-term plan through the committee structure of the institution, the department was, however, allowed considerable freedom to implement it so that gross distortions of structure, aims and philosophy were avoided. Rather different were the experiences of Middlesex, where the library staff dropped from sixty-eight to fifty-nine between 1980 and 1982 (recovering to sixty-three by 1986); and North East London Polytechnic, which dropped from eighty-seven to sixty-one between 1980 and 1986. In both institutions a more random approach was taken to the deletion of vacancies, and in both institutions one effect of this has been the virtual elimination of a senior management group. At Middlesex, the original Burnham team of seven, at one time planned to become nine in all, has decreased to just two. At North East London Polytechnic, the five-strong management team has also been reduced to two. Neither institution set out to eliminate its senior library managers, yet this is what has happened, and, with hindsight, is regretted.

Though it is clear that there has been a marked variation in the degree of autonomy given to libraries facing contraction, the reasons for the variation are not easily analysed. In some cases, the personal authority of polytechnic librarians within their own institutions appears to have been a positive factor; elsewhere, high regard for the library as an academic service seems to have been a major influence. However there are examples of institutions where the credibility and authority of both librarian and library service is unchallenged, yet where the luxury of involvement in the planning process has been denied. Too little is known of the varying approaches taken by polytechnics to overall planning and management to draw safe conclusions, though it is pertinent to point out that a change in committee structure or directorate can alter the institutional climate very quickly. It does seem fairly clear that those who had more scope to manage the process have been able to preserve better balances in their staffing. What we can not know, of course, is how different the situation would have been had alternative courses been followed.

Effects on services

So far this chapter has been concerned with identifying the scale of staff cut-backs where they have fallen and the institutional context in which they have happened. Although we shall consider the effects on staff roles and individuals in the system, the next section looks briefly at the ways services have been affected.

Abandonment of routine services

On the whole, polytechnics have tried to keep routine services operating, though from time to time, as libraries have been forced to hold vacant posts unfilled, some fairly basic services have undergone temporary suspension. A number of libraries have halted or at least rationed inter-library loans and reservations; some have closed separately-staffed service points handling audiovisual materials, periodicals or other special collections; many have reported backlogs in ordering and processing and the delays in stocking new material which result. Some have called a temporary halt to current contents listings, accessions lists and other routine Selective Dissemination of Information (SDI) services whilst others have cut back publications generally. One polytechnic librarian reported that user education was reduced by 12 per cent in 1982/83 because staff time could not be spared. Faced with an ever-demanding clientele, it is not surprising that the marketing of information services and the projection of a positive presence in the academic community are some of the first areas for attention, yet it is regrettable that polytechnics have been forced to retreat, at least in part, from the outgoing philosophy which was for many the hallmark of their service in the developmental years.

Where libraries have been able to acquire the necessary capital to develop their automated systems, the labour intensity of basic tasks like stock circulation have been reduced. As noted earlier in the chapter, the 100 per cent increase in 'services' costs are largely attributable to the increased use of automated procedures. For some, an area where automation has perhaps posed more problems than it has solved, is the provision of bibliographic and other information through the use of online databases. Ellard's *Directory* (1986) has noted, as might be expected, that online information services are now provided by every polytechnic library, but it is salutary to point out that some of these libraries have been afraid to promote these services as widely as they would wish for fear of being overwhelmed by the labour-intensive demand which could be unleashed. At Middlesex this is certainly an area the library is reluctantly having to keep the lid on, despite being only too aware of its importance. South Bank also records concern that staff may be unable to meet demand in this area.

Opening hours

One of the first things often chosen for reduction in libraries is opening hours. This is an easy cut and in 1982 twelve polytechnic libraries reported that they had reduced opening hours in order to cope with staffing reductions. Middlesex is one example, highlighted in the media by its own director in 1986, where regular evening opening of libraries is no longer possible and where Friday evening and weekend opening were abolished some years ago. A variant on the reduction in opening hours is shown at North East London Polytechnic where the libraries continue to open as before at 9.00 am for study purposes but where there is no staffed issue or enquiry service until 9.45 am.

Whether reductions in opening hours can be regarded as the most acceptable cut depends very much upon patterns of use, which may differ between institutions. Those with high concentrations of part-time students may find that to reduce evening opening makes the library almost totally inaccessible to a large number of their students. Most polytechnics are currently attempting to increase access in line with Department of Education and Science policy, and this tends to imply use by those other than full-time undergraduates and at 'abnormal' times of day. Hitherto, altering opening hours (dare one suggest sometimes to suit the preferences of library staff?) has been a fairly simple and obvious way of coping with fewer staff. Librarians may have to adopt more creative approaches to this area in the future, if polytechnic libraries are to remain in harmony with educational policy.

Closure of sites

All but three of the polytechnics operate a multi-site library service. Fourteen have up to four sites, a further eleven have between five and seven sites and two have eight or more. It is self-evident that a library service with multiple sites has a greater need of staff than a single-site operation. A COPOL Survey in 1985, for example, showed the total of weekly term-time opening in a single-site polytechnic to be around sixty-eight hours, whereas the average weekly opening for polytechnics with five or six sites was 283 hours. There is, however, no correlation between the number of sites and the ratio of library staff to students. Some polytechnics with one or two libraries are currently working at ratios of 1:140 or more whilst others in that group are working close to the average for all polytechnics of 1:118. Curiously, the same pattern is also true for those with six or more sites. Conyers' (1985) investigations showed that 32 per cent of Brighton's staffing costs could be saved if the service could be provided from one library instead of eight. For many, therefore, the configuration of their sites adds to the difficulties they face when cuts are demanded. Revill (1984) in his annual report stated that: 'staffing difficulties will persist until we are able to reduce the number of sites.' (Liverpool Polytechnic has ten sites.)

Polytechnics, like Middlesex, who have seven fairly similar-sized sites distributed across a wide geographic area have little scope for the closure of site libraries and the amalgamation of services, hence this strategy can not even be considered. Brighton has a more diverse range of site sizes varying from 2,500 FTE students down to two sites with only one hundred FTE each. The geographic disposition of its eight variously sized libraries provides little scope for amalgamation. Only two libraries, one serving 2,500 and the other 350 students just five minutes apart on foot, could seriously be considered for amalgamation. The difficulty in bringing about this obvious amalgamation is however one of space within buildings set alongside costs. The fact that the saving on such a move would be no more than the salaries of two library assistants (*c.*£16,000 pa) calls into question the capital spending on building alterations which would be necessary to effect the merger. This possibility is therefore reviewed periodically (particularly when further reductions are mooted) but the likelihood of its becoming a practical reality is quite small. North East London Polytechnic and Lancashire, conversely, have been rather good at reducing site libraries. The fourteen separate libraries North East London Polytechnic sported in 1978 have now been reduced to seven (shortly to be six), thereby mitigating in part some of the worst effects of its swingeing staffing cuts. Lancashire has also reduced from four libraries to one, thereby counteracting the loss of thirteen posts.

No librarians have had real freedom to close libraries when academic work has continued in buildings some distance from the nearest site library. In this area, the librarian has to follow the institutional lead. Until other pressures make institutions think more critically about their sites and buildings and the related costs, there is little likelihood of significant change. The critical thinking may not, however, be too far off since this area is one current concern of the National Advisory Board for Local Authority Higher Education (NAB), which is looking to bring about reductions in the premises costs of polytechnics.

Effects on staff

Generally speaking polytechnic librarians have endeavoured to maintain services where at all possible. Undoubtedly a few institutions were sufficiently generously provided with staff for this to be no huge problem even when cuts were substantial. For others even a small cut in staffing made service maintenance difficult. No matter what the starting-point, however, the effect upon staff is very similar. At the outset, word of cuts usually brings about personal anxiety in some and at least mild outrage amongst many, that the library should be threatened.

Although natural wastage has become the accepted technique for reducing staff in the public sector, the spectre of redundancy has hovered over some institutions bringing with it further insecurity and disquiet. At first sight it is easy to see why natural wastage has become the accepted practice; it is humane, no one actually loses their employment, and insecurity is minimised. However, where cuts have been made randomly through natural wastage, the possibility of retaining acceptable staff structures is limited by which staff move and which stay. As Wray (1985) has described, the consequences of natural wastage may be quite harmful. Within an organisation that is wasting naturally, the old will retire and the younger livelier members of staff with marketable skills will move on elsewhere, leaving those who are happily secure or who can not find jobs elsewhere to remain. Immediate prospects for promotion may not be high, but over time some of those who stay may expect to move gradually up the hierarchy. The long-term results of these events may not however be healthy as younger people, no matter what their abilities, find they are unable to get the first foothold on the professional ladder. New ideas are then less likely to be adopted and fresh ideas less likely to emerge.

Most polytechnic libraries had some, often senior, members of staff who had been absorbed from constituent colleges at the time of mergers and who were prepared to accept early retirement. Other staff have been motivated and able to find jobs elsewhere, and some will have left for domestic and other reasons. It appears from the pattern of reductions described earlier in this chapter that a number of junior professional staff will have been promoted leaving their former posts to be deleted from establishments. This erosion of vacancies at the junior end of staffing provides just the kind of block to new young blood which Wray (1985) predicted. In these circumstances it could be a very unbalanced and disparate collection of individuals who remain. So far the polytechnic sector of the academic library world does not appear to be suffering *too* adversely from the effects of natural wastage, though there have been some. New developments continue to surface, and a lively approach to change continues, but we are dealing with a relatively short time-scale here. The situation might be grimmer were we looking five years hence.

Senior management

An example of the deleterious effect of natural wastage has already been mentioned with reference to Middlesex, where the retirement of a number of Burnham-graded staff and the loss of their posts, along with the loss of those vacated by other senior staff who moved on to jobs elsewhere, has resulted in the loss of the second tier of management between the head of library services and the site/faculty librarians. This has brought about an isolated head of service with little support in the co-ordinating tasks particularly necessary in a multi-site setting. It is easy to think that cuts will always place greatest pressure upon the 'shop-floor', and indeed in some circumstances this has been so, but from this example alone it can be seen that it doesn't always work this way. At Brighton the senior management team has been maintained largely intact with some modest adjustments of responsibility to cope with the loss of one senior management post. It has, however, remained a static group over a number of years, and this may have a stultifying effect in due course.

The extent to which it is possible to make good the loss of senior posts depends heavily upon the abilities and goodwill of staff at the same level or in the next tier down and upon the support available to them. Taken at face value, it might appear to be quite exploitative to expect staff to take on increased responsibilities for no reward, and at times of staffing cuts there will be little scope for promotion. Looked at differently, though, it could be said that devolving responsibilities downward gives staff an opportunity to broaden their experience in a way which might otherwise have been impossible. In practice, some have responded positively and been willing to extend their roles perhaps in the hope that rewards or career advancement may follow, if not within their own institution then through their increased marketability. However, where aspirations remain unfulfilled for any length of time, tensions may result.

Some managers have taken the view that it is exploitative to expect staff to take on significant additional functional responsibility on a long-term basis (for example, responsibility for systems) and have instead commissioned smaller projects from members of their staff. The disadvantage here is that in something like systems development there is only limited value in getting an individual to carry out the investigative work which is the natural precursor to improving or setting up a system if the implementation is then either shelved or carried out with less management and co-ordination than desirable.

Subject staff

The statistical data earlier in the chapter indicated that polytechnic libraries had tried where possible to retain their middle to senior range professionals. Doubtless some loss in the technical services areas has been compensated for by the establishment of automated systems and matched by declining acquisitions. In reader services the maintenance of subject staff, albeit not necessarily on Burnham grades, appears to have been a major aim. Even where polytechnics have been subject to random cuts, this level has remained largely stable, indicating, perhaps, that the opportunities for promotion from this level have not been great and the scope for reduction through natural wastage small. Where vacancies have occurred it has been possible for some junior staff to be promoted, thereby leaving vacancies for deletion lower down the league.

Despite a desire to retain subject strength overall, there have undoubtedly been reductions in subject staff in some institutions, and individuals have been required to amalgamate responsibilities. Unlike the situation with senior management, subject staff have not usually been required to extend the level of their responsibility but rather the breadth of their subject coverage. Promotion possibilities are less obvious in this situation since it is fundamentally 'more of the same' or perhaps, more accurately, 'less of the same' in terms of in-depth service. At Brighton, where subject staff (course resources officers) were reduced from twenty-two to sixteen (subsequently to fifteen), the amalgamation of responsibilities was, for the most part, managed with minimum physical disruption to individual staff, and none was moved geographically since vacancies occurred throughout the system. Some, however, found that the number of staff and students with whom they had to work doubled over night. The reduction of subject staff can be a difficult area to manage involving delicate negotiations not only with individual members of library staff but with subject departments also. Curiously, although the latter often defend their own staff at the expense of staff from other areas (such as the library), they tend to be outraged when the direct consequences of their strategy actually hit them. One can readily appreciate the disquiet felt on both sides at the destruction or, at least, dilution of close and valuable relationships which have been built up over some years. That 'their' librarian should be replaced by half a person with limited or possibly no relevant subject background provides academics with understandable ground for concern. A major source of disquiet for subject staff who have taken on additional course areas has been the limitation which they have been forced to impose upon their involvement with departmental activities and concerns that fall outside the scope of straightforward library service. The expectation of course resources officers in Brighton that they might spend up to half their time outside the library working on a range of curricular activities in their subject departments had to be considerably readjusted. Most would say that this has significantly reduced the satisfaction provided by their jobs.

For some, one of the frustrations of their being spread more thinly is the inability to respond more positively to the potential demand for their skills and time which has arisen as a result of teaching staff seeking ways of coping with increased SSRs. As students are expected to take more responsibility for their learning and to work independently of lectures, the pressures on the libraries inevitably rise. For many subject librarians this is a situation they have welcomed and sought to encourage but, for others, the knowledge that they have little scope to handle further demand must make them view the prospect with concern.

At Kingston, where significant structural changes have been introduced (not in response to staffing reductions), subject staff have taken on additional responsibilities which formerly resided in the technical services section. They reported having found increased satisfaction in the challenges which arise from having a wider range of issues to deal with and more complexity in the prioritising of the components of their jobs.

Junior staff

The polytechnic libraries had thirty-one fewer non-professional posts in 1985 than they had in 1980. However, a majority of libraries (seventeen) either maintained a static number or increased their non-professional staff. Of the thirteen who lost posts, seven managed to restrict their loss to five or fewer, four lost between six and ten posts and two lost more than ten. Generally speaking, therefore, the picture is less dramatic than might have been expected. Comments from polytechnic librarians about the tightness of their staffing suggest much greater losses have been sustained. However, since many library services were already working at full stretch and some had planned increases which did not come to fruition, one must conclude that the combination of even a small loss of staff with growth in demand is likely to be uncomfortable. Interestingly, despite the 30 per cent growth in student FTEs, library issues – just one measure of demand for services – do not appear to have kept pace. Between 1982 and 1985, for example, COPOL statistics show a rise of just 11 per cent in average issues and a static state in inter-library loans. The evidence of one's eyes, however, belies the statistical evidence and one is forced to conclude that, even though the things librarians count may have risen less dramatically than was thought, the nature and complexity of demand has changed.

A factor that should not be overlooked here is the loss of posts from the junior professional group. Both more senior staff and junior colleagues will have been affected by the reduction of support arising from losses at this level.

Problems of motivation and morale

'Diminishing resources, uncertainty, sagging morale, increased stress and inter-personal conflict are all characteristics of organisational decline' (Jones, 1984, p.200). It is perhaps surprising therefore that only forty-eight out of eighty chief librarians from UK academic institutions who responded to a Centre for Library and Information Management (CLAIM) survey in 1983 expressed concern at the contraction of resources as a major problem for the future. More surprising still that only eleven mentioned understaffing specifically and just ten the problems of staff mobility and stagnation.

The annual reports of polytechnic librarians in the eighties, by contrast, all too often express serious concern about the adequacy of staffing levels and the effects of the relentless demand for services upon the too few staff who are trying to meet it. Cowley (1983) has echoed the views of a number of his colleagues at this time in saying: 'The common factor experienced at all sites was that too few people are struggling with too much work' (p.13).

Some librarians noted the ambiguity of roles which has arisen from imbalances in professional and non-professional staff following the process of natural wastage. Others described more bluntly the undesirable work patterns that have been forced upon them: 'senior staff were often spending up to half their time at the issue counter' (Jackson, 1985, p.1); 'too much professional time [is] spent on routine activity and assistants [are] pressed to the point of desperation in trying to maintain basic services' (Cowley, 1983, p.2). There is clearly fertile ground here for the growth of low morale and declining job satisfaction.

That staff are demoralised by their failure to produce the high quality of service they wish to achieve is specifically reported by a number of polytechnic librarians. Interestingly, though, most also speak of the tolerance and good humour of library staff determined to do their best in conditions of adversity. Jones (1984) has provided a useful and interesting review of the theory and counter-theory of job satisfaction indicating, as is well known, that there really are no truths in this area. He reported that research at the beginning of the eighties indicated a fairly high level of job satisfaction for librarians overall, though there is some evidence from a CLAIM survey in 1982 (Stewart, 1982) that polytechnic library staff were more dissatisfied with their jobs than colleagues in other libraries. Despite the unremitting level of demand being placed upon staff in those polytechnics that have fared particularly badly in recent retrenchment, staff still appear fundamentally to enjoy the world of academic librarianship and the 'sense of service' which is so frequently cited in the literature as an attraction. Although rare, some polytechnic librarians claim that their staff appreciate the challenges and creative pressure that have been thrust upon them. It is clearly a question of degree.

Of considerable concern to polytechnic library managers is the underlying discontent felt by staff at the lack of mobility occasioned by financial restraint across the education sector. Many have commented in recent reports that senior staff have little opportunity to move on, thereby blocking the promotion possibilities of younger, junior staff. A number of polytechnic librarians noted the anxiety they felt in encouraging young members of staff to qualify in librarianship knowing of the difficulty these young professionals will face in trying to secure permanent appointments in which they can practice their new-found skills. Frustration is in fact noted at all levels from the junior who can not get promotion, to the manager who is powerless to unlock the chain. Clearly, even in more buoyant times it could not be expected that the polytechnics alone would provide sufficient scope for the aspirations of all the ambitious in their midst. Thirty libraries with pyramid staff structures would always have provided a bottleneck for some.

In the context of frustration, polytechnic librarians naturally cite the importance of staff training and development activities as means of upholding staff interest and motivation. Earlier in this book, Conyers deals at some length with training in relation to professional stagnation and low mobility, citing a number of techniques such as job enrichment, job enlargement and job rotation as possible solutions. In systems where too few staff are struggling with too much work it is doubtful whether job enlargement would be an acceptable solution! With limited possibilities for promotion on a long-term basis one would also question how long new developments could sustain morale.

The severity of the problem of maintaining motivation and morale depends to a considerable extent on the age profile of staff in an organisation. Hunt (1979) has provided some interesting ideas about the way in which the goals of individuals change throughout their lives, depending on experience, the strength of their needs and the opportunities to satisfy them. For those at the younger end of the spectrum, getting a toe on the ladder will be the overwhelming concern. For those in their mid to late thirties who have been happy to make modest progress professionally the shock which may be occasioned by their reflecting upon the way in which they will spend the next twenty years of their working lives could be quite severe. For some the shock would be no less severe were job prospects plentiful, and it would certainly be misleading to think that problems of motivation and immobility were solely the product of an era of economic constraint.

The polytechnic libraries have a predominantly young staff, having retired a number of older members in the late seventies and simultaneously recruited young staff moving on in their careers. Clearly, from the outset, not all were motivated by strongly career-oriented needs and some will now merely be glad to have secure employment and be seeking more satisfaction from the jobs they are in. If we are to believe Hunt's (1981) argument, then those with moderate ambitions are likely to find that feelings of frustration diminish as they grow older and the profile of their needs changes. For others the adjustment to staying put may be harder, producing reactions from frustration to withdrawal. These are more disturbing consequences of immobility.

Conclusion

The effects of economic retrenchment have been felt throughout the polytechnic libraries; even those who have not lost posts from their establishments have faced increases in student numbers and growing demands on their services. New technology has cushioned some of this but most staff have had to cope with bigger jobs and greater pressures. For some the climate has provided scope for personal growth which might otherwise have stayed untapped; for others the diminishment of job satisfaction has been a major worry. Staff mobility in a declining market has been reduced, bringing with it the potential for frustration and tension. Since the problems of frustrated ambition are always more acute in periods of no-growth, we can probably expect this area to provide one of the significant challenges for library managers for the foreseeable future.

Note

1 Statistical data relates to the thirty polytechnics in England and Wales and excludes the former Ulster Polytechnic.

References

Committee of Directors of Polytechnics (1986), *Review of the year 1984/85*, London, Committee of Directors of Polytechnics.
Conyers, A. (1985), 'The costs of a multi-site library service: a study of Brighton Polytechnic', *Aslib Proceedings*, vol.37, no.10 (October), pp.395–403.
Cowley, J. (1983), *Annual report of the head of library services, 1981/82*, London, Middlesex Polytechnic.
Ellard, K.R. (ed) (1986), *Directory of information technology applications in UK polytechnic libraries*, Oxford, Council of Polytechnic Librarians.
Fulljames, D. (1985), 'Survey of opening hours in polytechnic libraries', Wolverhampton, Wolverhampton Polytechnic (unpublished paper circulated to COPOL members).
Hunt, J.W. (1979), *Managing people at work*, London, McGraw Hill.
Jackson, P. (1985), *Oxford Polytechnic library annual report, 1984/85*, Oxford, Oxford Polytechnic.
Jones, K. (1984), *Conflict and change in library organisations: people, power and service*, London, Clive Bingley.
Lindblom, C.E. (1968), *The policy-making process*, Englewood Cliffs, NJ, Prentice Hall.
NATFHE (1982), *College libraries policy statement*, London, National Association of Teachers in Further and Higher Education.
Revill, D.H. (1984), *Annual report of the polytechnic librarian*, Liverpool, Liverpool Polytechnic.
Revill, D.H. (1985), 'The polytechnics and their libraries' in J. Fletcher, *Reader services in polytechnic libraries*, Aldershot, Gower in association with COPOL.
Roper, V. de P. (1981), 'Contingency theory for polytechnic libraries', *Journal of Librarianship*, vol.13, no.1 (January), pp.25–36.
Stewart, L. (1982), *What do UK librarians dislike about their jobs?*, Loughborough, Centre for Library and Information Management, Loughborough University.
Wray, I. (1985), 'Is natural wastage really harmless?', *Guardian*, 14 August 1985, p.21.

7 The library assistant

KEN R. GRAHAM

Library assistants, like other groups of workers united by a common job title, are not the homogeneous group they appear to be at first sight. Individual personalities and the interaction of personalities influence the job content and the working environment generally. Senior management also has an important bearing on the nature of the library assistants through its recruitment policies, particularly through establishing minimum educational qualifications, and by the overall style of management, whereas middle management influences much of the day-to-day environment of the library assistant. As a result there is considerable potential for variation between library assistants, not just between polytechnics generally, but also between departmental or site libraries within a single polytechnic and ultimately of course between assistants in the same department.

Around 55 per cent of polytechnic libraries' staffs are non-professional. The majority of these will be library assistants. The range of backgrounds of library assistants is often surprisingly varied. Minimum requirements of four or five 'O' levels means the job is within the scope of many school-leavers. However high unemployment and the lack of alternative job opportunities has created a buyer's market for employers, and librarians are often able to choose from applicants with 'A' level and graduate qualifications. The choice lies between those who may be termed direct entrants (that is, those who satisfy the basic educational requirements but have no professional qualifications and who may or may not have further ambitions within libraries) and those who come via library school in which case they may or may not have previous library experience. Another possibility is all-graduate entry, as in the case of Manchester Polytechnic's graduate trainee scheme.

Graduates

This raises the question of what best meets the requirements of the service. Experience of working with assistants from each of these backgrounds shows that there are no hard and fast rules that apply and no seemingly best solution. One advantage of direct entrants with the basic educational qualifications is that they are arguably more suited and willing to perform the routine tasks which constitute much of the library assistants' work. They will therefore be more 'at home' in the job and more likely to stay long enough to become fully familiar with the basics of the job and eventually gain considerable experience.

In the present job market it is quite likely that graduates will apply for clerical posts. Some may be seeking practical experience before entering library schools. Others may simply want a job where their qualifications may have some relevance. Yet others will be graduates emerging from higher education as qualified librarians. As professional posts are relatively scarce, at least in the field of employment or geographical area chosen, then some graduate librarians may be obliged to settle for clerical posts at least as initial appointments.

Individual libraries will have their own policies on appointing graduates. To some, graduates *per se* may be seen as overqualified for clerical posts. Others may overlook problem areas and feel able to boast that all, or a majority of, their library staff are graduates. Such a claim may or may not be reflected in an improved service; there may be some political benefit, perhaps creating a different attitude towards the library.

Appointing assistants from library school has obvious advantages for the library in terms of higher educational backgrounds and a theoretical knowledge of the wider aspects of librarianship as well as providing a useful opportunity to assess their suitability for future professional posts. However it is necessary to draw a distinction between graduates with previous library experience and those who have none. On balance, graduates with previous experience seem preferable as they are, generally, quicker at settling into the job, a good deal of the basic routines being common to most libraries. They may be more readily accepted by the other assistants because they have a shared experience. Conversely, library school graduates, and graduates generally, without a library background need to be especially aware of the sensibilities of their fellow assistants, many of whom will possess considerable practical experience but will not have had the opportunity of further education and are therefore severely limited within the library in terms of their future prospects. One problem with newly qualified graduates is the quite natural desire to try out their new found skills. Their suggestions and criticisms may not be well received. Tact should be high on the list of desirable qualities sought when interviewing any candidate but particularly so in the case of graduate appointments to clerical posts. Assistants operate at their best working as a team: a team can do more to motivate itself than any amount of supervision from senior library assistants or professional staff; therefore, the rewards from maintaining a balanced and compatible group of assistants can be considerable.

Appointing graduates to clerical posts has obvious advantages. Equally, however, it has to be acknowledged that such appointments are not without some negative aspects. One possible drawback is that the expectations of clerical staff by professionals may be unconsciously but nonetheless unduly raised by the higher performance of one or two individuals. Were this to happen it would be extremely unfair and likely to cause resentment. Conversely it is not unknown for graduates to lose patience with the mundane detail of much clerical work. If this happens, mistakes may be made. Graduates may press for more involvement in professional tasks to the neglect of the more obvious and necessary housekeeping routines.

The effect of graduate staff on the earlier non-graduate professional librarians cannot be discounted as a possible cause of friction but the extent of such feeling is difficult to gauge. Certainly some non-graduate professional staff feel at a disadvantage. Similarly some librarians with a degree in librarianship may regard their colleagues who possess post-graduate library qualifications with some suspicion. Employers too may hold different attitudes towards those holding first degrees in librarianship and those with post-graduate librarianship qualifications.

Role of the assistant

Much will depend on what is expected of assistants: whether they are expected simply to perform a closely defined range of duties such as counter duties, clearing, shelf revision and shelf tidying; or whether they are expected to exercise a greater degree of their own judgement and initiative and undertake a wider role in the library, undertaking some of the more routine work and reader assistance. In some cases the role of the assistant is closely defined by senior management but in many cases it often rests with the professional staff in immediate contact with the assistant, and in such cases it is largely a matter of personal preferences. Some professional staff may feel more comfortable and perhaps less threatened in situations where there are well defined areas of responsibility, whereas others are quite happy to introduce wider training and let willing assistants operate to the limit of their ability. Equally, force of circumstance can to a great degree dictate the professional and non-professional roles within the library, particularly in smaller libraries with only a few staff where it is not possible, nor desirable, to have strict demarcation between specific roles.

Financial pressures, under which all polytechnic library services are now forced to operate, mean longer delays in filling vacant posts and difficulties in getting additional staff for new services – all of which throw increased pressures on staff at all levels. In such circumstances it is surely desirable to have resourceful and adaptable library assistants capable of meeting these needs.

The whole of this area appears to have been neglected as a subject for research. Individual opinion, perhaps even prejudice, rather than objectively recorded and judged performance, has characterised librarians' policies and practices. In these circumstances a few critical incidents may colour an employing librarian's attitude to whole categories of staff.

One problem that occurs when discussing library assistants is that it is difficult to generalise because the average library assistant does not really exist. There are many different roles for the assistant within a large polytechnic library service. The experience of someone working in a non-public central services or technical support department will be substantially different from that of an assistant used to working on an issues desk. There will be differences in the work of assistants in small isolated libraries compared with those employed in large centralised services.

The ability to adapt and fit into the existing work environment is an essential prerequisite in most jobs, and this is certainly true in the library. Clearly it is not only the content of a job which determines attitudes to a given job but also wider factors, taking into account the total environment, particularly the other staff. The importance of such factors increases in those jobs, such as the library assistant's, having a high proportion of routine work in situations where a few staff continually work in close proximity.

The library assistant is such a fundamental part of any library that it is surely impossible to imagine the library without assistants. This should not be taken to imply that they are more important than their professional colleagues.

The library assistant is a familiar figure to most people. To library users they are usually the first point of contact with the service and presumably in some cases the only contact with library staff. Even non-users have an image of the library assistant, albeit one that is often a hopelessly distorted caricature, as portrayed in novels, plays and television programmes such as *Sorry*. Added to the stereotype image is the fairly commonly held belief that anybody who works in a library is automatically a 'librarian', a view that distresses a great number of professionals. Within the library itself the picture is at least a little better. Most professional staff have at some time in the past worked as an assistant and, should anybody be in danger of forgetting this fact, it is quite common to hear protestations along the lines of: 'Don't forget that I was once a library assistant too you know!'. To give them their due most professionals continue to work in fairly close contact with assistants. Despite all this apparent familiarity, many people would be surprised by the range of library assistants' duties. The obvious source of enlightenment is the job description.

The largely mechanical nature of duties can lead to a lengthy job description as specific tasks are mentioned. The Library Association's list of professional and non-professional duties (1974) may be the basis of the job description. Professionals' duties tend to offer greater scope for interpretation and individuality; hence job descriptions may be more easily generalised. There may also be a fear on the part of management that, unless all tasks are mentioned in the job description, some individuals, in strongly unionised libraries, may refuse to perform some duties simply because they are not specifically mentioned. It is certainly the case that unions have objected to phrases such as 'and other duties as are allocated'. To counter the withdrawal of this catch-all item, managements may extend the job description in order to cover every eventuality.

Job descriptions, too, can be seen as giving the standard of minimal performance expected even when they are not described in performance terms. Seldom do job descriptions mention the quantities of work to be done in various time-periods. This presents something of a problem to management. The 'better' assistants may be seen as those who perform all their tasks correctly *and* who turn in exceptional quantities of work. At what point then can anyone say that a particular assistant is performing below the acceptable level? The job description may be the starting point for assessing staff but cannot, by itself, be used in staff appraisal. The real contribution of the assistant is often far wider than the mere performance of mechanical tasks. A job description type of approach fails to take account of the personality factors which are so important and make the difference between an assistant who is performing the basic duties and one who is really contributing to the overall performance and image of the library. What the assistant says and does on the day is, in effect, the library's policy despite what the chief librarian and the policy documents may say. Many factors influence the precise nature of the assistant's function in the library; diversity between polytechnic libraries is sufficiently wide to render all but the broadest generalisations meaningless.

Perhaps the single most important factor is the basic organisation of the library, for example whether it is a large centralised library service as at Lancashire or a widely dispersed multi-site system as in the case of Liverpool. In the same way the size of a subject department or site library is a significant factor in determining individual roles within that library. On balance smaller and less centralised libraries seem to offer assistants greater opportunity to undertake a wider and more interesting range of duties, mainly because of the smaller numbers of staff involved.

Equally important is the attitude of management towards library assistants, as their perception of the role will to a large extent determine the type of library assistant appointed.

Routine tasks constitute the major part of the assistants' working day. However, the routine nature of these tasks does not detract from their value and there can be no denying their essential importance. It is not uncommon for assistants to view themselves as the 'workhorses' of the library whilst professional staff appear to deal with the more glamorous but seemingly peripheral areas. This type of view is perhaps more commonly held at times of staff shortages. Such circumstances can on occasion be exacerbated by professional staff being unwilling or unaware of the need to pitch in and lend a helping hand with counter duties. It is unfortunately true that much of the assistants' work if left undone leads only to more work; for example, a reader faced with badly ordered and untidy shelves is not encouraged to return books to their proper place, whilst others may fail to find wanted items, thus destroying the efforts put into classification and cataloguing.

Assistants need to understand what their role is. It can happen that they interpret their jobs as keeping the records in order and the library tidy. The reasons why these jobs are necessary may not be seen as important. A confusion of means with ends can result where eventually, the readers are seen as interfering with tidy records and creating problems. Rules too can be interpreted literally and without alteration according to circumstances, as the assistant has not got the rank to modify them. Each assistant should be encouraged to see the job as making materials available to the maximum readership. Graduate staff may be better able to appreciate this distinction having been users on the other side of the counter.

The whole question of the relationship between educational qualifications and performance as a library assistant has not been sufficiently investigated. Does a library get better value from employing people with degrees or 'A' levels? Is there a higher turnover among more highly qualified clerical staff? Turnover costs money in replacement costs, losses of staff time and in training. Are the supposed benefits enough to compensate?

Being managed

As the 'managed' library assistants' contacts with senior polytechnic management are usually sparse, the directorate and governing body will appear to be remote bodies. Indeed some senior and other teaching staff may seldom be seen in libraries!

The polytechnic librarian should be better known yet much of what he does, his personal effectiveness, will be unknown. His role and the general managerial style of the system will tend to come across as a general feeling.

Assistants are better placed to evaluate the effectiveness of their own site or section librarian. One common weakness is that of personnel management. It is possible to sense uncertainty and lack of confidence, certainly in younger professionals, in dealing with their staff. The whole area of personnel management is a difficult one. Perhaps skill in personnel work arises more from experience and maturity than taught courses. Many will have chosen the career of librarian without fully appreciating the extent to which they would be involved in managing people. In this situation assistants and senior library assistants can exert a strong influence. The section librarian may be torn between a friendly approach within the team and preserving a social distance in order to maintain discipline. Good management is not just a popularity contest.

Stewart (1982, p.122) discovered that:

> The majority of employees expressed some degree of confidence and trust in their managers, whilst also expressing some dissatisfaction about the lack of explanation and information on management decisions.

The involvement of library assistants in internal management committees can range from a token gesture as observers to real participation. Even so library assistants will be outnumbered and outranked in such a forum. Their contribution will largely depend on the strength of their individual characters.

Most assistants would appreciate a voice on new appointments. They will be the ones who will have to work with a new member of staff, and carry any extra burdens. Small sites are particularly vulnerable as the odd mistake is less easily hidden. Involvement in selection could range from being a member of the interviewing panel to being consulted having met all the candidates.

Once appointed, it may be the case that new staff are assessed by their section heads, at least for the probationary report, but their peers are not often asked for their opinions. If they were asked, replies might be cautiously worded or 'coded' and would need interpretation. Even a favourable response may present problems. Managers must constantly bear in mind that the productive *working* group is not necessarily synonymous with the mutually chosen *social* group.

The professional/non-professional divide

If a study were done on polytechnic library assistants perhaps the findings would mirror Bowen's (1982) results on public libraries. Assistants studied experienced a 'distancing' of themselves by professional staff from non-professionals. Assistants tended to consult one another before approaching professional staff, who appeared to be too busy on other matters. Professional staff must appreciate the value of the assistant as the first line of contact with readers and the importance of assistants' abilities in personal relationships and communicating. The Library Association has reiterated the role of the library assistant (1984). The Association stated *inter alia* that: 'Much of their work will involve direct contact with the client and they are generally the first people with whom the client comes into contact. Interpersonal and communications skills are therefore essential.'

Library assistants expect their professional supervisors to have a good acquaintance with assistants' work but not necessarily a high competence as this requires long practice. A knowledge of what assistants do, the quantities of work reasonably expected and an understanding of the difficulties is necessary both in order to direct subordinates and to train new staff.

Organisation of the work offers various choices. Assistants may be required to do the whole range of available tasks or some special responsibilities could be allocated, in which case these jobs could be rotated after, say, six months. Making some tasks the special responsibility of individuals may increase their motivation, allow areas of expertise to develop and produce greater speed through familiarity. The negative aspects are that difficulties may arise during individuals' absences, the newest member of staff may receive all the unpleasant jobs and fresh approaches may be inhibited.

Job rotation is not without its problems. Some assistants may be displeased to inherit the work of a badly organised person. Their own good work may not receive recognition before it is passed to someone else. Job enlargement and job enrichment are also adopted on occasion. Bowen (1982, p.15) has warned that they: 'sometimes aggravated the situation, rather than improving it. It was as if these methods had been introduced more to prevent boredom setting in than to provide an effective service'.

Evidence from Stewart's (1982) survey 'indicates that . . .

the greatest conflict in libraries lies not between managers and employees, but between professionals and non-professionals'. Too great a divide between professional and non-professional staff can create in the latter the impression that assistants effectively manage the day-to-day running of the library. To the extent that professionals' jobs happen in offices and outside the library, their work may be misunderstood by library assistants. Sessions where staff can explain their roles and duties are invaluable in creating greater understanding and appreciation of each other's contribution. Joint sessions where professional and non-professional staff can discuss issues are also of benefit.

The clerical/professional divide tends to break down in smaller sites and may do so in larger libraries when they are under pressure. These situations create more interest for assistants but may frustrate professional staff when they are obliged to undertake a disproportionate amount of clerical work.

Impact of technology

Automated systems have introduced fundamental changes in assistants' work. The ways in which changes are introduced is important. Those who are affected by it should be involved from the earliest stages. There may be fears of redundancy, redeployment and even an inability to cope.

It can happen that a new generation of assistants arises, more familiar with the new technology than some of their older professional supervisors. Tensions can occur. Training is necessary in this area but needs to be associated with opportunity to practice. Being shown how to change a lens on a reader-printer, or access a data file from a terminal, may convince the trainer that an assistant can perform the task but unless the hardware is available, and is used frequently by the assistant, such training will be forgotten within a short period.

Training

Training can vary from being 'thrown in at the deep end' to a carefully structured and phased programme. 'Sitting by Nellie' appears to be the principal method. The tendency for polytechnics and their local education authorities to delay the filling of posts may mean that more recruits are now taken on at the beginning of sessions and therefore get a cursory introduction to their work. This should not be a very serious problem as long as the assistants are aware of their limitations and ask advice when unsure. Inducting new members of staff can also be a strain on existing members at these times. One of the most difficult aspects of the work relates to enquiries. Assistants may be keen to use their own subject knowledge but may lack knowledge of bibliographic tools. They may be capable of satisfying the enquirer but with a longer delay. Professional staff must encourage assistants to pass enquiries up and also be prepared to pass them down if this does not damage the relationship with the enquirer.

Library staff act as a pool of knowledge mutually dependent and should be unafraid to pass enquiries up or down the hierarchy. A professional librarian also is aware that an apparently simple enquiry could hide further needs. A superficially satisfying answer could be given as opposed to a reader going away highly satisfied. Assistants may not fully appreciate the subtleties of question negotiation.

Library assistants themselves sometimes find themselves having to train new members of staff. There may be dangers in allowing clerical staff to train their peers. An ability to do the job well does not necessarily qualify someone as a supervisor or trainer. Deviations introduced by their predecessors may be perpetuated; contexts may not be explained. Experienced assistants may be so familiar with the work that they cannot stand back sufficiently to analyse and therefore explain it.

Opportunities for assistants to undertake more formal training via City and Guilds or Business and Technicien Education Council (BTEC) courses are usually limited. To the extent that success on these courses may not result in salary increases or promotion, the motivation to undertake them may be lacking. Their value from the individual's point of view lies more in an enhanced sense of identity with the profession and greater commitment.

Comparisons may be drawn between the established rights relating to maternity leave and the relative inability to obtain leave of absence for courses varying in length from day release to one- and three-year professional courses. Having to resign in order to follow these courses is a pretty severe constraint and penalty. General pressures on staffing may be sufficient reason not to permit secondments but, as all poverty is relative, it may be seen simply as an excuse by management not to argue the case.

In view of the limited prospects available to the assistant, managements should at least award recognition for good work. They should also accommodate staff requests for sideways transfers, changes in duties and flexible working arrangements.

With multi-sites, staff turnover and the rapid changes occurring in higher education and its libraries, senior staff could easily lose track of who has been trained to do what. Managements should keep full records of who has been trained in what, by whom, when, and timetable refresher courses for the future. Assistants may be reluctant to point out their own deficiencies having nominally been trained once. Training might not be effective. Similarly asking assistants what their training needs are can be a fruitless exercise. It is difficult to know what one does not know until one has seen the whole spectrum of possibilities.

Conclusions

Management can seem remote. Indeed their remoteness can be a positive advantage! They should be available when staff want some action on a problem of their own. Management should be there to assist not simply control.

Tensions between staff do exist (House, 1985). Stewart (1982, p.127) found that:

> Relationships between individuals and departments, between manager and non-manager, between professional and non-professional, between experienced and inexperienced, all present opportunity for dissatisfaction.

Conflicts can arise. Managements should be aware of them even though there might be little to be done to resolve them. Recognition of their existence on the part of all staff and an honest approach to them is half way to a solution.

As assistants comprise the majority of staff, their roles, training, attitudes and expectations deserve further study. This chapter has suggested some of their concerns. Such matters should be considered by polytechnic library managements to see whether they apply in their systems and to investigate solutions and improvements.

References

Bowen, J. (1982), 'Shop floor experience of work in the public library', *Information and Library Manager*, vol.2, no.1 (June), pp.10, 15.

House, D. (1985), 'Managing the multi-site system' in J. Cowley (ed), *The management of polytechnic libraries*, Aldershot, Gower in association with COPOL, pp.135–56.

Library Association (1974), *Professional and non-professional duties in libraries*, 2nd edn, London, Library Association.

Library Association (1984), 'Duties and responsibilities of library staffs', *Library Association Record*, vol.86, no.8 (August), p.307.

Stewart, L. (1982), 'Relationships', *Information and Library Manager*, vol.1, no.4 (March), pp.122, 127.

8 The subject librarian

JEAN HIGGINBOTTOM

Any discussion of the role of the subject librarian must be prefaced by a definition of the term, but this in itself is no easy task. The bewildering array of titles that polytechnics give their subject librarians is indicative of the problem. 'Subject librarian' is most commonly used, but other variations on the theme include faculty librarian, school librarian, resources librarian, academic librarian, course liaison librarian (or officer), information officer, or subject specialist (the latter most often used in the literature to describe the 'genre').

The number and variety of duties assigned to subject librarians further complicates any definition. Harris (1974) has listed no fewer than fifteen, and they are by no means the same in all libraries. Whilst it may be reasonable to assume that such tasks as information and enquiry work and book selection would be included in the list, the same cannot be said, for example, of the inclusion of cataloguing and classification, which has been the subject of much debate.

Thus, any attempt to define the term subject librarian closely, is on dangerous ground. A suitably all-embracing definition of the subject specialist's role is given by Holbrook (1972) as: 'A member of the library staff appointed to organise library services in a particular subject field'. To that might be added the term 'exploitation' to reflect the more positive, one might even say aggressive, attitude towards making optimum use of library resources, as opposed to the more passive, custodial philosophy which was at one time prevalent in many academic libraries.

Development

Subject specialisation as it is now understood in polytechnics is a comparatively recent innovation in British academic libraries. Before the 1960s there were virtually no libraries organised by subject; instead the functional approach was used. The new universities did much pioneering work with subject specialist schemes, which were then further refined by the polytechnics.

In polytechnics, subject specialisation is something of a paradox in view of the conditions under which many of them operate. Holbrook (1981), in an article on school libraries in Bath University, has given as a prime reason for the success of the system 'the compact campus'. This is a rare luxury for polytechnics with their predominantly multi-site operation, often with sites separated by many miles. A second reason given is 'a tidy school structure'; again a rare luxury for polytechnics, which with their history of mergers have faced immense rationalisation problems.

Polytechnics have been unable to centralise on one site, because of mergers and lack of funds. Despite this inability, librarians have striven to follow Department of Education and Science recommendations (1972) to concentrate services as far as possible in one central library. These large central libraries were seen as more economic both in terms of staffing and in non-duplication of stock, but they did have the disadvantage of seeming impersonal to people who were used to the 'cosier' atmosphere of the smaller site libraries.

The new libraries were a major factor in the appointment of subject specialists. Their job was not only to provide the 'active' type of service required, but also to make the library appear less remote, especially where it was physically separate from the departments, and to create the impression of smaller libraries, giving a more personal service within the larger ones. Even with these new libraries, however, polytechnics are still faced with the problem of also running smaller libraries to serve the outlying sites. The 'compact campus' is not to be.

The multi-disciplinary nature of many courses in polytechnics would appear to militate against the adoption of a subject specialist structure and does indeed cause many problems. Who, for example, should be responsible for the combined studies degree or the BA humanities and social sciences? These problems are not insuperable. It may be for instance that the main input to the combined studies degree comes from the science departments, and so the course could logically become the responsibility of the science librarian. Alternatively, subject librarians could be responsible not for specific subject areas but for groups of courses, schools or faculties. Whilst this arrangement may not be tidy in terms of division of subject responsibility, it does reflect the organisation of polytechnics in general. After all, successive mergers have resulted in many anomalies, such as a technology faculty including a department of management, or an education librarian also having to cater for a nursing course.

What is of paramount importance in the successful operation of a specialist system with multi-disciplinary courses is that subject librarians should not work in isolation. They should talk, not only to their customers, but to each other, be ready to consult, and to accept the advice of those with greater expertise than themselves.

Technical services

With the adoption of subject specialist systems, one prerequisite became very clear, and that was the need to relieve staff of as many functional duties as possible so that resources could be concentrated on reader services.

In many libraries this has resulted in the division of staff into two sections, one concerned with reader services and one with technical processes such as acquisitions and cataloguing. The creation of centralised technical services has been largely dependent upon the adoption of standardised and, wherever feasible, automated systems. Although this makes more time available to reader services, it does, however, allow for little flexibility in certain areas which can, as will be discussed later, be a source of dissatisfaction and frustration among subject librarians.

Duties

Out of the manifold duties assigned to subject librarians, four main areas of activity can be identified. These are: enquiry and information work; user education; stock selection and editing; and liaison with teaching staff.

Enquiry and information work

'Accessibility' is the keyword in considering the enquiry and information role of specialists in polytechnic libraries, and it is directly related to the policy of promoting a more active, more visible library service. This is immediately apparent to the user by the number of separate enquiry points in many of the larger libraries, instead of one central desk. The decision to have staff working at enquiry desks, instead of tucked away in offices, went hand-in-hand with the transfer of functional duties to technical services sections in demonstrating the priority given to assistance to readers. So often, it seemed in the past, that only the most determined enquirer could find the person most qualified to help him.

The staffing of a number of separate enquiry points must be seen as the ideal. It is subject to many constraints, not least the number of staff required to cover for long opening hours. If subject librarians have additional functional duties which require time to work away from enquiry desks the ideal becomes even more difficult to maintain.

As an alternative a central enquiry desk may be used, staffed by non-specialist staff to answer simpler enquiries and to refer in-depth enquiries to the specialists. This obviously runs the risk of inadequate answers from the general staff, and provides a source of irritation to the reader who has to ask his question twice. Similarly, where a central desk is staffed on a rota basis by subject librarians then it becomes the 'luck of the draw' what sort of service the reader gets. Not only for this reason is it again important for subject librarians to communicate with each other. The inter-disciplinary nature of much of the work undertaken in polytechnics means that it is not unusual for an enquiry to require input from more than one person.

The importance to the library of the quality of the enquiry service cannot be overstressed. It is by this that the library as a whole is judged, and which ultimately can influence resourcing. It is important, also, not to be too critical of enquiry work which may not strictly be academically relevant. Finding addresses, helping to write job applications, finding information needed by a lecturer's child for a school project, or even a chat about holidays is not necessarily a waste of time – it can generate an enormous amount of good-will.

Current awareness and information services have undergone tremendous changes during the early 1980s, with increasing use of automated systems. This is especially so in subject areas such as science, where the literature has traditionally been highly organised and the quality and coverage of existing hard-copy indexes has been reflected in the proliferation of online databases. Conversely, in less well-documented subject areas such as art, there has been a slower growth in the availability of online databases. This has resulted in the need still for art librarians to spend much time compiling tailor-made bibliographies by traditional methods, whilst their science colleagues use online systems to conduct searches and construct Selective Dissemination of Information (SDI) profiles to be run on services such as Dialog.

The place of the intermediary in online searching has been the subject of much discussion and is likely to become an important factor in the future role of the subject librarian. Although there has been much speculation on the replacement of the intermediary by end-user searching, just how quickly this will happen is open to doubt. Certainly, in terms of factual data banks such as statistics or chemical structures, there seems little reason why users who are prepared to spend some time mastering the system cannot conduct their own searches. In terms of bibliographic databases, however, subject librarians with their knowledge of subject, literature, databases and host systems have a unique combination of skills that would be difficult to replace. Even supposing that more user-friendly systems do succeed in making the intermediary redundant, it is likely that there would still be a place for subject librarians to act as tutors and advisers in online searching. McLean (1985, p.255) in fact has taken the hypothesis further. He saw the proliferation of databases leading to a situation where even subject librarians may not be able to keep up-to-date with developments and may themselves need the advice of an information manager. This, he said, 'is certain to raise structural and organisational problems because it may challenge the supremacy of the subject librarian'. In one way or another information technology seems certain to have a profound effect on the role of the subject librarian.

User education

With the increasing size and complexity of polytechnic libraries much importance has been attached to the development of user education programmes, from the basic induction talks and tours for new students to comprehensive courses on literature searching for more advanced students. These can range from as little as an hour to thirty hours or more and include written assignments and examination questions.

To teach at the level required for thirty hours demands a thorough knowledge not only of the subject and the literature but also of the way in which the subject is taught, this latter being very much dependent on information gathered as a result of another of the subject specialists' duties – liaison with teaching staff. Using this information, specialists are well placed to tailor their instruction to the needs of the student both in terms of subject and level and also of optimum timing, such as the beginning of work for final year dissertations.

User education is a function of the library which relies heavily on the cooperation of teaching staff in setting time aside in courses for library talks. Some academics still fail to see the value of these sessions and librarians can encounter considerable resistance which requires all their powers of persuasion to overcome. It has to be admitted, however, that timetables for polytechnic courses can be very tight, making it difficult to fit in library talks. In the case of new courses, it is helpful if sessions can be written into the course submissions, so that the commitment is there from the beginning.

Some polytechnics have included tutor librarians in their staffing structures. This has the advantage of assigning user education to a group of people whose prime function is teaching and who can therefore develop the expertise and resources. However, it is the subject librarians, who by virtue of their enquiry work, are most likely to be aware of the difficulties encountered by students in their use of the library and who can adjust both the level and manner of delivery of lectures to suit their audience. Moreover, this division of labour negates one of the major benefits of the induction talk, that of being able to maintain, throughout later use of the library, the initial contact made between student and library staff. It is significant that in those libraries where tutor librarians were appointed, many posts are being converted to subject.

In times of stringencies, when staff are hard-pressed, it is tempting to cut back on user education. This can be counter productive as user education is a very time-effective operation. The more the students can be made self-sufficient the less are the demands made on enquiry desk staff for simple enquiries at the expense of the more complex queries.

A section of the polytechnic community frequently overlooked in any consideration of user education are the teaching staff themselves, especially new staff. Their requirements may be different from the students', but they can feel just as lost in a strange library and many would welcome a little tactful tuition. Apart from the benefit to their own research, lecturers who are themselves well informed of the library's resources will help and encourage their students to use the library fully.

Stock selection and editing

According to Harris (1974, p.307), stock selection should be 'firmly in the hands of the subject librarian'. Certainly, to leave this responsibility entirely to teaching staff runs the great risk of producing an unbalanced stock, not just in terms of too little or too much ordering, but because of the tendency for some staff to order material of interest, and of a level suitable, to themselves, whilst forgetting the needs of their students. Those staff who are mindful of their students' needs are invaluable to the library both by making their own recommendations and also by supplying the library with copies of reading lists, course syllabuses, and so on.

In such cases the subject librarian's task is mainly to supplement, to watch for gaps, for new editions, or the need for extra copies. Where there is little input from lecturers, the task of the librarians, who can be working virtually in a vacuum, is doubly difficult, and the feeling that one is expected to be a mind-reader is not uncommon! However, on a less cynical note subject librarians may take heart in the reassuring statement by Davis (1975, p.117) that: 'Once a department has gained confidence in the ability of the librarian, its staff will be prepared to leave a great deal of the selection to him.'

The situation with regard to stock selection in polytechnic libraries has changed radically in the last decade. In the early to mid seventies the emphasis was on stock building to serve the rapidly growing parent institutions, using increased but still not over-generous, resources. Then in the early to mid eighties the need instead was to make best use of drastically curtailed resources. Both situations demanded the expertise of the subject librarians to use book funds to best advantage, and as, hopefully, restrictions are eased this expertise will continue to be needed to make good the deficiencies.

Similar skills are important when applied to stock editing. In economic terms, libraries, with their limited resources for new buildings, cannot afford to allow their collections to grow indefinitely. In academic terms, collections dominated by old, out of date and little used material are unhelpful and off-putting, particularly in rapidly developing fields such as electronics and computing. Changes in courses and teaching staff can have a marked effect on the use of stock which needs to be constantly monitored. This applies especially to journals where a subscription can easily be continued long after a journal has ceased to be used. Consultation with teaching staff is just as important, if not more so, with editing as it is with selection.

Liaison with teaching staff

For the efficient execution of all their duties, subject librarians require detailed knowledge of the needs of the readers. Moreover, response to an existing need is not enough. For example, collections cannot be built up overnight. The library should also be in a position to anticipate needs. For this, good communication with departments is vital.

Information can be obtained through both formal and informal channels. The usual formal channels employed are the various boards and committees of the polytechnic. Academic boards do not normally feature representation from subject librarians; these are the domain of senior library management. However, senior subject or faculty librarians will serve on faculty boards, whilst all subject librarians may attend departmental boards and course committees. Much of the benefit of this form of involvement derives from the information gained on what is required from the library, but it also provides the opportunity for the library to influence the development of courses, particularly where resource-based learning makes exceptional demands on the library. It also encourages teaching staff to take into consideration the repercussions that their actions may have on the library. Attendance at large numbers of meetings is time-consuming and takes people away from other duties. Where this involves manning service points there can be serious problems. However, as a compromise, much can be gleaned from agenda papers and meetings attended as necessary.

A system of library representatives in departments can be invaluable to subject librarians, providing them with known contacts through whom to channel information and from whom to seek information and advice. The right representative with a willingness to understand the workings of the library can do much to enhance relations with the department.

Despite the various formal channels of communication available, many people prefer the less inhibiting atmosphere of one-to-one discussions. These may not necessarily be held in the library. Indeed more neutral ground such as the staff common room is often preferred, especially if matters appear to be in any way contentious. Even for librarian and lecturer to meet at all, when the library is in a separate building, demands a conscious effort, but such meetings can often achieve far more than lengthy committee meetings. There are, however, other places which may still suffice for the informal discussion. This writer, for instance, conducts a not insignificant amount of library business on the staff car park!

Publicity

Publicity and promotion of the library service feature strongly in many of the specialists' other duties, such as user education and liaison with departments. Additionally, they are responsible for a large proportion of the publications emanating from polytechnic libraries. The range of such publications is enormous, and sometimes of a very high standard.

The general library guide is the most obvious form of publicity, traditionally in printed form, but more recently other media such as tape/slide presentations or videos have been used. As an adjunct to user-education sessions interactive videos are now being developed. Publications most usually associated with user education at higher levels include guides to literature searching, the use of specific abstracts and indexes, lists of periodicals (confined to individual subject areas) and guides to special collections. Because of their special knowledge of the variations in the way in which subjects are studied, librarians are able to take this into account both in the contents and in the manner of presentation.

No matter how good a library's publications are, however, they are of absolutely no value if the promises contained in them are not backed up by the service itself. Through their own work and personalities, the subject librarians who are writing them have an important role to play in ensuring that an efficient service is provided.

Classification and cataloguing

Of all the duties that can be assigned to subject librarians none has been the subject of such dissension as classification. The basis of the conflict lies in the desire to relieve subject specialists of routine work against the belief that classification is a task that requires subject expertise.

It is significant that it is mainly in those libraries where there are highly-developed technical services divisions that classification is not the responsibility of the subject librarians. A prominent factor in this has been the adoption by many such libraries of automated co-operative cataloguing schemes such as Birmingham Libraries Co-operative Mechanisation Project (BLCMP) and South West Academic Libraries Co-operative Automation Project (SWALCAP).

The adoption of a standard classification is economically attractive to library management, especially in times of scarce resources, for classification is an expensive operation especially when undertaken by relatively highly paid specialists. To subject librarians the advantage in doing their own classification lies in their being able to interpret the schedules in a way that suits their readers, and in the detailed knowledge of the stock that the process of classification gives them. Against this there is the conflict between duties when time is short, the danger of backlogs building up, and discrepancies in classification which could be confusing to the users.

If classification is to be centralised in a technical services division, then there should be good communication between reader services and technical services. Class numbers can be vetted before books are processed; but thorough checking means much duplication of effort if not confined solely to those numbers open to doubt, and also leads to delays in getting books on to the shelves. Subject librarians should be made aware of the expense in changing class numbers, especially after a book has been processed, but they should be free to dispute a number if they feel it necessary. Far better, however, for them to be consulted first in regard to any problem numbers. Alan Bundy (1985, p.61) in a survey of polytechnic libraries, asked: 'Have you ever experienced any substantial conflict of loyalty between your responsibilities to the library and your users?' The prominence of classification as a problem shows that it is a source of dissatisfaction. In a survey of staffing structures for reader services (Higginbottom, 1981) the problem of classification was again a recurring theme.

The situation regarding cataloguing is rather less contentious as most subject librarians are content to be relieved of a time-consuming and, what many believe to be, a largely clerical operation. Flexibility with regard to added entries can overcome most problems in this area.

Multi-site operation

The introduction of new central libraries brought about the closure of many of the existing site libraries. Despite the economies of scale, rationalisation and easier communication within the library resulting from this, it was certainly not universally welcomed. Art librarians, in particular, have been vociferous in their opposition to the closure of separate art libraries, to the extent of issuing a statement by the Art Libraries Society (1979, p.45) in which ARLIS recommended that they should be kept separate. The reasons given included difficulties resulting from physical separation from teaching departments, the loss of a complete library staff solely devoted to art and design and the replacement of a small 'intimate' library by a 'vast, impersonal maze consisting of jewels widely scattered among dross'.

Whilst there is considerable validity in the arguments given in the ARLIS statement, it should be added that these are not applicable only to art and design. The need for proximity to departments applies equally to others, not least the chemist who finds himself in difficulty half way through an experiment. Separation from departments is a difficult problem to overcome, as is the loss of personal service, hence the emphasis on liaison in the subject librarians' duties. The advantages of a small collection to those whose subject demands the ability to browse, is undoubted, but this is at the expense of access to large collections of peripheral material which is only possible in central libraries. Moreover, the creation of multi-disciplinary courses means that no subject area can be isolated from others, and split site working creates considerable difficulties in supporting these courses.

The major disadvantage for subject librarians is that the size of a site library usually does not warrant the appointment of staff for specific functional duties, resulting in an 'everybody does everything' situation. Thus a site librarian, although being nominally responsible for a subject area, will find that time for subject duties is eroded by staff supervision, timetabling, circulation problems and a host of other duties that would be dealt with by other people in a larger library. Apart from work taken over by technical services units, there is a limit to what can be done to ease the administrative burden of site library staff. Against this has to be put the fear of loss of autonomy which is the basis of much of the argument in favour of site libraries.

Subject librarians within the library structure

For top management the removal of administrative duties from subject librarians can have undesirable consequences for the library as a whole. There is a great danger of conflict of loyalties to users and the library, and it is not unknown for polytechnic librarians to feel that their subject librarians identify more with the departments than with the library. The prime function of specialists is to provide an optimum service to their users, tailor-made to their requirements, and to fight for whatever is needed to achieve that. In doing so, however, they have to be aware of the constraints of working within the total library service. Extra demands made on the book fund will be at the expense of some other part of the library, and alterations to loan periods, and so on, cannot be made unilaterally if there is a perceived unfairness. Although they may not be as involved as others in the day-to-day running of the library, subject librarians need to keep in touch with developments through meetings, working parties, staff bulletins and so on.

Also of concern to chief librarians is that the lack of any administrative or managerial functions among subject librarians, who often comprise a very large section of middle management, leads to a serious gap in the managerial chain. Their isolation is most keenly felt where it is the practice for them to work independently. A rather more structured approach is to create teams of subject librarians working under the direction of a faculty librarian or equivalent, together with their own support staff of non-professional assistants to undertake the clerical work generated by the subject teams. Besides giving a more tangible chain of command, it provides the medium for management experience which is inherent in most site librarians' duties, but would otherwise be limited in a more horizontal staffing structure in central libraries. Senior subject librarians would then be involved in staff supervision, setting objectives and seeing them achieved, but still within the framework of their own subject responsibilities. The inclusion of support staff would also ensure that all professional staff gained expertise in staff supervision.

Subject librarians are at the 'front end' of the library service, and through their contacts acquire a wealth of knowledge on what is required of that service. As Crossley (1974, p.246) stated: 'They will have their ear close to the ground – in the library and in the teaching departments'. Thus it is essential that they should play a full part in planning, policy-making and budgeting. The benefit to the library is two-fold: the tapping of a major source of information on the users' requirements; and the additional motivation generated in the subject librarians by the awareness of the objectives of the library and the ability to influence their formulation.

According to Quiney (1985, p.86), subject librarians are:

> Naive about finance, partly because they have little administrative experience and are not directly involved in the planning process, and partly because some of them seem to take a pride in their dislike of paperwork.

Participation in financial discussions and preparation of estimates for their own sections should help in making subject librarians more aware of the full cost to the organisation of the service they provide; some tend to think solely in terms of their share of the book fund. Full understanding of the financial situation helps too to make sound judgements when discussing the implications of course developments with departments. The dislike of paperwork is shared by many but it is unfortunately an unavoidable part of management.

Career prospects

Although specialists may feel happier devoting their time solely to subject work, involvement in such financial and managerial matters not only contributes to the efficient operation of the library but it also helps to avoid the block on promotion through lack of such experience to which subject librarians are so vulnerable.

In a situation where suitability for promotion to senior posts is judged in terms of management expertise, subject specialists without the will or the opportunity to participate fully in the management of their libraries will find themselves at a disadvantage compared with their colleagues involved in more administrative-based duties. This applies especially when economic problems result in lack of movement of staff, no-growth situations and an ensuing fierce competition for a diminishing number of vacancies at senior level. However, the team approach to specialisation allows for some experience of personnel management at various levels, an increasing involvement in the general management of the library and a degree of scope for promotion within the team. The traditional duties of subject librarians also have much to recommend them, particularly liaison with departments. The expertise gained in dealing with teaching staff, plus the insight into the politics of an academic institution, are invaluable to prospective management.

Recruitment and qualifications

Subject librarians are normally recruited from the ranks of graduate professional librarians. They will therefore have at least a first degree, often with a post-graduate qualification in librarianship. The preference is usually for the first degree to be in a subject relevant to that with which the librarian will be dealing. This has the great advantage of in-built expertise in that subject area and emanating from that, increased credibility in the eyes of the readers, as librarian and academic meet on common ground with a mutual understanding of the needs of the subject. User education too, especially at higher level, is so much more relevant when the teacher is able to demonstrate the solving of the complex type of problem which is most likely to cause difficulty for the searcher.

There can, however, be disadvantages. Given the number and variety of courses offered by polytechnics, not to mention the increasing number of multi-disciplinary courses, it is unrealistic to expect to employ a subject specialist with a qualification suited to every course studied. Therefore, each specialist will have a wider area of responsibility than his or her degree befits, with the possibility of a rather biased level of service, resulting both from personal interest and from level of competence. It can also be seen as a contributory factor in conflict of loyalties between library and departments as specialists identify with certain departments. Lack of flexibility too can be a problem. If specialists are recruited on the basis of relevant subject qualifications, then in theory they can only be employed in pre-defined areas of the library, thereby limiting options to move staff around the library as need dictates and curtailing prospects of internal promotion except within subject teams.

Conversely, the subject librarian without relevant qualifications may be expected to have a more even-handed approach to service, although other factors such as personality may still influence this. Similarly, there is no barrier through subject qualifications to movement within the library. However, even then, the subject librarian of some years' standing will have built up a knowledge of stock, users and subject, albeit without the prior advantage of a relevant degree, which it could take a like number of years to translate to a different subject area. It could be argued that a good librarian should be capable of operating efficiently in any part of the library. Maybe, but the knowledge that makes a really good subject librarian takes time.

Academic librarians, like all academics, are under pressure to participate in continuing education and to up-grade their qualifications. Certainly, there is a trend for polytechnics to look for higher degrees from staff in higher management positions, and it can be seen as an increasing requirement for promotion to demonstrate an active willingness to keep up to date and to acquire skills in research techniques. Senior staff, too, will find themselves under mounting pressure from below as more and more junior staff are recruited with higher degrees.

Gradings, salaries and conditions of employment

As a result of the diverse origins of polytechnics, their libraries inherited many anomalies in staff structures. Fortunately, the rapid growth of the mid seventies gave them an opportunity to re-structure and achieve more consistency. The resultant structures show many similarities, with the division of staff into reader services and technical services sections predominant. There are, however, still inconsistencies with regard to applicable grades. In the absence of any precedent, polytechnics were forced to negotiate individually with their local authorities, so that staff at the same level can be paid on a variety of grades, both Burnham and non-Burnham.

The adoption of Burnham salary scales for senior library staff has, according to Revill (1985, p.25): 'Not been popular with many local authorities, principally on the grounds of costs and conditions of service'. It is, however, something that polytechnic libraries fought hard for, with varying degrees of success, not only as a means of adequate remuneration, but also as a part of the political fight to gain recognition for the library as an integral part of the academic process. The Burnham versus non-Burnham question has been the subject of much debate, particularly the adoption of hybrid posts combining Burnham salaries with National Joint Council conditions of service, and this is discussed in general terms elsewhere in this book. However, some discussion is warranted here, as the application or otherwise of Burnham scales has a direct bearing on the work of subject specialists and on the perception of their role in the library, not just by library management or by the users but also by the specialists themselves.

The imposition of Burnham grades carries with it the implication of an academic role, something of which subject librarians themselves are very much aware. It gives a status which they can relate to teaching staff and vice versa, an important factor in trying to integrate the library into the teaching function. It also identifies them in the minds of fellow lecturers as fellow academics with an understanding of and involvement in their work. Would it then be correct to assume that those paid on Burnham scales see themselves primarily as teachers whilst those on non-Burnham see themselves as administrators with no teaching function? Some may do, but so much of a subject librarian's work is not quantifiable, is dependent upon personalities, and on the ethos of the organisation as a whole, that assumptions are dangerous. It is reasonable, however, for a library to expect its academic librarians to undertake academic work, and it may well be under pressure from its parent institution to justify Burnham grading in such a way.

Hybrid posts have been unpopular with the unions as they cause them representational problems, which has resulted in a call from both unions primarily involved, for their replacement with either all Burnham (NATFHE) or all NJC

(NALGO) grades. The Library Association, in its recommendations on salaries (1985, p.3), did not accept hybrid posts because of negotiating difficulties, and advocated that librarians on Burnham or Scottish Joint Negotiating Committee scales 'should by virtue of their duties and responsibilities also be entitled to teachers' conditions of service'. In view of the hybrid nature of subject librarians' duties, hybrid grades have found favour with libraries as means of ensuring a high level of service all year round rather than just in term time. Because of the lack of agreement on suitable salaries and conditions for senior staff, it is unfortunate that polytechnics have been unable to negotiate an agreement similar to that made between the universities and the Association of University Teachers, as evidenced by Cowley (1978, p.19): 'For my own taste the AUT solution of providing full academic status and salaries for senior librarians but with special arrangements for conditions of service seems to be a fair compromise.'

Alternatives to subject specialisation

Subject specialisation has become the norm in polytechnics but what are the alternatives? The appointment of tutor librarians has already been discussed, and, as has already been seen, their function has largely been amalgamated into the subject librarians' duties. The concept of the tutor librarian is something of a hangover from the old college libraries when the chief librarian was appointed as a tutor librarian with a dual role of running the library and of teaching a subject on attachment to one of the departments.

Houghton (1976, p.19) has described the problems she encountered as a tutor librarian. These were mainly due to working apart from the rest of the library, resulting in difficulties in keeping up to date with stock developments and in frustration at not being able personally to implement any changes to the service for which feedback from tutoring might show a need. Another factor given as detracting from tutor librarianship, which is particularly important when there are restrictions on staffing, is 'that the tutor-librarian's role is to increase library use'; thereby leading to possible conflict with the professional staff who have to provide the back-up. At least when subject specialists conduct their own tutorial work, they do it with an awareness of the implications, as they will have to cope with the work they generate.

Staffing structures based on function were replaced by the subject approach because they were not compatible with the emphasis on exploitation. A concentration on administrative duties is usually at the expense of an active service to the reader, as much of the enquiry work is left to more junior staff whilst senior staff are closeted in offices. There is, however, the advantage to the staff that it provides a better career structure and the administrative experience needed for promotion.

The future

Polytechnic libraries are now past their era of rapid expansion and into a period of retrenchment, making the most of limited resources. Subject specialists have a valuable part to play in this, but their prime function is to encourage the use of the library. It could be hard to reconcile this with a situation where it is impossible to expand or even maintain services to the standards previously offered. The result is likely to be frustration and loss of morale.

The subject specialist structure itself is expensive to maintain. Holbrook (1981), writing in relation to university libraries, but still applicable to polytechnics, saw the possibility of subject posts being converted either to functional or to clerical posts as staff shortages occur in those areas. The number of subject posts would be reduced with the introduction of 'area' librarians covering a wider range of subjects. Another solution to the problem of shortage of staff, which is already happening in some academic libraries, is the grafting of functional responsibilities on to a subject specialist structure. This is more economical but runs the risk already identified, of the conflict between administrative and subject duties which usually results in the administrative work taking precedence over subject. Crossley (1974, p.243) made the same point when polytechnics were trying to release specialists from administrative work and added: 'The librarian who works under such conditions is striving to serve two masters, even if one may be less obvious than the other. Nobody works best under such conditions.'

Information technology is certain to have a profound influence on the future of subject librarians. They will have a growing role as intermediaries, but in the face of greatly increased and more complex systems may lose some of their autonomy by coming under the direction of an online adviser. In the introduction to their survey of 'Subject specialisation in British university libraries', Woodhead and Martin (1982, p.94) said: 'In retrospect, we may be seen to have recorded the high-water mark of subject specialisation in British university libraries.' In view of similar cuts in resourcing, the same could well be said of polytechnics.

References

Art Libraries Society (1979), 'Art libraries in polytechnics', *Art Libraries Journal*, vol.4, no.1 (Spring), pp.36–46.

Bundy, A. (1985), *A study of the role of subject librarians in British polytechnic and Australian institute of technology libraries*, Underdale, South Australia, South Australian College of Advanced Education Library.

Cowley, J. (1978), 'Polytechnic librarianship: state of the art', *COPOL Newsletter*, no.17 (February), pp.17–24.

Crossley, C.A. (1974), 'The subject specialist librarian in an academic library: his role and place', *Aslib Proceedings*, vol.26, no.6 (June), pp.236–49.

Davis, K. (1975), 'Book selection' in J. Cowley (ed), *Libraries in higher education*, London, Clive Bingley.

Department of Education and Science (1972), *Polytechnics: planning for development* (Design Note, no.8), London, Department of Education and Science, Architects and Building Branch.

Harris, K.G.E. (1974), 'Subject specialisation in polytechnic libraries', *Libri*, vol.24, no.4, pp.302–9.

Higginbottom, J. (1981), *Staffing for reader services in polytechnic libraries*, Loughborough, Loughborough University of Technology, Department of Library and Information Studies, MLS dissertation.

Holbrook, A. (1972), 'The subject specialist in polytechnic libraries', *New Library World*, vol.73, no.867 (September), pp.393–6.

Holbrook, A. (1981), 'School librarians at Bath University Library: a social science case study', *Aslib Proceedings*, vol.33, no.1 (January), pp.23–31.

Holbrook, A. (1984), 'Subject specialists in university libraries: fossils or forerunners?', *University College and Research Section Newsletter*, Library Association, February, pp.7–9.

Houghton, B. (1976), 'Whatever happened to tutor librarianship?', *Art Libraries Journal*, vol.1, no.4 (Winter), pp.4–19.
Library Association (1985), *Recommended salaries and conditions of service for library staff in colleges and polytechnics* (Salary Guide, no.5), London, Library Association.
McLean, N. (1985), 'Library management and the development of information technology' in J. Cowley (ed), *The management of polytechnic libraries*, Aldershot, Gower in association with COPOL.
Quiney, L. (1985), 'The social sciences, business, management and law' in J. Fletcher (ed), *Reader services in polytechnic libraries*, Aldershot, Gower in association with COPOL.
Revill, D.H. (1985), 'The polytechnics and their libraries' in J. Fletcher (ed), *Reader services in polytechnic libraries*, Aldershot, Gower in association with COPOL.
Woodhead, P.A. and Martin, J.V. (1982), 'Subject specialisation in British university libraries', *Journal of Librarianship*, vol.14, no.2 (April), pp.93–108.

9 The systems librarian

GRAHAM K. L. CHAN

What is a systems librarian?

Systems librarians are the people responsible for managing computerised library systems. Other library staff often do not know what systems librarians do, but are very impressed by them because they speak an incomprehensible language and are surrounded by machines which only they seem to be able to bring to life. Uncertainty about their role is heightened by the fact that not all systems librarians are called systems librarians. Some still go by the earlier title of automation librarian, while some libraries make no mention of either systems or automation. Instead they hide their systems librarians behind titles such as deputy librarian, sub-librarian or development librarian. However, whatever they are called they can all be regarded as systems librarians as they all carry the responsibility for their libraries' computerised systems.

This does not mean they are responsible for *all* the library's computerised systems. Their main areas of responsibility are usually the major housekeeping operations; typically circulation, cataloguing and acquisitions. These are normally the most complex and expensive computerised systems in the library, and they are increasingly being provided by integrated systems running on powerful stand-alone minicomputers. Other housekeeping operations, such as serials control and inter-library loans, may also fall within the systems librarian's purview, especially if they use the same integrated system. However, in polytechnics more reader services oriented operations, such as online searching of external databases, viewdata, and special local database systems, are more likely to be developed by site or subject librarians. Systems librarians will probably be asked for advice and assistance in these areas, but their role is likely to be restricted to providing the facilities and perhaps some training, while the major development and use of these facilities is left to others. There is no intrinsic reason why this should be so; it simply reflects the fact that in many libraries the large housekeeping systems take up so much time that the systems librarian is unable to give much attention to anything else. In libraries where the large housekeeping systems have stabilised and no major new developments are under way, the systems librarian will have more opportunity for greater involvement in reader services operations.

Aspects of the systems librarian's work

Whole books have been written about how to tackle library automation so no attempt will be made here to describe in detail everything that the systems librarian should do. Instead the general areas of concern will be discussed with a view to illuminating some of the practical considerations across which the literature tends to draw a discrete veil.

Choosing a new system

Choosing a new system usually involves two processes: firstly an objective analysis of the technical requirements, and secondly a pessimistic assessment of other, non-technical factors which may prevent the choice of the technically best system. Often these non-technical factors make the final choice very easy by restricting the field of potential candidates to a very few who can then be quickly sorted out on technical grounds. Logically the technical factors should be considered first, but probably in practice technical and non-technical factors tend to be jumbled together.

As regards the technical requirements, every library must obviously have some idea of what it wants from a system, but there can be almost infinite variation in the level of detail it chooses to specify. At the very least the system will have to support the existing level of operations, so the usual statistics in the polytechnic librarian's annual report can provide a base from which to start drawing up a specification: number of service points, loans, books catalogued, and so on. Normally the pressure on the library will be increasing every year, so suitable allowances for increases in the number of sites and volume of transactions will be added on to the existing figures. In addition, the library will probably want the system to provide some services which are not currently available or need to be improved, in particular more management information, which in practice means every statistical and financial breakdown the library staff can think of. Useful additional pointers to the items which need to be included in a system specification will be provided by system suppliers, who will indicate what information they need in order to prepare their proposals.

If a system is being developed in-house, the library will have to provide a very detailed specification, but if a commercially available system is to be purchased, the level of detail required will depend on how flexible the library can be. If it feels, for example, that it absolutely must have a particular type of screen display or filing order, it will have to include that in its specification. If on the other hand it is willing to change, it may prefer to see what the suppliers can offer rather than be very specific from the start. The more flexible a library can be, the fewer problems it is likely to have. Although the system is not supposed to dictate what the library does, the more it insists on special software or changes to existing software, the more delays and malfunctions it will inevitably suffer.

The systems librarian's role at this stage will be to draw up the technical specification after consulting other library staff to determine what they want the system to do. The systems librarian will have to act both as a source of information for the staff and as a collector of information from them, as often they will not know what is feasible nor what questions need to be asked. The systems librarian will therefore have to guide their deliberations, pointing out what needs to be specified and what can reasonably be expected from suppliers. As the staff will never all agree on what they want, the systems librarian will have to act as arbiter and together with the polytechnic librarian, must reserve the right to make the final decisions. Those staff who disagree with the final decisions will complain either that they were not consulted or that the consultation process was a sham because it did not result in what they wanted. However, being the main source of information about what is possible, systems librarians are in a strong position to guide the staff's discussions in the direction they want and confine the opposition to, hopefully, just a few incorrigible malcontents.

Having agreed on what the library needs, the next job will be to investigate the reasons why it cannot have it, and it is here that the non-technical factors tend to come into play. The most obvious is money. The kind of stand-alone, minicomputer system which a polytechnic library will want is likely to cost at least £50,000 and for the larger polytechnics with many sites it could easily be over £1 million. A request for this kind of funding will probably be met with at best total incomprehension and at worst outright derision by polytechnic administrators and academics as well as by local authority officials and councillors. Even if they are sympathetic to the library, polytechnic administrators and academics will see it as simply a source of books and journals and will want to spend any money available for computers on the polytechnic's central computing facilities or on minis and micros for their own departments. Local authority officials and councillors will tend to be suspicious if not hostile towards the polytechnic, and in any case they will see computerisation as no more than a few BBC microcomputers which they are accustomed to buying for schools. It is easy to ridicule such attitudes but those who hold the purse strings do have a duty to be sceptical. Librarians will talk about needing computerisation because their existing systems are breaking down, when what they mean is that they cannot send out overdues or cope with reservations or get the statistics they want. To the library users nothing is breaking down: they can still borrow books, that is all they want from the library, and any available money should be used to buy more books. The costs of library computerisation therefore raise political and moral questions: how much can the library realistically request if it wants to be taken seriously and even if it thinks it can get what it wants, would this really be the best way to spend the money? These questions should be considered by all the library staff involved, but, because of their central guiding role, systems librarians should be most acutely aware of them and should ensure that they are fully discussed. Paradoxically, having been appointed to lead the computerisation programme, systems librarians may often find themselves trying to restrain more enthusiastic colleagues who do not appreciate the costs involved.

In addition to deciding how much money to ask for, the systems librarian must consider how much time is likely to be available in which to spend it. As funds can never be carried over from one financial year to the next, the library may have to choose a system which can be installed and paid for before the end of the financial year. Very often this allows only a few weeks, as the money is not made available until near the end of the financial year when the polytechnic or the local authority releases funds hitherto reserved to cover anticipated budget shortfalls or expenditure on items such as building work which will not be completed before the end of the year. By the time the library obtains the money to buy the system it originally proposed, newer and better systems may be available, but because the money must be spent within a few weeks there is no time to start again. The systems librarian must have the orders constantly ready to be signed and sent to the supplier as soon as the money is granted, and, even though that supplier may have been chosen several years before, the library must still order their system or risk losing the money.

These considerations are political as much as financial, and local politics may influence the choice of system in other ways as well. The local public library may also be seeking a computerised system, in which case there may be some advantage in joining forces to submit a proposal for a system which can serve both. With their multiplicity of sites, limited research collections, and increased involvement in community information services, some polytechnic libraries may be very similar to public libraries, and politically a joint request may stand a better chance of success with local councillors who see no political, social or educational advantage in spending money on a polytechnic. Equally the polytechnic may be suspicious of or hostile towards the public library, but whatever the outcome the systems librarian will probably have to consider the possibility, as someone is bound to suggest it. Both the public and polytechnic libraries will also probably have to consider suggestions that they use the local authority computer. Indeed, local councillors are likely to question the necessity for the polytechnic to have either its own library or its own computers, so the systems librarian has to be prepared for many long and difficult arguments ranging far beyond the initial issue of a computerised library system.

Obtaining approval for a new system

Having decided which system to buy, the systems librarian can look forward to spending at least two years trying to get it, unless he or she has been appointed to install a new system which has already been approved. Even then approval may only have been given 'in principle', and there will still be a long way to go before the money can actually be spent. Systems librarians can never predict when they might be allowed to proceed, who might veto the proposal, or what hurdles they might have to overcome, and they must be ready to move immediately final approval is given, not only because the money must be spent before the end of the financial year, but also because at any moment someone may have a change of heart and put everything back to square one. Not until an irrevocable official order has been sent to a supplier can the systems librarian be sure that anything will really happen.

Obtaining approval means writing reports, or more accurately variations on the same report, which are sent to every individual and committee who could conceivably have some influence in the matter. The reports must assume that anyone reading them knows absolutely nothing about libraries, so they must start by explaining what a catalogue, circulation system, and so on, is and why the library needs one. They must then prove that only a computerised system can provide what the library needs and present a range of options which the library could choose. Having discussed the advantages and disadvantages of each option, the systems librarian will finally recommend one as the most suitable on the basis of how closely it matches the library's requirements and its cost.

In these reports, the systems librarian must prove that the most suitable option is also the least expensive. This is likely to be the most vital but also the most difficult part of the report. It is the most vital because, no matter what their public utterances may be, local councillors of all parties will only be interested in ways of cutting the costs of the polytechnic. Even within the polytechnic, lecturers and administrators, faced with pressure on all sides to cut costs and increase services, will want to see any money they give to the library spent on books and journals. Proving that the desired option is the least expensive is difficult because it is almost certainly not true. The least expensive option is probably the existing manual or in-house computerised system running on the polytechnic or local authority computer. With a manual system the conventional argument is that it is extremely expensive when staff costs are taken into account, but librarians know perfectly well that computerisation never results in staff savings. Even if staff are redeployed, the total wage bill remains the same. Apart from simply telling outright lies, all the systems librarian can do is to demonstrate that, in order for the manual system to provide the same level of service as a new, computerised system, additional staff would have to be employed whereas the new system would not require any additional staff. The flaw in this argument is that the library would never be given the additional staff so the additional expense would never be incurred. However, as there is no other alternative, the systems librarian is forced to use the argument and hope no one notices the flaw.

Similar difficulty arises with an in-house computerised system running on the polytechnic or local authority computer. Unless the library is charged for computer time, which is very unusual, it is probably cheaper than any possible alternative although it provides nowhere near the desired level of service. The systems librarian has to add on the notional cost of computer time to show how expensive the system really is, and then also adds the cost of additional computer time and programming to bring the service up to the desired level. Again the flaw in the argument is that these costs would never actually be incurred because the resources needed to improve the system would never be available. Typically, however, the existing computer is being replaced by a new machine which cannot support the library system, at least not without extensive reprogramming and additional hardware. The systems librarian can therefore argue that simply continuing with the existing system is impossible and transferring to the new machine would be more expensive than buying a new system.

The report should be as short as possible, because the longer it is the less likely anyone is to read it. It will gradually grow in size as people point out areas which are not included in it and which they think need to be considered, but it is impossible to foresee everything that the critics will raise, so any attempt to forestall them by including every possible aspect of the subject in the report is bound to fail. It is better to keep it short to begin with; the systems librarian can then concentrate on the specific points raised by the critics without wasting time and energy on areas they have overlooked.

In fact, hardly anyone will read the report, although the polytechnic librarian will always be told to submit a report whenever the matter is raised. As most people will not read it, it is perfectly safe to submit basically the same report every time, simply revising the dates and addresses and incorporating any changes suggested by the few people who have read it. A word processor is invaluable as it can store the basic report and repackage it to look like new every time. It also makes it easy to extract the essential parts to produce a condensed, one or two page version. This will eventually be required by the polytechnic administrators, local authority officials and councillors who, having repeatedly told the librarian to submit a report and having repeatedly been given it and ignored it, will eventually tell the librarian they have no time to read a report and what is needed is a short statement specifying what is required exactly and concisely. This may evolve into a cyclical process, as having received the exact, concise version, they may say they need more information and tell the librarian to submit a report. In time, they will gradually grow used to the idea that the library needs some money for computers, and the library will get it either when a financial windfall means there is a need for large capital items to mop up the money quickly or when the library has been on the list of funding requirements long enough for people to be too embarrassed to turn it down yet again.

Even when permission to spend has been given, any order for anything to do with computers will automatically be referred to the computing department and, if approved by them, it will be sent to the local authority's central purchasing department, which will want to know why the library is trying to order a computer which is not on their approved list from someone who is not one of the local authority's contracted suppliers. The systems librarian must therefore make some effort to prepare the ground in advance. From the start, advice must be sought from the head of the computing department, and the systems librarian should incorporate any suggestions from the head of the computing department in the library's reports, constantly point out how helpful the computing department is and how anxious the library is not to overburden it (which is why the library must have its own system), and ideally obtain the head of department's signature on any orders that are sent out. This is not simply a cynical exercise, since the computing department often is very helpful and can give the library valuable advice as it has to go through similar procedures to obtain its own funds. In fact, the library and the computing department often face very similar needs and difficulties, so mutual sympathy and understanding are not unusual.

The intervention of the central purchasing department is not necessarily bad either. It can obtain many items at a discount and this may even apply to the library's computer system, or at least parts of it. Once it has been explained to them that the library must have a specific system with specific hardware which is only available from a specific supplier, they will usually be perfectly willing to co-operate and may still be able to negotiate a lower price. Again, this means that the systems librarian must make an effort to keep the central purchasing department informed, and the eventual orders must be accompanied or followed up by an explanatory note pointing out that this is what the systems librarian has been talking about.

Implementation

The systems librarian should try to prepare the necessary orders, site plans, wiring diagrams, and so on, well in advance, keeping them constantly up to date so that when final approval is obtained they can be sent out to the system suppliers, polytechnic maintenance department, British Telecom, and so on, without delay. Every opportunity should also be taken to have any possible site preparation work done in advance. Installation of additional electric sockets, resiting or modification of issue desks, purchase of new furniture, are examples of items which can sometimes be accommodated within existing budgets or justified as additional minor works without any mention of computers. It is also now normal for libraries to begin bar coding stock long before approval is obtained for an automated circulation system.

After the orders have been sent out, there may be a slight lull when to the library staff nothing seems to be happening. The systems librarian will however have plenty to do, working out detailed system parameters, timetables for data input and stock preparation, and so on. Delivery times for hardware will be three to six months and inevitably there will be price increases because of currency fluctuations. When hardware does arrive it has to be tested, and some peripherals (VDUs, light-pens, and so on) will be found to be defective. However, initially the major problems are likely to be in site preparation and installation of telecommunications links, both external British Telecom lines and internal cables and communications equipment. Although deadlines will be set, at least some will not be met and slippage in one area may delay work in other areas. 'When planning the timetable for the implementation of the system, the librarian should bear in mind that no computer system yet has been installed which has not been subject to some slippage' (Leeves, 1984, p.17). To a large extent systems librarians are at the mercy of others in this process and, apart from making constant phone calls to ask what is happening, they can do little other than wait for electricians, carpenters and telephone engineers, to turn up. If any work has to be done by the local authority's direct labour force, the time estimates should be at least doubled.

Systems librarians must ensure that all the site preparation work required is specified clearly and completely on the orders and accompanied by plans and diagrams whenever possible. They should also prominently label all the required locations of electric sockets, cables, telephones, and so on and ensure that other library staff and caretakers know where they are so that they can point them out to the workmen if the systems librarian is not available. Systems librarians should make dozens of copies of the orders, plans and diagrams to give to the workmen who arrive to do the work and who will never have seen them before or will not have bothered to bring them. They must also try to be on site as much as possible when any work is being done and constantly check on its progress. Often this checking need be no more than a casual stroll through the area on the way to somewhere else, but the systems librarian should not hesitate to query anything, as, if anything is installed wrongly or in the wrong place it may be extremely difficult to get it corrected afterwards.

As the deadline for going live approaches, the systems librarian is likely to become increasingly worried about data input and stock preparation. The programme will probably have begun quite optimistically, but gradually enormous piles of anomalies and exceptions will accumulate, more and more refinements will have to be dropped, and increasing numbers of complications will have to be put aside to be dealt with later. Some of the problems will work themselves out if left long enough, for example if some batches of student data are input wrongly it will not matter after a few years when they will all have left the polytechnic. Some problems, however, the library will have to learn to live with, for example mixtures of upper and lower case records, as there will be no practical possibility of correcting them.

If existing machine readable data is to be loaded into the new system, programs will have to be written and run to convert it into the required new format, typically by the polytechnic's computing department. The systems librarian must specify exactly what records and fields are present in the existing data, what is to be done to them, what new records and fields are required, and how any necessary values must be calculated. The programmers will repeatedly claim that the programs are finished when they are not, so the systems librarian must insist on exhaustive debugging and test runs using large amounts of data deliberately designed by the systems librarian to include as many types of error and defect as possible.

As far as stock preparation is concerned, a particularly pernicious problem is unreadable bar code labels. They tend to be unreadable either because of poor quality printing (laser-printed labels should be used if possible) or because incorrect algorithms have been used to generate them. Because bar coding usually begins well before the library has any equipment to test the bar codes, the problem is often not discovered until just before or soon after the system goes live, which means there has to be a crash programme of relabelling at the worst possible time.

When the hardware has been delivered, the system supplier will send someone to install it who, after carrying out some initial tests, will say that everything is working and depart as quickly as possible, leaving the library to discover all kinds of problems and defects. This will be a particularly fraught time for the systems librarian who will still be struggling to sort out the existing problems and get the site preparation, data input and stock preparation completed. On top of this, the systems librarian will need to begin extensive testing of the software (at least some of which will not work) and staff training, and because of missed deadlines the time available for this will have been drastically reduced. Of course this presupposes that there is an absolute deadline for going live which cannot be extended. This is most likely if circulation is being automated, as the new system usually has to be running by the start of the academic year since no provision has been made to maintain the existing system beyond that point; besides which the polytechnic librarian and possibly other senior library staff will be unwilling to allow further delay if at least the basic functions can be made to work. If circulation is not involved, implementation can probably be more leisurely and in any case there will be fewer problems, but eventually the systems librarian will have to decide to go live with some problems still unresolved and some parts of the system still unusable.

Resurrecting existing systems

A systems librarian is often appointed specifically to implement a new system, but there may already be a computerised system in operation which has to be kept going until the new system is installed. Also, as most polytechnic libraries are now automated to some extent, it is likely that in future, systems librarians will increasingly be appointed to manage and develop existing systems rather than to bring in completely new ones. In both cases there will probably be considerable delay before the new systems librarian arrives, during which the most basic operations may have been maintained but some applications will have fallen into disuse, and a long list of problems and requests for changes will have accumulated.

Resurrecting an existing system is more difficult than implementing a new one, as everyone expects the new systems librarian to know everything and fix every problem immediately, and they will start grumbling if no obvious improvements are visible within a month at the latest. If the existing system has been developed locally, probably little or no documentation will be available, and what there is will be out of date and sometimes misleading. Commercially supplied systems are often no better, and even if it is a widely used system there will be local variations, parameters and procedures. In any case, there will probably be no time for systematic study of the documentation. The systems librarian should ask the polytechnic librarian to send any available documentation as early as possible and should try to become familiar with it before taking up the post. Otherwise there will probably be time to do no more than read odd snatches of manuals and system specifications which have a bearing on the particular problem in hand.

As systems librarians are expected to be miracle workers they must try to work some miracles very quickly in order to retain credibility. This means they will have to work very long hours, at least initially, without complaint and possibly without publicity, as it is better if they can seem to work their miracles with no apparent effort. A great deal of luck is involved in trying to predict areas which will yield the greatest gain for the least effort, and there will always be problems which are so important that they must be tackled immediately irrespective of their likely susceptibility to miracle cures. A concentrated and sustained attack on the major problem areas is likely to result in some progress and maybe even a dramatic breakthrough when the systems librarian can suddenly announce the solution to a problem that has been causing trouble for several years. However, the miracles need not necessarily be so significant or far-reaching, as long as they are things that no one else in the library would even attempt to do and which preferably meet a long-standing need. For example, the staff will be impressed if the systems librarian simply gets a VDU or printer to work which has been gathering dust in a corner for months, or produces a special print-out which a site librarian has been requesting for years. Even if such matters do not have high priority, they are often worth spending some time and effort on, because they can provide highly visible, tangible successes which will boost the confidence of other library staff in the systems librarian and create a breathing space in which to tackle more serious problems.

Development

Implementation of a new system or resurrection of an existing one merges imperceptibly into system development. At the start, no system works properly or has all the planned features, and it will probably be about two years before the library has something close to what it originally wanted, running reasonably smoothly. During this time, new software will be loaded to correct errors and provide additional facilities which may or may not have been envisaged at the start. Also, additional terminals and possibly other hardware such as memory or discs will be installed to meet increasing demand, additional sites will be brought into the system, and adjustments will be made as sites are moved from one location to another. This can all be regarded as development, but the systems librarian will be fortunate to be allowed six months, much less two years, before library staff start to exert pressure for what *they* regard as development, which will be a major new system such as circulation, if cataloguing has just been automated, or an online public access catalogue (OPAC), if circulation has just been automated. As soon as anything is installed, everyone will want more and no one will appreciate how much time and effort is needed to get systems working or to make changes to them. The pressure from the polytechnic librarian will be particularly relentless, as polytechnic librarians tend to be very anxious to keep up with new technology and they know that they must include major items in capital bids at least two years in advance.

This situation may change in future if systems librarians start to become polytechnic librarians, but in the meantime systems librarians have to resist this pressure as long as possible, otherwise they will never have time to get anything working properly before they have to turn their attention to something else.

Eventually, however, the systems librarian will be forced to begin working on the next major development because the polytechnic librarian will start drafting proposals and specifications for the systems librarian to comment on. Being by definition the expert on these matters, the systems librarian is unlikely to be happy with what the librarian has written, and will therefore have to rewrite it, thereby being inexorably drawn once again into the cycle of report writing and lobbying required to obtain the necessary funds.

System development therefore involves a continuous programme of gradual improvements within existing budgets, punctuated every few years by major spasms of large-scale capital spending. The two overlap to some extent, as some items included in capital requests will be funded from existing revenue budgets when the capital fails to materialise. This will not reduce the size of the capital requests as the systems librarian will add new items to them to replace those already acquired or use the difference to cover price increases. After, at most, five years the system will be obsolete and after, at most, ten years the hardware will be worn out, so the whole cycle will have to start again from the beginning.

Maintenance

A systems librarian should carry a small screwdriver at all times. Most of the library's hardware will be covered by maintenance contracts, but there are always minor repairs which systems librarians will need to do themselves, such as screwing in plugs and sockets which have come adrift or freeing jammed keys on VDU keyboards. A screwdriver is also invaluable for routine operations such as manipulating the tiny switches on the backs of VDUs and printers, coaxing open the back doors of the computer after the key has been lost, or breaking into the machine room when all the operators have gone to lunch. If the systems librarian can deal with such matters personally there will be less delay than if the maintenance company has to be called.

After the initial teething troubles, major problems with the computer itself should be infrequent, although when they occur it may take several days to trace and correct the problem. If computer defects are very frequent, there is probably an environmental problem such as a dirty power supply or inadequate air conditioning. System suppliers so often fail adequately to specify the environmental requirements that the library should try to make them contractually responsible for ensuring that these requirements are met. Although they are unlikely to agree to this, it may at least force them to specify in detail what the requirements are.

Problems with VDUs and light-pens will be much more frequent. Although the maintenance company may offer a fast-response contract at a higher price than usual, there is no point in taking it, as the response will not be any faster. The company has only a limited number of engineers and, no matter what the contract says, it will not give high priority to a broken VDU if someone else has a CPU defect which has knocked out their entire system. This underlines the need for systems librarians to try to effect minor repairs with their own screwdrivers. Ideally the library should keep some spare terminals which can be temporarily swapped for broken ones, but this is difficult in multi-site libraries, although the systems librarian can try to make use of other library staff, especially the polytechnic librarian, who is likely to be travelling frequently between sites by car.

The weakest link in the library's system will probably be the internal telecommunications network. Increasingly libraries are connecting their systems to switching devices or local area networks installed by the polytechnic's computing department. For the library this is cheaper than installing its own dedicated telephone lines and modems and provides more opportunities to widen access to the library system and access to other systems from the library terminals. However, interfacing problems can arise, particularly if a local area network is involved, and it can be very difficult to pinpoint defects. At the University of Reading, for example, interfacing problems are thought to have caused frequent freezing of VDUs (Lovecy, 1985) and Oxford Polytechnic has suffered similar experiences. Moreover, the computing department's technicians will not only be hopelessly overstretched, but also, being used to academic computing where if a terminal or even a whole terminal room is not working the user can go somewhere else or do the work later, they will not appreciate the need for the library's system to be running continuously every day. Consequently, they may take a long time to respond to service calls and will often shut down parts or even all of the system without warning, possibly not bothering even to switch it back on again if it is in the vacation. The systems librarian therefore has to be prepared to scour the whole polytechnic to find the technicians and badger them unmercifully until they fix the problem. The only real answer, however, is to ensure that at least some of the most heavily used terminals are hard-wired into the library computer.

Programming

It is often assumed that a systems librarian must be a programmer, but this is not necessarily so, although every systems librarian is likely at least to dabble with the occasional BASIC program and will probably be involved in using packages. As libraries increasingly abandon locally developed systems in favour of commercially available ones, there is likely to be less and less need for systems librarians to do any programming, but nevertheless some programming knowledge can help the systems librarian to understand how a system works and to specify requirements to systems analysts and programmers employed either by the system supplier or by the polytechnic computing department. Also, most systems can be extended by user written programs so systems librarians who can write them will be able to enhance their systems much faster than if they had to rely on others.

There is one major area where it is still a great advantage to have a systems librarian who can program: file transfer from one system to another. Systems librarians who can write the programs themselves will probably do a better job than other non-library programmers, as the systems librarian will have a more intimate knowledge of what needs to be done than anyone else. There will also be less risk of misunderstanding or misinterpretation if they do not have to try to transfer this knowledge to another programmer. Moreover, another programmer, particularly one from the polytechnic computing department, may have little or no experience of dealing with files of such size and complexity, with the problems of different magnetic tape formats and character codes used by different machines, or with the need for special, non-printable control codes to be inserted in the data. A high-level language such as COBOL-74 can usually deal with all the problems quite simply, but the programmer is quite likely to be unaware that there is a problem, or, not knowing how to deal with it will claim that it is someone else's responsibility to solve it, or will simply ignore it and leave the systems librarian to discover that the resulting data is full of errors or even completely unusable.

Budgeting

Budgeting for capital expenditure on equipment is usually not difficult as the system suppliers will provide cost estimates, as will British Telecom for telephone lines, the polytechnic maintenance department for site preparation, and so on. However, recurrent revenue costs are often related to level of use, and not only is this impossible to predict but in co-operative network systems the charges fluctuate according to the number of members and the total activity throughout the network. A library's monthly Computer Output Microfiche (COM) charges, for example, may vary according to the total number of fiche produced for all the network members during the month. Moreover, the provision of additional terminals or additional facilities such as key-word searching during the year may result not only in dramatic increases in use but also unforeseen additional maintenance, software development or processing charges. It is particularly difficult to draw up revenue budget estimates for the first year of operations with a new system, as there is no prior experience on which to base the estimates. Some guidance may be obtainable from the system supplier and from other libraries of similar size using the same system, but in the first year the estimates will be largely guesswork. Thereafter it should become slightly easier as the systems librarian can add a percentage for inflation to the previous year's figures together with further estimates to cover any likely new developments during the coming year. Expenditure, however, always has to be monitored very closely and the systems librarian may have to suspend some activities temporarily to avoid serious over-spending. Like everyone else involved in budgeting, the systems librarian will try to overestimate costs so as to provide a cushion to absorb unexpected expenditure and to buy books on library automation, programming manuals, and minor items of equipment after the library's book and equipment budgets have been exhausted.

Polytechnic libraries usually have to meet the recurrent costs of their automated systems from their book funds, and the systems librarian will have to withstand constant complaints from other senior library staff about the high proportion of the book fund being consumed by the automated systems. These complaints often come from the same people who are most vociferous in their demands for more computerisation. Their usual refrain is that there should be a separate budget head for computerisation; they seem incapable of understanding that the polytechnic has a finite sum of money and that transferring some of it to a new budget head will not increase the amount available to buy books. Nevertheless, the impact on the book fund is often not adequately considered when computerisation is being discussed, and the systems librarian must constantly hammer home the message that even if all they want is another VDU it will mean fewer books. The systems librarian can also offer to cut costs by taking away their terminals, reducing the number and frequency of COM catalogues, discontinuing accessions lists, statistical reports and selective catalogue listings, and so on. This will usually still the criticism at least for a while.

Staff management

A systems librarian may have general staff management responsibilities, for example as head of technical services or deputy librarian, which involve the same kind of personnel work as any other department head. In addition, since their work impinges on virtually every other department and site in the library, systems librarians must become adept at securing the co-operation of large numbers of staff, often very widely scattered over a multitude of sites, often suspicious or jealous of each other. They must also ensure that other library staff are sufficiently well trained to operate the computerised systems on their own.

The first essentials are to keep staff informed about what is going on and to involve as many as possible in the planning process. Apart from frequent informal discussions, systems librarians will probably have to chair committees or working parties charged with drawing up recommendations, give talks at staff meetings and write articles in staff newsletters. As usual, no one will listen to what they say or read what they write, so staff who are interested will repeatedly ask them the same questions while those who are not interested will try to ignore it all. However, systems librarians must make the attempt if only to satisfy the enthusiasts and protect themselves from accusations of not consulting anyone.

Similarly it is good public relations to arrange for staff to visit other libraries to see computerised systems in operation, in particular those which the library is considering for its own use.

Staff training will be an ongoing requirement as new staff are appointed and new facilities are made available. While some written instructions must be provided, no one will read, much less remember very long documents, and hands-on experience is essential. Workshops in which people are given set exercises to perform, perhaps after a short initial demonstration, are ideal. In setting these exercises, systems librarians should remember they are likely to be dealing with complete novices who will, for example, type 'RETURN' on the keyboard if instructed to do so rather than press the RETURN key.

As soon as possible the systems librarian should start to spread the training load by involving other staff in it, partly because it will introduce more variety into their jobs and help to maintain their interest and partly because otherwise there will be too much for the systems librarian alone to do. Initially these staff can be asked to assist in running workshops, for example, and eventually the systems librarian should be able to delegate most of the routine training to them. Anyone who has taken a particular interest in an aspect of the system or a package should be encouraged to take the initiative and organise training sessions themselves.

Inevitably automation will give rise to claims for staff regradings and complaints about health hazards of VDUs. There will always be someone who will claim that they should be paid more to use computers and someone who will claim that using a VDU will make them go blind or sterile. Once one person makes these claims, others will follow. They will all be supported by the union, and no one, not even those who were most enthusiastic and eager, will start using the system until an agreement has been reached. These matters should therefore be raised and agreement should be reached well before any system is installed. In theory, negotiations should be conducted by the personnel officer, but if the systems librarian can deal with it there is more chance of it being settled quickly. Automation rarely justifies regrading, as the level of skills required from the staff is usually no higher than their existing skills, and, since automation normally makes their work easier and more interesting, they should not expect to be paid extra for something that is already a benefit to them. Health hazards will normally be dealt with by a new technology agreement covering all local authority employees. The hardware will usually already comply with the requirements of the agreement, and initially the only problem is likely to be the maximum permitted hours of VDU use, commonly four hours per day. Someone may claim this means they can only work for four hours a day, but the systems librarian will have to argue that library staff are engaged only in intermittent VDU use which does not in total exceed four hours a day. The initial agreement will not of course be the end of the matter, as claims under the new technology agreement, typically for free eye tests and spectacles, are likely to be made before the local authority or the polytechnic has laid down any procedures for dealing with them, so the systems librarian will probably have to become involved in devising and implementing the necessary procedures. Moreover, no matter what the agreement says, both new and existing staff will raise the same arguments repeatedly, especially those about hours of work and eyesight, but at least the agreement will allow the system to get started.

Personal relationships

Systems librarians are heavily dependent on others to supply, install, maintain and use the systems in their charge, so they have to deal with people as much as with machines. In particular, they are in almost daily contact with three main groups of people: library staff, computing staff and system suppliers.

With library staff, systems librarians must be patient, co-operative and sympathetic. They must be prepared to explain and demonstrate the same things again and again, to listen to people's problems and accommodate their special requirements whenever possible. Most online systems are now flexible enough to allow a great deal of variation, so it is no longer necessary to attempt to impose the kind of rigid standardisation, for example in classification of books held at different sites, demanded by the early, offline systems which tended to upset site and subject librarians. The systems librarian must, however, be firm with senior staff when they ask for software to be changed or for new software to be written. They never appreciate the difficulties or the dangers involved in this, nor the amount of work required, so the systems librarian must try to act as a filter, screening out the requests that would be likely to cause more problems and delays. Despite the systems librarian's best efforts, some staff will never reconcile themselves to automation and will always have as little to do with the system as possible. The systems librarian will soon recognise who they are and should waste no more time on them. The time will be far more productively spent supporting and encouraging the enthusiasts who will be equally easy to identify. Although it can be very disheartening when staff are constantly reporting problems and asking for advice, the naive faith in the systems librarian which they sometimes display – a belief that the systems librarian can fix anything – is in a way the best possible compliment.

In their relations with the computing department, systems librarians must be quietly persistent. The more they can do themselves the better, from punching cards and mounting tapes to writing and running programs, as apart from speeding up the work this will gain them more respect from the computing staff who, ideally, will begin to think of the systems librarian almost as one of them and also as someone who will only bother them if it is really essential. Systems librarians will be uneasily aware of the pressure on the computing department, which like the library will always be overstretched, but nevertheless, when their help is needed, the systems librarian will often have to prod them repeatedly as they may not appreciate the urgency of the situation or they may simply be overwhelmed by the other demands being made on them. From time to time there may be opportunities for the systems librarian to help the computing department, for example by ensuring that the library buys books they want or by relieving them of mundane though straightforward jobs such as sorting and labelling the library's magnetic tapes. Obviously there has to be a limit to this, but small favours like these can pay dividends if, when problems arise, the computing staff actually want to do all they can to help instead of merely being obliged to because it is their job.

Systems librarians can and frequently should be much less restrained in their dealings with system suppliers who are often simply appalling. Particularly with stand-alone minicomputer systems, they typically rush to market with systems which are poorly designed, incomplete, full of software bugs, have little or no documentation, and are backed by hopelessly inadequate technical support staff. They sign up as many libraries as they can as quickly as possible and only attempt to get the systems to work properly when some or all of their customers threaten to pull out. The difficulties experienced at Brent Library Service (English and Jurkowski, 1985), where the users had collectively to exert considerable pressure on the system supplier before any satisfactory documentation or system support was provided, are unusual only in that they have been documented so honestly and publicly. Possibly because they do not want to admit to having made a mistake or to having been too gullible, librarians often seem to close ranks and become extremely defensive about their computerised systems, glossing over the problems and taking the line that, while there may have been difficulties initially, everything is much better now. Also different members of staff are likely to view the situation in different ways. Some will be perfectly happy with the system and say it causes no problems, because they themselves do not have to deal with any problems. When anything goes wrong they simply report it to someone else, and they may not even be aware of how much time and effort has to be expended to keep the system running. Typically the someone else who has to deal with the problems is the systems librarian, and the façade only cracks when systems librarians meet together and exchange horror stories.

Sometimes librarians themselves are partly to blame for being too eager to buy the latest, untried system, or for being too impatient in pressing for additional facilities, or for insisting on too many special modifications and believing the supplier who claims to be able to deliver them all with no trouble. Nevertheless, librarians tend to be much too ready to be understanding and forgiving. A report on Kent County Libraries stated that: 'downtime has generally been the result of software difficulties' (Harrison and Masters, 1983, p.12), as though this is nothing to worry about when in fact it is precisely the problem: the hardware is usually highly reliable, the software is often rubbish. In many instances libraries spend hundreds of thousands of pounds on these systems, and they have every right to be angry if the systems do not work. There is no point in being polite and friendly if, as has repeatedly been demonstrated, only harsh words and threats will galvanise a supplier into action, and if systems librarians are unhappy with a supplier they should never hide it. Systems librarians are often asked for advice about systems and may move to other libraries which are looking for new systems, so they do have some influence in the marketplace even if there is no prospect of their current libraries changing their systems in the near future, and system suppliers should never be allowed to forget this fact.

Qualities needed to be a systems librarian

Although some systems librarians may spring fully formed out of library school, it is better if they emerge gradually from the ranks of the library staff after a period of years in which, by accident or design, they have become increasingly involved with automated systems. They are responsible for making dramatic changes in the way a library operates, so they need the kind of experience and understanding which they can acquire only by performing those operations in the front line themselves. It is often assumed that a systems librarian must be almost a fully qualified computer scientist, but probably none of them are, and, while technical knowledge and programming ability are obviously desirable, wide experience of routine library operations at a junior level is just as important.

Technical knowledge and programming ability can actually be disadvantages if misapplied. Systems librarians must always guard against the danger of becoming too fascinated by their machines and, for example, should not spend their time constructing online databases when the job could be done more quickly and efficiently by a cardfile. They must also try to dissuade other library staff from making the same mistakes. Moreover, while a systems librarian who is a good programmer is invaluable, one who is a bad programmer can be a disaster. A bad programmer is likely to leave a legacy of unfinished, undocumented systems that never work properly, no one understands, and are impossible to maintain. Good technical knowledge and programming skills, properly applied, will make for a more effective systems librarian, but such knowledge and skills are acquired not by attending a few training courses but by spending long hours, largely outside normal working hours, studying manuals and writing and running test programs. Those who are not prepared to make this effort will have to accept that they will be less effective than someone who does.

Programming is often assumed to require a science

background, but in fact the only requirement is the ability to think and apply rules in a rigorously objective and logical manner. Whether they do any programming or not, systems librarians must have this ability as they have to analyse and document exactly what needs to be done and work out how to make the automated system do it. They will constantly have to read, understand and use flow charts, system specifications and manuals, and sometimes have to write them themselves. They must not, however, be cold, emotionless automatons, as they have to manipulate and preferably charm a greater number and variety of people within and outside the polytechnic than anyone else in the library except perhaps the polytechnic librarian. If they cannot manage charm, they must at least display infinite patience, tact and understanding, except of course towards system suppliers. System suppliers are the only people with whom systems librarians can lose their tempers; with everyone else they must be calm and collected even when everything seems to be collapsing around them. It also helps to have a sense of humour.

Systems librarians – who needs them?

Systems librarians have evolved quite recently, and many libraries with automated systems do not have systems librarians or do not appoint them until after the system has been installed, so they are obviously not always essential. However, the kind of stand-alone minicomputer systems that most polytechnic libraries are or will eventually be using require someone to look after them on a full-time basis, and sooner or later if a new post is not created there will at least have to be a rearrangement of duties so that someone in effect becomes the systems librarian even if the title itself is not used. The systems librarian's work will overlap with that of the heads of those sections which are the major users of the system, but they will expect the systems librarian to take the lead in planning and developing it and in dealing with problems.

It is desirable for systems librarians to be appointed at the very beginning, before any new system is chosen, so that they can guide the investigations and have as long as possible to familiarise themselves with the system that is eventually installed. This also ensures that they have no one else to blame if the wrong decisions are made. However, many libraries will choose their system first and then appoint a systems librarian to implement it, and of course when first appointed a systems librarian will inherit the existing system, so a good systems librarian must be able to take any system and make it work.

Whether systems librarians will always be needed is uncertain. Eventually as computer systems become increasingly user friendly and computing expertise becomes increasingly widespread, systems librarians may become extinct. If this does happen, it could be argued that at that point everyone will be a systems librarian, so the species will have achieved the ultimate success. In any case, library automation is advancing so rapidly and systems are becoming so complex that systems librarians are likely to be needed more rather than less for at least the next decade.

References

English, A. and Jurkowski, C. (1985), 'Urica: the Brent experience', *Vine*, no.59 (July), pp.48–53.

Harrison, D.J. and Masters, B. (1983), 'Progress with Plessey online at Kent County Libraries', *Vine*, no.47 (March), pp.8–13.

Leeves, J. (1984), 'Selecting and installing an online, stand-alone circulation system: a guide and checklist for public libraries', *Vine*, no.56 (December), pp.3–36.

Lovecy, I. (1985), 'A library implementation of a LAN', *Vine*, no.59 (July), pp.33–9.

10 The polytechnic librarian

DON H. REVILL

This final chapter examines the role of the polytechnic librarian. Whatever title he or she may have – chief, head of learning resources, or director – he or she is concerned with all the matters covered in earlier chapters of this volume.

The librarian will have an idea of the structure he wishes to develop. He must plan to achieve it, albeit the actual result will inevitably be a compromise between the ideal and the attainable, given the many constraints. The institutional context will strongly influence the librarian's ability to act. Internal politics will affect his capacity to manage, plan and market library services.

Having established a presence, and hopefully an influential one, he must consider his role, and style, as leader of the library service. Decision-making is an essential element within leadership and command. He may adopt a participative management style in which staff can, themselves, influence events. He will realise that the effectiveness of library service is crucially dependent on the quality and numbers of staff, therefore staffing of the library will be a prime concern. This involves not only developing an adequate structure but also establishing good relations with trades union, staff development and consideration of his own professional development and involvement in professional activities. Finally the librarian must obtain resources, essentially in terms of cash for staff, book fund, buildings and automation. Each of these points will be developed below.

Perrow (1961) has argued that any organisation has four main tasks:

1. capital acquisition;
2. acquisition of activity legitimation;
3. skills acquisition;
4. co-ordination of the organisation with the external environment.

The first and second tasks are a prime responsibility of the polytechnic librarian, albeit shared by others. Skills acquisition includes recruitment of staff, a suitable structure for those staff and their development. The fourth task is a large part of the librarian's job. He has to manage the unit's relations with, and interdependence on, others parts of the organisation.

Edwards (1975) sees the function of library management as different from the function of librarians performing as professionals. He believes library organisation is rooted in bureaucracy. There is some truth in this yet. Without becoming involved in the librarian versus manager controversy, there is a strong case for the professional librarian as manager. He has to obtain resources and allocate them to fulfil professional ends. He has to direct and lead the library – hence must have professional knowledge and legitimacy. He has to explain and justify the library to others. The librarian is also responsible for analysing and studying the effectiveness of the library. Efforts in this direction may sometimes be against the wishes of staff who may prefer to be left alone 'to get on with the job'. However, cases are seldom won on advocacy and assertion alone. Basic data is still needed if only to reassure top management that the library is effective in fulfilling its purpose.

Organisational design and effectiveness

Silverman (1970) defined system effectiveness in terms of an organisation's capacity to survive, adapt, maintain itself and grow. A more conventional definition would stress the attainment of objectives at least cost. In the case of libraries, the design intentions are to serve effectiveness, yet the inability to reach the optimal design may oblige the system to approximate more closely to one concerned with efficiency; efficiency in this case being equated very largely with minimal cost. Pfeffer (1978, p.223) has argued that the critical question: 'is not how organisations should be designed to maximise effectiveness, but rather whose preferences and interests are to be served by the organisation . . . What is effective for students may be ineffective for administrators.' Mintzberg (1973) too identified one of a manager's purposes as being to ensure that his organisation serves the ends of those who control it. The ends served by the polytechnic should relate to the success of students on courses of study. However, the latent intent may be rather closer to minimising costs and avoiding conflict with the local authority.

Lee (1977, p.399) has reported library directors as feeling:

> Caught in the middle, trying to maintain a balance between the demands of academic staff and students, central administration and their own staff. Many of the directors . . . felt that a disproportionate amount of their time must be devoted to educating the administration, to articulating and interpreting library matters to their newly installed superiors.

O'Connor (1980, p.45), in discussing problems faced by heads of American university libraries, where the demands of the President's Office and the central administration 'were the source of many frustrations', thought that the same problems had appeared in British library systems. 'The general outcome was a declining ability of the library to meet needs, a lack of goals and planning, and inability to accommodate educational changes quickly' (p.46). This latter is crucial. Libraries grow and change. It may take up to three years to negotiate necessary change through polytechnic and local authority structures. This is far too long. By the time those changes are agreed, they will have largely been superseded by other requirements. Thus the librarian could satisfy the directorate and the governors while providing a less than effective service to students and academic staff. Users are more or less remote from the top decision-makers. Their influence through the committee and consultative structure can only extend so far.

One can only agree with Pfeffer (1978, p.241) that 'organizational design outcomes [are] both causes and consequences of underlying political forces'. There is seldom one 'best' organisational approach:

> Enterprises with highly predictable tasks perform better with organizations characterized by the highly formalized procedures and management hierarchies of the classical approach. With highly uncertain tasks that require more extensive problem solving, on the other hand, organizations that are less formalized and emphasize self-control and member participation in decision-making are more effective (Morse and Lorsch, 1970, p.62).

Wilkinson (1978, p.26) has observed:

> The modern library is clearly not a homogeneous organization, either in terms of its objectives, the demands it makes upon its personnel, or the mental set it requires to achieve its goals. Why, therefore, attempt to impose

> a single authority structure, a single communication pattern, or a single personnel policy throughout a library? Why not instead let those parts of the library that develop complex objectives be organized along highly participative (if not collegial) lines . . . let those parts that develop routine, task oriented objectives requiring adherence to regulations and subordination to administrative authority be more structured.

Perrow (1979, p.166) characterised the differences between clerical and professional tasks fairly well:

> When the tasks people perform are well understood, predictable, routine and repetitive a bureaucratic structure is the most efficient . . . Where tasks are not well understood, generally because the 'raw material' that each person works on is poorly understood and possibly reactive, recalcitrant or self-activating, the tasks are non-routine. Such units or organizations are difficult to bureaucratize.

This same dichotomy can be seen reflected in the concepts of mechanistic and organic structure as identified by Burns and Stalker (1966) with clerical roles having a mechanistic orientation and professional staff adopting an organic mode. Thus the library service has two distinct modes of operation. Lawrence and Lorsch (1967) have suggested that organic and mechanistic structures can co-exist within an organisation. Library assistants' tasks are characterised by classical features of bureaucracy, the files (the issue, the stock on the shelves) and rules (loan categories, alphabetical order, regulations). Professional librarians' jobs have greater scope for judgement (enquiry work), discretion (interpreting rules) and initiative (tuition in library use, feeding information to lecturers). Relations with academic staff are, in this respect, critical. Organisational design must recognise this. The effectiveness of the library is inextricably involved with the actions of teaching staff. Hence library staff are obliged to seek partnership with them. However, academic staff seem indifferent to partnership (Ford, 1980, p.346). Libraries' problems start in the classroom, if not before; hence any structure must place great emphasis on liaising with, and influencing, academic staff.

Most polytechnic libraries seem to have adopted designs based on subject, the primary division of polytechnics' teaching departments, by recruiting subject librarians, many of whom enjoy academic salary grades. Some local education authorities have been unsympathetic to this idea. Pressures appear to be growing to reduce the number of library staff on academic grades both because of costs and the fact that they now count against staff-student ratios. Nevertheless professional staff soon find that teaching departments, student groups and book selection revolve around subjects, therefore library staff have to adopt a similar structure. A cyclical process develops where library staff liaise with academics in order to anticipate learning needs, and instruct students in the use of the literature of their subjects in order to make them relatively independent in library use. Failures in the library, and common problems discovered via students' enquiries, can be analysed and fed back to academic staff and the library's own courses of tuition in library use, book selection and deployment. Any break in the cycle can seriously affect the library's effectiveness. These relationships have a natural progression not always appreciated by polytechnic higher management.

In order to be effective, the library needs to know about forthcoming courses, changes in courses, teaching content and style, particular emphases on subject coverage and the phasing of teaching programmes. Without this knowledge, the library acts, or rather reacts, blindly. To be effective the library needs to be able to anticipate and be pro-active. Only through the closest involvement in academic planning and by having an intimate knowledge of courses can library staff properly fulfil their function. This is the proper role of most professional library staff.

Technical services staff share some of the features of the organic/mechanistic, professional/bureaucratic typologies. The appropriate pattern of clerical and professional functions is contingent on the nature of the work to be done and the needs of the people involved. Nevertheless conflicts between the two sectors can occur. The traditional area is that concerning conflict between staff and line (Dalton, 1950). Bundy (1966) has seen bureaucratic organisation, with antagonism between professionals and the bureaucracy, as the primary cause of conflict in libraries. She particularly referred to division of work by function and argued that the typical division into technical and readers services creates the conditions of conflict. The librarian may be able to mitigate this problem by arranging that staff spend part of their duties on technical services and part in readers services, even though there might well be a separate technical services department. Further automation may allow the complete decentralisation of these functions.

Another form of conflict, apparent to some extent within systems, is that which could be labelled 'cosmopolitan' versus 'local' (Gouldner, 1957). In the library context Rayward (1969) has pointed out the problem of conflict between staff who emphasise the library's participation in the bibliographical universe and management who emphasise the library's institutional dependence. Within academic libraries, further support for another distinction between staff comes from Whitworth (1974), who found that college librarians could be distinguished by their attitudes towards 'extended' role activities including involvement with audiovisual materials and tuition in library use compared with traditional, purely 'library', activities. Librarians with an extended role orientation were found to be more cosmopolitan and those with a restricted role orientation more local.

Changes in design

Changes in design to meet shortcomings and anticipate change can be difficult to negotiate. The most immediate problems stem from government restrictions on spending in higher education, national policy and local authority control. Libraries can do little about these. The storing of resources against future contingencies is a strategy employed by organisations. The slack can be used 'to buffer the effects of environmental fluctuations' (Pfeffer, 1978, p.136). Libraries seldom have 'slack' in terms of surplus space, staff or funds. 'Smoothing environmental fluctuations' (Pfeffer, 1978, p.157) is a possible strategy. In libraries' terms, this could mean influencing readers' behaviour through tuition in library use and persuading academic staff to liaise more closely. There is no obvious mechanism whereby demand can be encouraged to transfer to off-peak time other than congestion obliging the reader to try later. In this latter case it is likely that the reader will not pursue his need (Urquhart and Schofield, 1972, p.238). One could take the advice of Burns and Stalker (1966, pp.251–2) and retain a degree of flexibility while risking what may appear, superficially, to be the very denial of management:

> The firms which absorb innovation best have practically scrapped the rules about organisation charts. They do see to it that people know one another in a personal sense, but they are not put out if several people seem to be doing the same job, if no one is quite sure who his boss is, if policy is changed unpredictably and no one is officially told about it . . . It flows through, over and around obstacles which would halt a tidier kind of organisation. It also uses men better – those who don't like it leave it . . . those who stay are thrown into situations of responsibility, they strive to cope.

Politics of the job

There is a political dimension to the job. Staff might not realise the extent to which a polytechnic is a political system. Politics, in this context, is concerned with obtaining and allocating scarce resources and with the control of conflict.

The librarian will be a member of the academic board which is supposed to be the main policy-making body. His position on the board is somewhat unusual. While running a largely service organisation, he has some of the characteristics of an 'officer' of the institution quite unlike heads of teaching departments and other academic staff on the board. His interests are polytechnic-wide yet academic, administrative and supportive. He does not control student enrolments. The library's interests may, on occasion, be seen to conflict with those of teaching departments. The computer manager will be in a similar position yet able to muster strong arguments, and data, for resources. He has the information technology climate in his favour at present. The librarian needs to gain the support of the computer manager. They share many concerns yet, with a limited cake, could be seen to be in competition. In this respect the library, as the more familiar resource, may lose an advantage.

There will be some allies. Those departments such as law and social sciences that regard the library as their 'laboratory' can usually be relied upon to make the librarian's points for him. Similarly the engineers and scientists will resent any suggestion that their need for good library services is any less vital.

It is in this interplay that the library can gain. Speaking always, and solely, on library matters on the academic board and its committees can lead to the librarian being fatally typecast. He must take a larger view, let others make his points for him, speak on a wide range of academic matters of which he is knowledgeable and only press library concerns out of necessity.

Within the academic board it is possible, certainly in times of retrenchment, for a scale of priorities to operate which might exclude the library. The individual academic's course comes first, then his department, and his faculty. Teaching departments may feel that they have more in common, or more to gain collectively, than in supporting a library cause. The 'allocation of benefits, if not costs, is weighted in favor of faculty and staff' (Raffel, 1974, p.418), reflecting the power and influence of status holders, élite groups, or individuals.

The librarian may prefer to adopt a low profile for a quiet life without flak, yet to be ignored will do little to improve the library. The central administration and directorate may be relieved not to hear from the library. They have other problems. Inaction in not pursuing the library's case, the acceptance of being unimportant, will have an adverse affect on the library's finances and services:

> People don't ignore calls from people they want to talk to, and they don't 'trust' individuals whose performance they consider crucial to their own success. Our managers ignore us because they don't care, and because they don't perceive that they have any responsibility to assist us (White, 1981, p.68).

It takes skill, persistence, time and patience to raise the library to a level at which it gets its fair share of attention and resources.

The librarian must talk to top management, persuade, cajole and educate them to agree what is to be done and then talk about how to achieve it and the costs. It is necessary first to establish what it is right to do. At least then, if cash support is not forthcoming, management will know why things are not done. They will have some responsibility in the matter. It is imperative that the librarian makes himself heard. A degree of aggression may be necessary. A 'number of management studies indicate that . . . is exactly what bosses expect – from top-notch subordinates. They expect their worthwhile subordinates to be full of ideas and initiatives, to be impatient and perhaps even a little abrasive' (White, 1981, p.69).

A further problem is that the library has relationships outside the polytechnic, but it will also have educational objectives which may go beyond individual course objectives. The library is part of a larger bibliographical and library network. It is affected by events at national and international levels. While this larger context is well recognised for teaching departments, it may not be so apparent to those in authority where the library is concerned. The library may have objectives on students gaining the ability to find out and keep up to date in their subjects through the trained use of information sources. Such objectives are not always seen as formal course objectives. They may be implied but not often explicitly stated. The librarian will adopt a proselytising role on such matters.

Funding

One of the most important functions of the librarian is to get funds. If he does not achieve his fair share there is the excuse, but little consolation, that the director has not obtained the 'right' level of funding for the entire institution. The librarian must also exercise a strong influence on the allocation of library funds:

> The academic librarian is hard put to it . . . to make his budget serve his needs. As the range of disciplines in education continues to fragment and become specialized, he is under greater pressure to satisfy his main client, the student user (O'Connor, 1980, p.36).

Funds are needed for staff, books and buildings. At one time a polytechnic librarian with a high professional reputation would have had a large staff, many on academic grades, a high book fund, a large part of the library's activities computerised and a new building. These were the attributes of success. In recent years there have been large variations in the fortunes of individual libraries on these four distinguishing properties. Continual and continuing improvement is no longer guaranteed. More realistic attitudes now prevail. The ability of individual librarians cannot be regarded as the single most important factor. It has to be conceded that national and local events and policies have a stronger influence. At one time one may have believed that once a system had obtained its new library then all would be well. This appears not to be the case. The attitude may become:

'You've got your new library, be satisfied with that'. Pressures on book fund and staffing may increase.

Power and influence

Library power, as described by Thompson (1974), is not guaranteed simply through the power of the written word. Pfeffer (1978, p.198) has contended that there are at least four bases for influence in the organisation:

1 the possession of or ability to control critical resources;
2 the control of or access to information and information channels;
3 legitimacy of the desired position or actions;
4 formal authority, as derived from the formally designated organisational structure and constitution.

The librarian may have a strong or weak control over resources. Allocations to subjects or departments may be mediated through more senior positions or committees. However, the librarian should be in a strong position to influence the direction of resources. He provides the data on which decisions are taken. The library may not be able to bring in a great deal of outside money, but it has a great deal of internal money to dispense. The problem is that the library may allocate in a covert rather than in an overt manner, and those who benefit are largely students rather than heads of department and senior staff. The benefits are seen and enjoyed in the library not in the teaching departments. Hence the evidence of authority, power and influence is lacking. It is a largely invisible influence. A scheme to use the considerable book fund in a secondary allocation to reward teaching departments for doing the right thing *vis à vis* the library was attempted at Liverpool. The reasons why it failed would make an interesting case study. One argument was that it would give the library too much power!

It might be thought that as information is an important resource then the library would be in an ideal position to exercise influence. However, senior polytechnic management often require the kind of information that is mediated via central and local government ministers, elected members and officers, rather than published information. Academic staff and students require published information but the institution's library is not the sole provider. Alternatives exist. Nor is the locus of power at the level of students and the generality of teaching staff.

A librarian can use his ability to 'buffer, filter and selectively provide information' (Pfeffer, 1978, p.19) in presenting cases to committees. Presentation of cases can be difficult. The Churchillian one side of A4 may be ideal. It will be read, but Churchill could get away with it. He was the supreme policy-maker. Policy can be stated briefly. Arguments and data to support that policy tend to produce lengthier papers. There appear to be two views. One is that sheer force of personality, and dogmatism, challenging dissent, will carry the day. The other is that it requires reasoned argument fully backed by research and fact. To the extent that academic institutions are not entirely rational bodies, the former may be successful. It all depends on the institutional climate.

There is also the dilemma over how much to put into documents. Two classic academic challenges are risked: 'There is not enough information here for us to make a decision' and 'There is too much here to understand in the short time we have had the papers'. Both tactics lead to reference back and no action. The major ploys are still those described in Cornford's *Microcosmographia academica* (1953). A re-reading of Dale Carnegie (1938) could also be of benefit.

The 'legitimacy of the desired position or actions' is seldom in doubt. The value of, and necessity for, a good library service is strongly supported by academic staff although they may not be so forthright in supporting all the prerequisites of staff, machines and buildings as well as 'books'. Priorities enter into it.

The librarian's formal authority resides in his position as a head of department. Access to and control of channels of communication is a further source of power, hence the value of unique knowledge derived from membership of key committees. Noble and Pym (1970) have pointed out that professionals on committees that vetted other committee decisions were in a powerful position, while inter-locking committee membership conferred disproportionate influence on the professionals concerned. The librarian will seek to gain membership of such committees. One indication of the possession of power is when one can stop some particular development. This has happened, almost by accident, in a few polytechnics where the librarian's name was included on a form certifying the availability of the resources needed by teaching departments before new courses could be offered. The librarians, on occasion, refused to sign the form, thus giving them the power of veto.

The chief librarian has at least one advantage over those of his staff who also become involved in internal committees:

> When faculty members attend committee meetings, they do so during the time they are not teaching, and enough time is provided for this activity. When librarians attend committee meetings, their work continues to accumulate. It was assigned on the premise that they would be there all the time (White, 1985, p.6).

Only the polytechnic librarian, generally, is a partial exception to this rule. He is the only 'spare' man around. This freedom of action allows the librarian to 'badger' top management and anyone else who needs to be moved. Similarly the librarian should also act as a buffer to protect his staff against some of the excesses perpetrated by more senior decision-makers. 'Badgering' will include encouraging and educating senior academics in library matters via papers, presentations, and bringing examples of good practice to their attention. One can invite senior academics as interviewers in staff selection (this may be a requirement anyway for senior library posts), or invite them to visit the library to see behind the scenes and meet the library staff. Their perceptions will be altered, hopefully favourably. Yet despite all this White (1981, p.69) has contended: 'Ultimately managers only get credit for two areas of accomplishment: innovation and marketing.'

Innovation

Innovation involves change and planning. Planning for change requires a knowledge of higher education in the UK and a crystal ball. Education is experiencing a period of rapid change and uncertainty. Time is needed to inform and involve oneself in those changes affecting one's own institution. This is all part of establishing credibility as an academic, as a colleague and not simply as a librarian.

Morein and Webster (1977) have suggested areas that should be examined in terms of changes that will affect the institution. These are equally pertinent to the UK:

1 economic
   (a) increased cost of material
   (b) higher salaries
2 technological
   (a) computer cataloguing
   (b) computer circulation
   (c) audiovisual
   (d) microforms
3 social
   (a) declining birth rates
   (b) attitudes towards college
4 higher education
   (a) demand for vocational education
   (b) more independent study
   (c) life-long learning.

Management is concerned with planning for change. The greater the uncertainty perhaps the greater the need to plan. Yet there are so many possible future scenarios that there could be a retreat from planning. Any plan may become merely a reference point against which one can only compare the present position. O'Connor (1980, pp.37–8) has supported the view that:

> There now appears to be a major state of disequilibrium owing to the effects of decisions usually taken outside the immediate closed system of the libraries' own determination. No longer can the librarian succeed in his planning and control without acknowledging the immense upheavals that external economics and inflation in particular can have on his system. Managing open systems presents its own problems and calls for special skills which may take time to acquire.

Automation

To some extent computerisation and information technology in general have become major constituents of innovation. New services have arisen as responses to technological opportunities. Video in all its forms, online searching and Prestel are now common in polytechnic libraries. Many elements of library operations have been computerised. Polytechnic libraries now seem to be planning for the next generation in terms of stand-alone, fully integrated, systems. The polytechnic librarian need not be a technical expert but must be able to argue convincingly for institutional support in this area. Veaner (1985, p.295) has pointed out that new technology, automation and computerisation 'has forced resource expenditure into high levels of visibility'. Resource questions are now more political:

> In connection with costs, it will be up to academic librarians to convey to higher levels of administration the true costs of computerized information systems. We should be long past the seductive hope that great cost reductions in computer hardware will bear any relationship to trimming a service institution's budget. Any 'savings' realized will be more than offset by far more significant increases in other costs, which will result in a larger, not a smaller, total expenditure (Veaner, 1985, p.301).

This is a gloomy forecast and a daunting task for any librarian. The opportunity cost of automation can be very large. Nevertheless libraries must prepare themselves for the full onslaught of new technology. It is difficult to conceive of a library in the year 2000 which does not have its major systems fully computerised. Not least of the problems is that of replacing, and therefore rejustifying, expensive computerised systems when they are 'only' five or ten years old. This is a new field for most librarians. It is problematic how their institutions will respond. 'The profession needs to teach itself to freely abandon tools that have become superseded, even if not worn out' (Veaner, 1985, p.297). This may be easier said than done.

Marketing

Marketing is attracting greater attention. The polytechnic librarian needs to become more closely involved in marketing. To some it is just the old problem of providing services to meet needs yet it can offer new perspectives. Change and growth can take place in the areas of:

1. market penetration. The library can increase its market share of potential users. Further efforts may be made to increase usage by part-time students;

2 market development. New missions for existing products, new services, formats, involvement with educational development services;
3 development of new products to add to the range or replace others such as new media, online services;
4 diversification. New products and new missions for example video facilities, bookshops, film booking service, copyright clearance office.

The particular problem of the polytechnic – indeed any academic – library is that of encouraging use. Readers are seldom obliged to use the library. Alternatives do exist for students from book purchase, and the use of other libraries, to dependence on lecture notes. Teaching departments can impose duties on students, including reading; the library, itself, cannot. Librarians can encourage use to the point where staff cannot cope. Even so what statistics there are do not seem to indicate that library use then falls back to a level at which the library can cope. Recent years have seen a decline in input factors (staff, book funds' real purchasing power), yet a sustained growth in outputs such as book issues and enquiries.

Leadership and command

The role of polytechnic librarian includes leadership and command. Leadership is not the sole prerogative of the librarian. Library staff heading sections of the library will also exercise leadership within their own areas. Dragon (1979, p.64) has observed:

> Libraries are unique social institutions with staff characteristics, clientele and mission quite unlike any other . . . but, the library's leaders must plan, organize, control and lead their organizations in much the same way as leaders in hospitals, banks, insurance companies or universities.

A requirement then is to understand the concept of leadership and apply this knowledge. The librarian also needs to acquire self-knowledge on his personal rating as a manager and a leader. McGregor (1966, p.67) writing of his former belief that a leader could operate successfully as a kind of adviser to his organisation, said:

> I could not have been more wrong . . . I finally began to realise that a leader cannot avoid the exercise of authority any more than he can avoid the responsibility for what happens to his organisation . . . since no important decision ever pleases everyone in his organisation he must also absorb the displeasure, and sometimes severe hostility, of those who would have taken a different course.

In some circumstances, hopefully only temporarily, the leader could become a focus of disaffection. It may sometimes be better for people to hate one man than one another! The departmental scapegoat has his functions. Most managers in higher education nowadays feel that they have little control over staff grades and salaries. Librarians cannot easily optimise the mix of book fund, staff and buildings. In expansionary times interesting things happen. Career progression is more possible. In times of retrenchment managers can be blamed for the lack of opportunity. They need to have sufficient confidence not to feel personally threatened by disagreement and criticism.

Strong leadership is necessary in order to control a dispersed professional organisation and to mediate with the controlling hierarchies. The librarian must have the ability to command the various styles of leadership in the appropriate circumstances. Influence is not identical with leadership, but the leader should influence more often than others and create the expectation that he will exert his influence.

Leadership styles

There have been many styles of leadership identified. The conventional typology cites a sequence of autocratic, authoritarian, persuasive, consultative, participative, democratic and, ultimately, *laissez-faire*. Different situations require different styles except that the days of the autocratic or authoritarian leader are hopefully over. The manager should have the ability to command many styles according to the circumstances. He could adopt a consultative style on conditions of service, a persuasive style on getting change accepted.

There are differences of opinion as to whether leaders should maintain a certain social distance from their staff. Growth in size means that personal contact cannot always be maintained with subordinates. A social distance is created whether it is wanted or not, yet it should not result in lack of knowledge through remoteness. Any leader is compelled to remain in ignorance, or feign ignorance, of some actions or developments. He may not agree with every decision made. These decisions may depart only marginally from what he would do or from policy. If it varies more than fractionally then the manager should be concerned and investigate why the decision was taken. There may be some justification for it. It is often so because policy is seldom taught. No manager can remain ignorant of certain endemic conflicts in organisation, for example that between staff and line functions and inter-site competition (House, 1985). Whether he can resolve these conflicts is another matter. Acknowledgement of their existence, on the part of all staff, is half way to a solution.

Any leader is in a very good position to retain his leadership. In a new situation that 'requires' a certain type of leadership or style, which the existing leader does not have, then the leader can delegate. He produces the new skill via someone else. This is related to the idea that a leader often steers a group towards skills, and preferences, akin to his own or which he can satisfy, or he defines the situation to the group in his terms to stress the relevance of his skills in arriving at a solution. This reinforces his position. Such a leader is also likely to react against tasks imposed from outside, not of the leader's choosing. Delegation is not merely a protective device. Delegation is necessary in order to give staff the autonomy many seek, to share responsibility and authority and fully use their skills.

Qualities required

O'Connor (1980, p.46) has considered that a chief librarian must be:

> Flexible and adaptable, willing to accept change as a way of life, and open minded about alternatives. He must be stable and have an equable temperament, have endurance and be exceptionally persuasive. In short he needed to be a leader, not just an authority.

O'Connor (p.67) also listed the symptoms of the failing, or 'anxious', manager. Any manager must be aware of his own weaknesses and whether his performance is deteriorating. Interest and enthusiasm may be difficult to sustain sometimes, while illness, mental or physical, or domestic problems can lead to poor decisions and worsening relationships.

Hicks and Gullett (1981, p.307) have argued that leaders arbitrate over disagreement, suggest ideas rather than issue orders, supply objectives and priorities, act as catalysts to start or increase a movement, provide security, and are positive and optimistic. They represent their organisations. A favourable impression of the leader will probably lead to a favourable impression of the library and inspire others that the work is worthwhile and important. The manager should develop an attitude to his own personal availability in the interests of managing his own time. He must ask himself whether he should adopt an open door policy or insist on papers and an appointment. His own and his staffs' time is a valuable resource and it should not be wasted.

Self-rating

It is useful if, on occasion, library managers compare qualities found in themselves with those found in successful executive heads. Argyris (1953) has listed the following:

Successful executive heads:

1 exhibit a high tolerance of frustration;
2 encourage full participation to the extent that they permit people to tear apart their decisions without feeling personally threatened;
3 continually question themselves without being constantly critical of themselves;
4 express hostility tactfully;
5 accept victory with controlled emotions;
6 are never shattered by defeat;
7 identify with groups, thereby gaining a sense of security and stability;
8 set goals realistically.

Various self-rating forms have been devised. One of the earliest of these was Blake's managerial grid, a conceptual device to give points of reference for discussion (Blake and Mouton, 1964). The grid has a quantitative suggestion, but it is in reality completely qualitative. Participants discuss where their management philosophy falls in relation to this grid. As the whole experience can be traumatic, a helpful principle to adopt is that no one should assess anyone else until they themselves have been assessed. The experience should not form part of formal staff appraisal or promotion exercises. Dragon (1979) has described the Ohio State

Leadership Model where two factors became regarded as critical. These factors were consideration (concern for people) and structure (concern for the task). Their Leader Behavior Descriptive questionnaire can be used to measure the behaviour of supervisors as described by subordinates. Fleishman (1973) followed a similar course. The Fleishman questionnaire involved staff in assessing their superior on about fifty points using a five-point scale. The superior also assessed himself using the same items. A true understanding of personal style should result in minimal differences between the group's and the individual's assessment. Scores for 'consideration' and 'structure' are derived. Other leadership questionnaires for self-assessment have been compiled by Goodworth (1984) and Townsend (1984). Townsend's list was short but to the point. 'A good leader is available, humorous, fair, lets people in on information, decisive, humble, objective, tough, effective and patient' (Townsend, 1984, p.122). 'As for the best leaders, the people do not notice their existence. The next best, the people honor and praise. The next, the people fear; and the next, the people hate . . . when the best leader's work is done the people say, "We did it ourselves"' (From Lao Tzu, quoted in Townsend, 1984, p.123).

A good librarian should be a source of ideas. There is a need to strike a proper balance between pursuing the librarian's own ideas and acting on ideas and proposals from staff. A danger sign is when all the ideas are coming from below and are being rejected, or when no new ideas are forthcoming from anyone. Managers should also watch out for the situation where ideas appear to be their own but have in fact been sown in their minds, some months earlier, by subordinates. The originator will not generally be pleased and would prefer recognition. The librarian himself will act in the same way by placing ideas in the minds of his superiors. If they eventually act on them, assuming that they are their own, then the librarian experiences quiet inward satisfaction and overlooks the lack of recognition.

Decision-making

Leadership involves decision-making. Vroom and Yetton's (1973) five management decision styles, paralleling leadership styles, give a basis for considering how best to make decisions. They are autocratic, benevolent dictatorship, consultative (individual), consultative (group) and democratic. May (1978) has provided a simpler and clearer exposition. The situation determines which style to adopt. Time is the major constraint. A more autocratic mode results if there is insufficient time for consultation. Staff have to learn to live with this. If there is trust in the manager no harm need be done. Decisions may have to be taken which are unpopular with some staff. The whole system's needs must take priority over individual sections or interests.

The classic prescription for decision-making where a problem is defined and analysed, information is gathered, alternatives are considered and action evaluated is challenged by Lindblom (1959) who has argued that decisions are actually made in a much less structured way. Managers seldom have complete information on, or analyses of, a problem. In practice most managers make a choice from a few known alternatives. Lindblom called the process 'incrementalism'. Cates (1979) has argued that incrementalism limits both risk and change and is best suited to a stable environment. Cates proposed that better solutions can be arrived at by substituting creativity for rationality. Lindblom (1979, p.520) in his reassessement stated that: 'incrementalism . . . is not, in principle, slow moving. It is not necessarily, therefore, a tactic of conservatism. A fast-moving sequence of small changes can more speedily accomplish a drastic alteration of the *status quo* than can an only infrequent major policy change.'

Many decisions in librarianship can be of this nature. A consensus develops as librarians tackle similar problems. Through membership of professional bodies and publication, a view develops that is acceptable. To this extent the librarian's job is simplified. This is not to say that the odd aberrant opinion and practice should be shunned. The deviant or creative individual can be a catalyst for fresh thinking.

Participation

Some decisions and tasks cannot be carried out successfully unless there is full support on the part of those engaged to do them. It is probably impossible nowadays not to involve staff in decision-making. Staff demand it. Insisting on a purely hierarchical response structure could be dysfunctional. Blau and Scott (1962, p.183) have argued that the presence of a number of professionals undermines the possibility of a rigid hierarchy of control. Noble and Pym (1970) found that professionals' claim to control areas within their competence also extended into general organisational planning. It would seem unwise therefore to exclude them from decision-making. An authority structure much closer to what Weber (1947, p.402) described as 'collegiality' is more likely and more appropriate.

However a balance is necessary between allowing collegial authority to determine every decision and professional oligarchy or dictatorship (benevolent or otherwise). As Weber (1947, p.39) argued: 'collegiality unavoidably obstructs the promptness of decision, the consistency of policy, the clear responsibility of the individual', while Noble and Pym (1970, p.440) pointed out that: 'in respect of rapid decision-making the organization appears more efficient the further we leave behind the formal, collegial authority structure and approach the oligarchy which has evolved within it.' Collegial authority may present something of a mismatch under local control.

> The organization's accountability to the external public authorities for the use of its funds . . . threaten[s] the collective autonomy and individual discretion of the professionals. A collegial authority structure is not well adapted to meet this environmental pressure (Noble and Pym, 1970, p.441).

The means to moderate the dysfunctional effects of both bureaucratic forms and the use of professionals in the library, and to benefit from their potential contribution, includes the use of a participative management structure coupled with strong leadership.

McClure (1980, p.39) saw the absence of information as a key factor in decisions to involve staff in participative decision-making, yet the 'imposition of participatory management styles in an organization with unequal information contact among members is likely to result in greater differences of power between the two groups', hence participation reinforces inequality. The theme that participation is bad for staff is a common one. Criticisms range from participation as pretence to it being a part of organisational control. 'Group decision-making is occasionally little more than a sham, in which the workers are reduced into thinking they have participated in making a decision, which turns out to be what management wanted to do in the first place' (Pfeffer, 1978, p.232). Dickson (1981, p.159) too believed that:

> Participation represents an extension of organizational control over employees rather than . . . a means of employee influence over upper level management. Organizational control is achieved through establishing a framework for participation which limits the issues that can be raised and the influence that can be exerted upwards.

It is used to 'provide a means of containing conflict and restoring order and legitimacy to those in authority' (Dickson, 1981, p.172). However, the original motive for introducing participation may be genuine and altruistic. Certainly it could help control, but this argument is circular. No one would introduce participation if it damaged the organisation. Staff ask for participation. Should a polytechnic librarian then deny them this on the grounds that it enhances management's control and is bad for them? Such an attitude suggests a perpetuation of the management and labour dichotomy and antagonisms. A participative structure could be seen as modelling the library on the academic institution it serves, all members having an equal voice and vote as is supposed to occur in teaching departments and boards of study. To some extent this is a misreading of how an academic institution actually works. There may be surface democracy but there is undoubtedly surface and hidden autocracy. The academic board is not the final arbiter on very much. National authorities, the local authority, the director of the polytechnic and the governing body all have the power to accept or reject academics' opinions.

Not all staff wish to 'participate'. In the USA, Flener (1973) found that less than 50 per cent of staff were interested in participation. The view was expressed that administrators were paid to take decisions and should do so. As Cayless (1978, p.107) has pointed out: 'the implication here is that the "managed" group, whilst not actively opposing participation, can see no advantage in it for them'. Potential disadvantages of participative styles must be recognised and met (Kaplan, 1975). Participation can be easily misunderstood. Some decisions cannot be taken in a democratic or even consultative way. Expectations may be raised that cannot be met. Staff must realise that a decision agreed in the library has to get approval at many higher levels before it becomes reality. Rejected minority opinion holders may be alienated by the process. Group decision-making may be frustrating to some, and group cohesiveness may be turned against management. Group decisions may be poor ones because no one feels really responsible. Compromise may water down or prevent an effective decision.

Participation can lead to demands (on salaries, staff numbers) that the controlling authority cannot or will not grant. Some members may need to be educated in the realities of institutional life. Similarly the subtle differences between participation, consultation and democracy may need to be spelled out. Each problem for decision will have to be approached in a different way depending on the constraints surrounding it.

Participation need not lead to improved productivity. Stewart (1972) studied the relationship between participation and performance in libraries. He concluded that a direct relationship did not exist. However, the librarian adopts participation with other motives. It may assist productivity indirectly in getting change accepted and permitting the workforce to know what is going on. The workforce may feel better informed and more in control of its own destiny. Participation is part of treating people properly and may raise morale.

Morale

Plate and Stone (1974) have shown that Herzberg's motivation–hygiene theory is relevant to libraries. Their findings indicate that the factors producing job satisfaction and motivation were concerned with the actual job content and work processes; those leading to dissatisfaction (hygiene factors) were factors relating to the context in which the job was done. Even so, as Heller (1972, p.160) has pointed out, some principles can be contradictory – 'security and appreciation in one corner and challenge and testing in the other' – while 'one man's hygiene is another man's motivation'.

An interesting point is raised by Morse and Lorsch (1970), who have suggested that competence in tasks can become a more reliable and consistent motivator than salary or benefits. Competence is produced when there is a fit between tasks and organisation. This sense of competence continues to motivate, proceeding to higher goals as lower ones are achieved. However there appears to be no necessary causal relationship between job satisfaction and performance. Locke (1970) has suggested that: 'satisfaction should be regarded primarily as a product of performance . . . and only very indirectly as a determinant of performance'.

Librarians have little control over many of the factors that encourage high morale. There is a limit to the extent to which the conditions of the job can be improved, and salaries raised. Library managers tend not to have the independence to create a promotion and succession plan. Other than recognition, the most tangible reward is through promotion to vacancies at a higher grade but usually only after a competitive interview involving external candidates. Yet too many internal promotions can create problems. Vacancies may not be filled. The impetus from new appointees is lost.

There are no easy answers to staffing problems. It is wrong to assume, as much of the literature of personnel management does, that there is an amicable and satisfactory solution to all personnel problems. Just as it is too simple and glib to attribute a single technology to an organisation, so it is to assume that actors' perceptions will be similar within each technology or hierarchical level. It is likely that people will have varying attachments to the organisation regardless of its bureaucratic or professional complexion.

The role of the librarian in fighting for benefits for his staff, from promotion to getting vacancies filled quickly, can be undermined by trade union activity. He may find himself obliged to adopt a 'management' stance while privately his loyalties are with his staff. However, it may be that the union is more successful in providing these benefits. If skillfully used, the relationship with the union can be beneficial, leading the librarian in the direction he already wishes to go. Nevertheless the converse can also be true. A 'them and us' attitude can develop to the detriment of all. The librarian may then find that his staff communicate their problems via channels that bypass his office.

Staff development

Staff do not always know their own deficiencies or needs. It is probably too simple to ask them. Possibilities and opportunities must be offered to them. Staff development can tend towards the permissive rather than positive or directive. Management may allow people to attend courses but seldom direct staff, however persuasively, to courses where the skills offered would benefit the library. As job mobility decreases, there is a greater need for staff development in order to create new ideas and reduce complacency. Some people do not grow with the system. They may not keep pace with academic changes, and new technology.

Senior management too should not be exempt. In this respect the polytechnic librarian benefits enormously from membership of the Council of Polytechnic Librarians (COPOL). COPOL is a means of trying to influence the librarian's environment via 'political' action, a source of valuable information, and a valued community of colleagues where experience can be shared. Senior library management can be expected to pursue their own development via higher degrees, attending and speaking at professional courses, through publication, research and professional reading. Exchanges of post at this level tend not to happen. A scheme has been proposed whereby polytechnic librarians spend a day with their opposite numbers in other institutions. Examining and discussing others' current problems, papers, internal memoranda, diaries and meetings would give opportunities to understand management styles and provide useful comparisons and ideas.

The librarian may not be required to do any of these things. There are few pressures to act in this way and little reward or recognition for doing so. Nominally it might be expected, as an academic, that the librarian make some effort in this direction, but his rank and position would seldom be threatened if he did not. Librarians engage in these activities more because of internalised values than from necessity.

The librarian should be very conscious of the length of time he has spent in the same job. Many years' experience can be beneficial except to the extent that one additional year brings little incremental learning. It is sometimes said of managers that they are most effective between five and eight years in office. Other than the advantages of a 'new broom' and the honeymoon period often enjoyed by a new manager, it may take five years to get established. Within three more years the librarian may have achieved all that he could. There are nevertheless some advantages of sheer duration. Continuity and knowledge of the system are provided. An understanding of the institution's history can provide powerful arguments and information. Time leads to useful contacts, techniques for coping, self-confidence and a strong professional identity. The converse is that battles long since fought and lost might not be rejoined when new opportunities present themselves. A newcomer might do so and succeed in the changed circumstances. The risks of ossification are reduced where the librarian's own superiors change office. Having a new boss can often produce new incentives, initiatives and the same or new problems to be tackled.

Conclusion

The polytechnic librarian's role is to give direction, to lead, but more importantly it is to create the conditions in which his staff can do their work. Similarly the top management of a polytechnic should see their task as the creation of the conditions that allow the polytechnic librarian to do his job. Unfortunately 'control' seems to be a major concern of governors and directorate. The librarian must demand time from the directorate in order to promote innovations, discuss ideas and get problems solved. The librarian alone cannot do it. The institution should be able to do so.

Libraries are still a people problem. The most important task for library professionals is still the interaction with fellow professionals both inside and outside the library – 'the greatest emphasis will be on people-oriented people, who can plan, interact, articulate and persuade' (White, 1985, p.168).

Some comfort can be gleaned from Drucker (1970), who has suggested that a well managed organisation is dull and boring because all the crises have been ironed out and converted into routines, and that a large workforce can spend more time interacting than working, while a symptom of bad organisation is too many meetings.

Peck (1984, p.272), writing about successful small colleges, may have provided the prescription for successful libraries. The seven characteristics are:

1 administered through people rather than through organisational structures;
2 decisions about the future and change made largely by intuition;
3 dominated by a commitment to mission and purpose;
4 effective, not merely efficient;

5 extremely well run at the operational level;
6 highly innovative and creative;
7 opportunistic in the best sense.

Finally, if the polytechnic librarian has done a good job in recruiting the right people, training and developing them, there is further comfort in a thought, which initially may appear to be the very denial of management, that the essence of good management is leaving good people alone.

References

Argyris, C. (1953), 'Some characteristics of successful executives', *Personnel Journal*, vol.32, no.2 (June), pp.50–5.

Blake, R.R. and Mouton, J.S. (1964), *The managerial grid*, Houston, Texas, Gulf Publishing Company.

Blau, P. and Scott, W. (1962), *Formal organizations*, London, Routledge and Kegan Paul.

Bundy, M.L. (1966), 'Conflict in libraries', *College and Research Libraries*, vol.27, no.4 (July), pp.253–62.

Burns, T. and Stalker, G.M. (1966), *The management of innovation*, London, Tavistock Publications.

Carnegie, D. (1938), *How to win friends and influence people*, Tadworth, Surrey, World's Work.

Cates, C. (1979), 'Beyond muddling through: creativity', *Public Administration Review*, vol.39, no.6 (November/December), pp.527–32.

Cayless, C.F. (1978), 'Staffing in college libraries' in G. Jefferson and G.C.K. Smith-Burnett, *The college library*, London, Clive Bingley.

Cornford, F.M. (1953), *Microcosmographia academica*, 6th edn, London, Bowes and Bowes.

Dalton, M. (1950), 'Conflict between staff and line managerial officers', *American Sociological Review*, vol.15, no.150, pp.342–51.

Dickson, J.W. (1981), 'Participation as a means of organizational control', *Journal of Management Studies*, vol.18, no.2 (April), pp.159–76.

Dragon, A.C. (1979), 'Leader behaviour in changing libraries', *Library Research*, vol.1, no.1 (Spring), pp.53–66.

Drucker, P. (1970), *The effective executive*, London, Pan.

Edwards, R.M. (1975), 'The management of libraries and the professional function of libraries', *Library Quarterly*, vol.45, no.2 (April), pp.150–60.

Fleishman, E.A. (1973), 'Twenty years of consideration and structure' in E.A. Fleishman and J.G. Hunt (eds), *Current developments in the study of leadership*, Carbondale, Illinois, Southern Illinois University Press, pp.1–40.
Flener, J.G. (1973), 'Staff participation in management in large university libraries', *College and Research Libraries*, vol.34, no.4 (July), pp.275–9.
Ford, G. (1980), review of C. Oldman and G. Wills (1978), *A reappraisal of academic librarianship*, Bradford, MCB Publications in *Journal of Documentation*, vol.36, no.4 (December), p.346.
Goodworth, C.T. (1984), *How to be a super-effective manager*, London, Business Books.
Gouldner, A.W. (1957), 'Cosmopolitans and locals', *Administrative Science Quarterly*, vol.11, nos.3, 4, pp.281–306, 444–80.
Heller, R. (1972), *The naked manager*, London, Barrie and Jenkins.
Hicks, H.G. and Gullett, C.R. (1981), *Organizations: theory and behaviour*, London, McGraw-Hill.
House, D. (1985), 'Managing the multi-site system' in J. Cowley (ed), *The management of polytechnic libraries*, Aldershot, Gower in association with COPOL, pp.135–6.
Kaplan, L. (1975), 'The literature of participation: from optimism to realism', *College and Research Libraries*, vol.36, no.6 (November), pp.473–9.
Lawrence, P.R. and Lorsch, J.W. (1967), *Organization and environment: managing differentiation and integration*, Cambridge, Mass., Harvard University Press.
Lee, S.A. (1977), 'Conflict and ambiguity in the role of the academic library director', *College and Research Libraries*, vol.38, no.5 (September), pp.396–403.
Lindblom, C.E. (1959), 'The science of "muddling through" ', *Public Administration Review*, vol.19, no.2 (Spring), pp.79–88.
Lindblom, C.E. (1979), 'Still muddling, not yet through', *Public Administration Review*, vol.39, no.6 (November/December), pp.517–26.
Locke, E.A. (1970), 'Job satisfaction and job performance: a theoretical analysis', *Organisational Behaviour and Human Performance*, vol.5, no.1 (September), pp.484–500.
McClure, R. (1980), *Information for library decision-making*, London, Aldwych.

McGregor, D. (1966), *Leadership and motivation*, Cambridge, Mass., MIT Press.
May, J.D. (1978), 'Should your staff help make decisions?', *Audiovisual Instruction*, vol.23, no.7 (October), pp.35–7.
Mintzberg, G. (1973), *The nature of managerial work*, London, Harper and Row.
Morein, P.G. and Webster, D.E. (1977), *The academic library development programme: a guided self-study for the small and mid-sized academic library*, Washington, Council on Library Resources.
Morse, J.J. and Lorsch, J.W. (1970), 'Beyond theory X.', *Harvard Business Review*, vol.48, no.3 (May/June), pp.61–8.
Noble, T. and Pym, B. (1970), 'Collegial authority and the receding locus of power', *British Journal of Sociology*, vol.21, no.4 (December), pp.431–45.
O'Connor, M.J. (1980), *Research in library management* (British Library Research and Development Report, no.5550), London, British Library.
Peck, R. (1984), 'Entrepreneurship as a significant factor in successful adaption', *Journal of Higher Education*, vol.55, no.2 (March/April), pp.269–85.
Perrow, C. (1961), 'The analysis of goals in complex organisations', *American Sociological Review*, vol.26, no.6 (December), pp.854–66.
Perrow, C. (1979), *Complex organisations: a critical essay*, 2nd edn, Glenview, Illinois, Scott, Foresman Co.
Pfeffer, J. (1978), *Organization design*, Arlington, Illinois, AHM Publishing Co.
Plate, K.H. and Stone, E.W. (1974), 'Factors affecting librarians' job satisfaction: a report of two studies', *Library Quarterly*, vol.44, no.2 (April), pp.97–110.
Raffel, J.A. (1974), 'From economic to political analysis of library decision-making', *College and Research Libraries*, vol.35, no.6 (November), pp.412–23.
Rayward, W.B. (1969), 'Libraries as organizations', *College and Research Libraries*, vol.30, no.4 (July), pp.312–26.
Silverman, D. (1970), *The theory of organisations: a sociological framework*, London, Heinemann, ch.4.
Stewart, H.R. (1972), *Staff participation in the management of college libraries and its relationship to library performance characteristics*, Bloomington, Indiana, Indiana University, PhD thesis.
Thompson, J. (1974), *Library power: a new philosophy of librarianship*, London, Clive Bingley.

Townsend, R. (1984), *Further up the organization*, London, Michael Joseph.
Urquhart, J.A. and Schofield, J.L. (1972), 'Measuring readers' failure at the shelf in three university libraries', *Journal of Documentation*, vol.28, no.3 (September), pp.233–41.
Veaner, A.B. (1985), '1985 to 1995: the next decade in academic librarianship, Part II', *College and Research Libraries*, vol.46, no.4 (July), pp.295–308.
Vroom, V.H. and Yetton, P.W. (1973), *Leadership and decision-making*, Pittsburgh, University of Pittsburgh Press.
Weber, M. (1947), *The theory of social and economic organization* (translated by A. Henderson and T. Parsons), New York, Free Press.
White, H.S. (1981), 'Management communication – or don't call me, I'll call you', *Information and Library Manager*, vol.1, no.3 (December), pp.68–9.
White, H.S. (1985), *Library personnel management*, New York, Knowledge Industry Publications.
Whitworth, T.A. (1974), *The college librarian: a study in orientation and role incongruence*, Sheffield, Sheffield University, School of Librarianship and Information Studies, MA thesis.
Wilkinson, J.P. (1978), 'The psycho-organizational approach to staff communication in libraries', *Journal of Academic Librarianship*, vol.4, no.1 (March), pp.21–6.

Index